THE DOMESTICATED
AMERICANS

Books by Russell Lynes:

THE DOMESTICATED AMERICANS

CADWALLADER

A SURFEIT OF HONEY

THE TASTEMAKERS

GUESTS

SNOBS

THE
DOMESTICATED
AMERICANS

by

RUSSELL LYNES

Illustrated

HARPER & ROW, PUBLISHERS

New York, Evanston, and London

FIRST EDITION

H-N

LIBRARY OF CONGRESS CATALOG CARD NUMBER: 62-14538

To Mildred Akin Lynes

CONTENTS

ILLUSTRATIONS

With their sources

ix

Robert Monroe for Suburbanite Home Builders, Pontiac, Mich. (*photo Krantzen Studio, Inc., courtesy* The American Home, *copyright* VTFO, *the Curtis Publishing Company*)

Following page 212

Early 19th-century kitchen (frontispiece, *The New England Economical Housekeeper*, Mrs. E. A. Howland, 1847)

Stove (*The American Woman's Home*, Catharine E. Beecher and Harriet Beecher Stowe, 1869)

An electric kitchen (*The House and Home*, Vol. I, 1896)

Kitchen in the Theodore Sutro house, New York, N.Y., 1899 (*photo Byron Coll., Museum of the City of New York*)

Model for Westinghouse electric stove, 1909 (*photo Westinghouse Electric Corporation*)

First electric range marketed by Westinghouse, 1914 (*photo Westinghouse Electric Corporation*)

Kitchen table in home of Calvin Coolidge, Plymouth Notch, Vt. (*photo William H. Schleisner, courtesy of Gottscho-Schleisner, Inc.*)

Drawing by George Platt of the parlor floor of his house in New York, N.Y., about 1850 (*coll. the author*)

Parlor of the W. A. Farnsworth house, Rockland, Maine (*photo Cervin Robinson for H.A.B.S.*)

"Look on this picture, and on this," from an advertisement of Magoun's window screens, about 1866 (*Bella C. Landauer Coll., New-York Historical Society*)

"They are only collecting the usual fans and gloves," drawn by Charles Dana Gibson (*Life*, 1897)

Dressing room alcove of the 1860's reconstructed in the Brooklyn Museum, Brooklyn, N.Y. (*photo Brooklyn Museum*)

Advertisement by Paine's of Boston, Mass., of a folding bed (*Warshaw Collection of Business Americana*)

Advertisement of Gould's Double Acting Force Pumps for house use (*Palliser's New Cottage Homes and Details*, 1887)

Advertisement for Pears' Soap (*Harper's Bazar*, 1887)

A Greek Revival bathroom from an advertisement of Dusenbury Plumbing, about 1845 (*photo Museum of the City of New York*)

Advertisement of Standard Porcelain Enameled Ware (*Life*, 1907)

Bathroom in a Long Island, N.Y., house of 1957 with fixtures by Sherle-Wagner (*photo Lisanti, Inc.*)

Following page 276

A domestic party in Boston, 1855 (*Culver Pictures, Inc.*)

Five-o'clock tea, 1885 (*Culver Pictures, Inc.*)

"Blowing the Feather" and other parlor games (*Bella C. Landauer Coll., New-York Historical Society*)

"Baseball on Television" by Glenn Grohe from a series of beer advertisements entitled "Home Life in America," reproduced in *Life*, 1948 (*courtesy of the United States Brewers Association*)

Advertisement of the Estey Organ Co., about 1890 (*Bella C. Landauer Coll., New-York Historical Society*)

Listening to the phonograph, about 1885 (*Culver Pictures, Inc.*)

"Playing the Dummy," drawn by Harrison Fisher (*The Harrison Fisher Book, 1908, copyright by Charles Scribner's Sons*)

Conversation pit in the residence of George Weissman, Rye, N.Y., designed by Ulrich Franzen, 1957 (*photo Michael A. Vaccaro, copyright Look Magazine*)

"The Habits of Good Society" (*Appleton's Journal, 1872; Culver Pictures, Inc.*)

"The Inner Man—Buffet Supper," drawn by Gluyas Williams (*The New Yorker, 1940*)

"A Reminiscence of the White Sulphur Springs," drawn by C. S. Reinhart (*Harper's Weekly, 1888*)

The family of Dr. I. W. Drummond on the back porch of their house in New York, N.Y., about 1875 (*photo Museum of the City of New York*)

Tea hour on the porch of a New England home, about 1900 (*photo The Bettman Archive, Inc.*)

Living room and terrace of the George Weissman residence, Rye, N.Y., designed by Ulrich Franzen in 1957 (*photo Michael A. Vaccaro, copyright Look Magazine*)

Aerial view of Los Angeles, Calif., 1960 (*photo William Garnett*)

Endpapers: "The Perfect Vehicle for a Trip through the Mountains" *Life*, October 21, 1886 (*Coll. New York Society Library*)

PART ONE

Manners, Hovels,
and Houses

CHAPTER I

What This Book Is About

... Much of the character of every man may
be read in his house.
A. J. Downing, *The Architecture
of Country Houses*, 1850

This book is an attempt to throw a small beam of light on the
American experience and character by looking at and poking
around in the houses in which Americans have lived either by choice
or because they could not help themselves. It is partly a discussion of
manners, partly an opinionated critique of domestic architecture, and
partly an exercise in social history, but it is not, I hope, an antiquarian
view in any respect. I am interested not in Americana but in Americans. This book is intended to be a companion volume to another
book of mine, *The Tastemakers*. That book, obviously, was concerned
primarily with taste; this one, less obviously, is concerned primarily
with manners.

There have been a great many forces that have helped to shape
the American household and the buildings that have kept it dry and
warm and in some cases embellished it. The process of our domestication (some people might call it our becoming civilized, others our
being tamed) has in some respects been slowed and in others hastened
by our inability to stay put either physically or socially. Our mobility
has revealed itself in our tastes in architecture, in our manners in the
living room, and in the uses and characters of our parlors and dining
rooms and kitchens. So, of course, has the wastefulness in which a nation overly rich in natural resources can indulge. So, too, has the inventiveness that has made our houses into museums of gadgets which
replace servants that we have been, at least theoretically, rather em-

3

barrassed as good democrats to employ. Our beliefs in equality and our flouting of them have shaped our houses as surely as have our plentiful forests, our fascination with technology, and the surges of immigration of inexpensive labor from countries less fortunate than our own.

It is at these sorts of contributions to the American household that I invite the reader to look with me. I have found them in many respects fascinating, frequently surprising, but above all unified. There is something persistently American about the American character that shows in his household; I am glad to leave to the reader's judgment just how admirable this is. I would call it a continuity of cussedness. In doing so I might be doing it an injustice, but the fact is that while the American will take a good deal of pushing around and leading by the nose, his independence (that is, his cussedness) continually keeps him from giving in. He will go just so far to please the tastemakers, the real-estate interests, the writers of books of etiquette, and others who have tried to make him behave according to their lights. Then he balks. He has balked ever since the Age of Jackson when this book begins.

CHAPTER II

The Movers

> Tear away from your mother's apron strings;
> and don't squat down between a rock and a
> stump, just under the eaves of father's back
> door. Get away from the paternal homestead.
> Go where people will see and appreciate your
> virtuous manhood. . . . Locate among strang-
> ers.
> Sereno Edwards Todd, *Country Homes*, 1876

On a winter afternoon in 1842, Charles Dickens, who had a marked talent for setting the teeth of Americans on edge, took a train from Boston, a city of which he had generally approved, to Worcester, a matter of fifty odd miles. There was a quality about the landscape that he saw from the windows of the train that surprised and amused him. "All the buildings," he wrote in his *American Notes*, "looked as if they had been built and painted that morning and could be taken down on Monday with very little trouble." Dickens, of course, was used to stone houses in the English landscape, houses that looked as though they were as permanent as the hills about them. A New England village where "every house is the whitest of white" and where "the clean cardboard colonnades had no more perspective than a bridge on a Chinese tea cup" made him wonder if Americans ever intended to settle down. Not only did the houses look impermanent; they looked unprivate. ". . . those slightly built wooden dwellings," he noted, "behind which the sun was setting with a brilliant lustre, could be so looked through and through, that the idea of any inhabitant being able to hide himself from the public gaze, or have any secrets from the public eye, was not entertainable for a moment."

One of the reasons why Mr. Dickens got under the skin of so many

5

Americans was that his observations were so frequently and so uncomfortably accurate. It was easy enough to explain, of course, that Americans built of wood rather than of stone because wood was so cheap and so available, but that did not explain either the disregard for privacy or why, as Dickens noted of the suburbs around Boston, American houses looked to be "sprinkled and dropped about in all directions, without seeming to have any root at all in the ground." Indeed, it appeared to him as though "the whole affair could be taken up piecemeal like a child's toy, and crammed into a little box." It was something more than white clapboards that gave America a here-today-gone-tomorrow look. It was more than just the newness of the houses and the fresh white paint, the meadows, "rank, and rough, and wild." It was something in the American character that, though Dickens did not define it, he seemed to discern: a restlessness, an urge to move on, a sense of there being unlimited space to be used or wasted, an unwillingness, in spite of all protestations to the contrary, to put down permanent roots.

The truth of the matter is that ours is a society as mobile as wheels, ambition, almost unlimited expanses of land, and an itch to sample the grass in the next pasture can make us. To move is as natural to the American as maintaining roots is to the European. Our restlessness and mobility are in our metaphors. In England a man *stands* for Parliament; in America he *runs* for the Senate. The American prides himself on his "get up and go." We think of progress as "covering ground" and we admire the man who "makes it under his own steam." The bright young man of promise is "a young man who's going places." The failure in our society is the man (or the institution, for that matter) who "stands still." The most famous exhortation in the American vernacular is "Go west, young man." We sing: "Where do we go from here, boys? Where do we go from here?" and "Don't Fence Me In," "How You Gonna Keep 'em Down on the Farm?" and "It's a Long, Long Trail."

There is more truth than humor for the American in the aphorism "Home is where you hang your hat." It is part of our mythology, rather than of our history or of our longest memories, that the American homestead is the symbol of family continuity and stability and the stronghold of democratic institutions. We associate the homestead with the virtues of family unity and solidarity, the sacrifices that the family makes for its members, the peace and reassurance of the hearth, and the sharing of pleasures and tragedies. No legend, no nostalgia, is without some basis in fact, but enduring homesteads have been few in our history compared with the vast number of transitory homes, pickings-up and puttings-down, homes that were expected to be only stepping stones to something better. Our romanticized notion of the homestead reflects actuality about as accurately as a cheerful Currier and Ives print reflects nineteenth-century life on a farm. Americans are nomadic.

It is not possible to understand the relationship between the American and his house, which he is more likely to regard as a piece of equipment than as an institution, without considering the conflict that has been in progress for more than a century and a half between foot-loose Americans and those who have tried to get them to settle down and put permanent roots into the community. Some of the pressures that have kept us moving have been practical ones, some have been romantic. Sometimes our motives have been greed, sometimes escape, sometimes hope, sometimes despair, and sometimes merely the restlessness of boredom or loneliness. We have moved in order to avoid the snapping of an economic trap sprung by a failing industry or worn-out soil; we have moved because someone a long way off needed our skills and because nobody at home any longer did. We have moved because the character of neighborhoods changed and we no longer felt at home in them. We have moved because of divorce or because our children had been fledged. We have moved because of our social aspirations or because of our loss or gain in financial status. We have moved for the fun of it, because we got tired of the view from the terrace, because of another child in the family, or because we wanted a house with a picture window. We have moved for no reason at all, except for the sake of moving.

The pressures to make us stay put have come from politicians and architects and clergymen and social workers and others who have been concerned with the home and the family's identification with the community as a stabilizing and domesticating force. We have had the virtues of home ownership preached to us by the real-estate interests; they talk about permanency, though it is obviously to their interests to encourage a profitable degree of mobility. But, though the pressures for settling down have often been eloquent, they have rarely been effective. The conflict between our restlessness and our belief (for it is a belief) in a permanent home explains a great deal about the nature of American domesticity and about the degree to which the American has become domesticated.

It was the foot-loose and the adventurous who came to this continent first, and they were followed by religious zealots, by malcontents, by nonconformists. Some came of their own free will, some because Europe wanted to be rid of them; some came to avoid political or religious repression; some came to convert the heathen, some to exploit them; some came to flee from famine, some to escape from militarism, some to invest in land, some in search of a quick profit. Some came in chains. Many came looking for the peace and comfort of a new home, but few came with any illusions that such a state of well-being could be achieved without sacrifice and struggle. They came to settle a new continent, but settle scarcely seems to be what they did. Some, of course, stayed where they first stopped and did put down roots so that towns and eventually cities grew where huts and forts had been, but they were bench marks in a landscape that surged with the movements of people, clearinghouses for those who were headed elsewhere, points of entry from the Old World, distribution centers for the New.

By the time Andrew Jackson became president the trek to the West was in full swing. More and more families were deserting the Eastern seaboard for the country "beyond the mountains," and by 1830 a third of the populace of America were proud to call themselves "men of the Western Waters." Forests were falling before the axes of farmers, sod in the prairies was being cut into bricks to make houses, and cities were growing at a rate which foreign visitors could scarcely believe. "All at present is energy and enterprise," observed the novelist and adventurer Captain Frederick Marryat in 1837. "Everything is in a state of transition but of rapid improvement. . . . Ten years in America is almost equivalent to a century in the old continent." Cincinnati, which had first been laid out five years after the Revolution, was a "beautiful, well-built, clean town, reminding you more of Philadelphia than any other city" only forty years later. Detroit in the mid-1830's, a muddy settlement of log cabins, grew from two thousand to ten thousand inhabitants in six years. A New York newspaperman, Charles Fenno Hoffman, who was traveling in the West in the winter of 1833, arrived in the pioneer town of Chicago to find a community of "two or three frame buildings and a few miserable huts." They had been built in such a hurry during the preceding summer that they were "mere shells" and they were so cold inside that the ink froze while he was writing his report to the New York *American*. Eighteen months later he came back to Chicago and was astonished to discover "five hundred houses, four hundred of which have been erected this year, and 2,200 inhabitants." There were, moreover, five churches, two schools, and "numerous brick stores and warehouses." Even more spectacular was what happened to the town of Buffalo, New York. It had been attacked by British troops and their Indian allies on December 30, 1813, and burned. Only two buildings in the town remained standing. Seventeen years later the redoubtable Mrs. Frances Trollope of London found it the "queerest looking" of all the towns she had seen in America. ". . . all the buildings have the appearance of being run up in a hurry, though everything has an air of great pretension; there are porticoes, columns, domes and colonnades, but all in wood." Captain Marryat, on the other hand, when he arrived there only seven years after Mrs. Trollope, found it "one of the wonders of America." "It is hardly to be credited," he said, "that such a beautiful city could have risen in the wilderness in so short a period." Mrs. Trollope was at least half right when she said, "Surely this country can be said to spread rather than to rise."

"Time to an American is everything," observed another English visitor, "and space he attempts to reduce to a mere nothing." One of the ways in which he captured time and reduced space to suit his need to be on the move was to build roads and turnpikes and the nineteenth-century equivalent of the throughway, canals. The four main routes to the west (the Genesee Road through the Mohawk Valley to Buffalo, the Forbes Road from Philadelphia over the Alleghenies to Pittsburgh, the Cumberland Road out of Baltimore, and the Wilderness Road through Virginia and over the Cumberland Gap to Kentucky) were too slowgoing. By comparison the Erie Canal, which was completed in 1825, was a speedway; it cut the traveler's time from New York to Buffalo from about twenty days to six. And then as now, nothing was permitted to stand in the way of America's need to keep moving. Americans were careless then, as they are today, about tearing down anything that detained the foot-loose. "I have been told," said an upstate New York lawyer to a visiting English peer in James Fenimore Cooper's novel *Home as Found*, "that in England there are difficulties in running highways and streets through homesteads and dwellings; and that even a railroad or a canal is obliged to make a curve to avoid a church-yard or a tombstone." This was in 1838.

To be an American was in many respects to be a "mover," and Cooper, like many of his thoughtful contemporaries, was fascinated and disturbed by his countrymen's inability to settle down. He explained it in the following three-cornered conversation between the lawyer, the English peer, and their city host.*

Lawyer: The Western fever has seized old and young, and it has carried off many active families from our part of the world. . . . Most of the counties adjoining our own have lost a considerable part of their population.

Host: And they who have gone, do they belong to the permanent families, or are they merely the floating population?

Lawyer: Most of them belong to the regular movers.

Peer: Movers! Is there any material part of your population who actually deserve this name?

Lawyer: As much so as the man who shoes a horse ought to be called a smith, or the man who frames a house a carpenter.

Peer: We love to continue for generations on the same spot. We love the tree that our forefathers planted, and the roof that they built, the fireside by which they sat, the sod that covers their remains.

Lawyer: Very poetical. . . . It must be a great check to business operations, however, in your part of the world, sir!

And later in the conversation the lawyer comments:

"I have found some trees much pleasanter than others, and the pleasantest tree I can remember was one of my own, out of which the sawyers made a thousand feet of clear stuff, to say nothing of middlings. The house I was born in was pulled down shortly after my birth, as indeed has been its successor. . . ."

Nothing seemed to stand still; houses that weren't pulled down were frequently picked up and put somewhere else.

"One of the sights to stare at in America," wrote Mrs. Trollope in her *Domestic Manners of the Americans* in the early 1830's, "is that of a house being moved from place to place. . . . The largest house that I saw in motion was one containing two stories of four rooms each; forty oxen were yoked to it. The first few yards brought down the two stacks of chimneys, but afterwards all went well. This locomotive

* This conversation has been reduced to dialogue for the sake of brevity.

power was extremely convenient in Cincinnati, as the constant improvement going on there made it often desirable to change a wooden dwelling for one of brick; and whenever this happened we were sure to see the ex No. 100 of Main Street, or the ex No. 55 of Second Street creeping quietly out of town, to take possession of a humble suburban station on the common above it." Mr. Dickens was similarly surprised in the town of Lebanon, near St. Louis, a few years later. "During one halt," he wrote, "I walked into the village and met a *dwelling house* coming down hill at a good round trot, drawn by some twenty oxen!"

An ox with a house on its back might well have been the symbol of the age when the "Western fever" gripped so many Americans. Oxen drew Conestoga wagons across the Alleghenies and across the plains; they hauled barges carrying families with all their goods and chattels along the waters of the newly opened Erie Canal. They hauled logs to clear land and make cabins.

But moving was not merely the prerogative of those who headed west to seek their fortunes or to escape from their debts. City families, who had no intention of ever being anything else, also refused to stay put and their restlessness was even more whimsical than that of their country cousins. May 1 was "moving day" in Eastern cities. Families poured out of their houses with baskets of crockery and mirrors and tables, and piled them into carts or stacked them on sidewalks where drays waited to rattle them over cobblestones to a new address a few houses or a few blocks away. Maidservants untacked the Brussels carpets and the straw matting from parlor and bedroom, stuffed the feather beds into wardrobes, and piled the kitchenware in barrels along with washbasins and slop jars. The streets were a clattering shambles of displaced furniture and families frantically playing the annual game of "move all," a sort of spring madness that seized the populace. A poet implored the muse to explain it:

> Sing, heavenly muse! which is the greatest day,
> The first of April, or the first of May;
> Oh, ye who moot nice points in learned schools,
> Tell us which breed the greatest crop of fools!

Country folk, who moved less often but, when they did, traveled much longer distances, looked upon the city dwellers who "moved every year from one good, finished, right-side-up house to another" as living, according to Abigail Dodge of Hamilton, Massachusetts, in a place that was only "an exaggerated trunk into which they pack themselves annually." And furthermore, she said, "They don't strike roots anywhere. They don't have to tear up anything. A man comes with a cart and horses. There is a stir in one house,—and they are gone; there is a stir in the other house,—they are settled,—and everything is wound up and set to run for another year."

This annual stir in the cities was by no means a uniquely nineteenth-century folly. Anyone who can remember even so recent a decade as the 1930's, a hundred years later than the verses quoted above, can see the furniture stacked on the sidewalks of many cities and the moving vans at work on "moving day," which in recent years was not only May 1 but October 1 as well. Thousands of families still picked up their belongings and moved to different apartments. They moved because they had found a place for less money or because their landlords were disagreeable about repainting the dining room, or because they wanted to take a step up the social ladder or sometimes, as in the Depression, a step down it. The housing shortage caused by the Second World War put a stop to that particular kind of whimsical mobility, but nothing seemed to be able to stem the tide of our restlessness. "One out of five Americans changes his residence each year," the *New York Times* reported in 1958, but the pattern differed from the days of the first Age of the Common Man. Then it had been Easterners shuffling about or moving west; in 1958 it was families in the West that were the most restless. Northeasterners have become the most stable population in the nation.

As we have seen, this ebb and flow of people, which to a very considerable degree we have come to take for granted, was a matter of very grave concern to many thoughtful men and women who worried a century ago about the character of the family and of the home. There were other kinds of restlessness and instability besides picking up stakes and moving that bothered them. They were concerned because there seemed to be no strong ties that held families together. They were worried about the number of young couples who, instead of settling down in homes of their own, chose to live in boarding houses. They were bothered by the fact that so many young women had no training in the skills of running a house, and they worried about the frailty and ill health that afflicted so many of them and about the

shocking rate of abortion even among those who could afford large
families. Physical mobility and instability were closely identified in
the minds of those who worried about the home. They worried about
mobility as an escape from parental responsibilities and about how,
in the name of "gentility," social mobility led people to live ostentatiously and beyond their means.

"Everything is moving and changing," wrote Catharine Beecher in
her *Treatise on Domestic Economy* in 1842. "Persons in poverty are
rising to opulence, and persons of wealth are sinking to poverty. The
children of common laborers, by their talents and enterprise, are
becoming nobles in intellect, or wealth, or station; while the children
of the wealthy, enervated by indulgence, are sinking to humbler stations. The sons of the wealthy are leaving the rich mansions of their
fathers, to dwell in the log cabins of the forest, where soon they bear
away the daughters of ease and refinement, to share the privations of a
new settlement."

Catharine Beecher, who was the older sister of the famous preacher
Henry Ward Beecher, and of the even more famous author of *Uncle
Tom's Cabin,* Harriet Beecher Stowe, was a woman of uncommon
good sense and inventiveness, where the house was concerned, and
one whom we shall meet frequently in the pages of this book. She was
all for having the sons of laborers rise and become "nobles," as she
put it; but no one believed more strongly than she in the stability of the
home.

She was, of course, by no means alone in this. Many voices were
raised to proclaim the virtues of home ownership, and more especially
of the home that would remain the family seat for a succession of
generations. The house itself, its physical presence, was a symbol of
virtue in the last century as it surely cannot be said to be in this one.
We believe in the continuity of the family, but we no longer set
much, if any, store by whether it stays in one place for any considerable length of time. The nineteenth-century attitudes were different.
"We believe," said Andrew Jackson Downing, the editor of *The
Horticulturist,* in 1850 "above all things under heaven, in the power
and virtue of the individual home. We devote our life and humble
efforts to raising its condition." To Downing and to many of his contemporaries and immediate followers the house was less a symbol of
status than of character, of the solid, republican virtues rather than of
ostentation. "A house built only with a view to animal wants," Down-

ing wrote, "will express sensuality instead of hospitality . . . gaudy and garish apartments will express pride and vanity."

It was the urge to move that militated against the house of character. "The many inducements," wrote L. F. Allen, the author of *Rural Architecture,* in 1852, "held out to our people to change their locality of residence, in hope of bettering their condition is a strong hindrance to the adoption of a universally correct system in the construction of our buildings; deadening . . . that home feeling which should be a prominent trait of agricultural character." And he added what was in so many of his contemporaries' minds: "An attachment to locality is not a conspicuous trait of American character, and if there be a people on earth boasting a high civilization and intelligence, who are at the same time a roving race, the Americans are that people; and we acknowledge it a blemish in our domestic and social constitution."

To build for oneself was not enough; one should build for one's children and their children, and mere shelter was not enough, beauty was the civilizing agent that must accompany it. "It is not for ourselves but for the sake of our children, that we should love to build our homes, whether they be villas, cottages, or log cabins, beautifully and well," wrote Calvert Vaux, Downing's protégé. "Men and women can go abroad and take their pleasures elsewhere; but the young people are mostly at home; it is their store house for amusement, their opportunity for relaxation, their main resource; and thus they are exposed to its influence for good or evil unceasingly. . . . They soon learn thoroughly to enjoy every possibility of enjoyment it possesses, and their unspoiled instincts for the good and true are perpetually seeking in it for gratification of their nascent perceptions of the beautiful."

It was, of course, to the advantage of architects to persuade families to build sturdily and beautifully for posterity, and they were among the most vigorous proselytizers for the virtue of substantial homes. "Let it be considered that in building our country homes," said the Woodward brothers in 1866 in their book of *Country Homes,* "we are not simply providing for ourselves, but for our children—we are constructing a homestead. It is for want of this consideration that we have so few *homes* in our country, so few home associations, around which our deepest and purest affections are entwined."

By and large those who were worrying about the problems of the home concentrated their attention and their fire on rural and small-town dwellings. The nation was predominantly agricultural and the farmer was considered its backbone, but even as early as the 1840's the suburbs around great cities like New York had begun to grow as a network of railroads brought the countryside within commuting distance of the financial and commercial centers. To those who believed that home ownership could overcome the evils of mobility, the suburbs looked, as they still look to real-estate developers today, like the answer to prayer.

The reasons that the advocates of home-ownership could find for deserting the city for the suburbs were as numerous as the flies in a typical unscreened country kitchen. The city was a place of "overcrowded, unhealthy, dirty, cheerless abodes" where the housewife was prey to the "rapacity of tradesmen and shopkeepers" and her husband to the "inordinate and extortionate charges of landlords." It was a place where only a thin layer of social and financial cream floated on a sea of pale and vitaminless souls. "Envy not the smartly dressed clerk, nor even his rich employer, surrounded by the splendors of city life," wrote Sereno E. Todd in *Country Homes* in the 1870's. "The brightness of the outside wrappings is not always a guarantee that there are cheerfulness and peace of mind within. Many of them may more justly envy you your sound sleep of nights, of which their overanxious and overwrought brains so feverishly defraud them." Furthermore, there were the infamous temptations of the city— women, gambling, drink, the theater, low company, dance halls, sharpers of every sort and description lying in wait to fleece the innocent. "How I wish some good angel would guide my pen," said Todd, "while I portray the dark side and the wonderful disadvantages of city life!"

Less hortatory and more urbane men than Todd took a somewhat cooler view of the city, but they were no less convinced of the advantages and pleasures and proprieties of life away from the clatter of drays and omnibuses, the cries of street callers, the smoke and soot of chimney pots, the garbage and pigs and rats in the streets, and the inconvenience of climbing four or five flights to one's constricted abode. Why, asked one of them, should a family pay a thousand or twelve hundred dollars rent in the city when for six thousand dollars it could buy not only two acres of land in the suburbs but build a house as well—"a centre and gathering place for his domestic interest and affections." The annual interest on his investment would be only four hundred and twenty dollars. And how much pleasanter than "the

narrow house in the crowded street, where every sense is offended—
with no open sky or distant horizon tinged with the glories of the
dying day or rising morn—no grassy lawns, or waving trees or fragrant
banks of flowers."

The advocates of the rural life were not asking their readers to
move into the deep country or turn from merchants, clerks, or lawyers
into farmers. They were merely urging them to try life in the suburbs,
and the arguments they used a century and more ago are the same
ones that have been used ever since. "We know of localities," said the
Woodward brothers, "which can be reached from Wall Street in as
many minutes as it would require to go to 50th Street, where land
can be obtained for about five hundred dollars an acre, where there
are all the conditions of health, good water, pure air, extensive and
attractive views and whatever else is desirable in a country house."
Not only that but "there are at least twenty railroad trains which stop
daily at convenient stations, between the early morning and ten
o'clock at night." And furthermore, do not overlook the advantages
to children and the "wholesome associations" of country living for
them. "There is nothing like a piece of land, with cheering prospects
of a happy and respectable home to develop an ambitious boy or man
into a good citizen," said Todd.

The forces of progress—the joining of the two coasts of the continent by railroads, the development of widely scattered industries, of
mines and mills, the arrival of hordes of immigrants from Europe, the
growth of river and canal traffic, and the increase in urbanization
after the Civil War—all tended to encourage the foot-loose and
presented the custodians of the home with new problems. "The ease
with which a place of abode is changed and the growing habit of
travel," reported a committee of the General Conference of Maine
in 1883 on the subject of divorce, "weakens the power of home life
and relaxes many healthful and moral restraints." With an increase
in luxury came an "aversion to economy, drudgery, and housework.
When young men are unwilling to bestow any effort in making their
home attractive, and young women prefer the cotton mill and shoe
factory to their kitchens and drawing rooms, the results cannot be
good." A few years later the National Divorce Reform League noted
that "The instances of persons moving from place to place who are
ostensibly married but who are really living in violation of legal
marriage, are somewhat numerous." The boarding house, one of the

more tangible symbols of nineteenth-century mobility, was also a threat to the family, especially those families of which the husband was a traveling salesman who found "temptation" in the form of unattached young women in the boarding houses in which he stayed. The ease of travel, it was also contended, encouraged bigamy.

But worse than any of these, it was believed, the American incapacity to settle down threatened the nation with socialism. In 1892 the Reverend Daniel Merriman in a report of the Committee on Marriage and Divorce reported, according to Arthur W. Calhoun in his splendid three-volume *Social History of the American Family*, "The family, if not based on, is yet intimately connected with present forms of private rent and property; and when private ownership ceases and the individual is wholly lost in the state, it is difficult to see what possible security there is for the permanence of the conjugal relation or what space is left for the home. . . ." And Calhoun himself adds: "What seems to be mere love of change and impatience of control, 'the easy movement of population which makes "home" often but an attachment to the moving van . . . The rule of personal desire and individual idiosyncrasy'—all these are preliminary to a recentering of society; they are the clearing ground for a broader socialization."

There is no denying that America has taken long strides in the direction of socialization since the Rev. Mr. Merriman made his dire prognosis in 1892, but in recent years the advocates of home-ownership have shifted their ground slightly. "Ownership of homes," wrote W. W. Jennings in 1938, "is the best guarantee against communism and socialism and the various bad 'isms' of life. I do not say that it is an infallible guarantee, but I do say that owners of homes usually are more interested in the safeguarding of the worthwhile things of life and the traditions of our national history than are renters and tenants."

This questionable supposition, for it is no more than that (it was once assumed that property owners were Republicans to a man, but it has recently been demonstrated in the new suburbs that this is no longer true) is a favorite not only of real-estate promoters, but of their political supporters as well. "The security of the country," proclaimed Governor Lowden of Illinois at an Own-Your-Home Exposition in New York in 1920, "depends in a large measure upon the number of homes owned by the dwellers therein. Family ties grow strongest in the house, however modest, which the family calls its home. Love of home is at the root of love of country. Increase the number of home owners and you increase the number of patriots of any land. We shall measure our progress during the years that lie ahead by the increase in the number of homes our people own."

If Mr. Dickens were to visit America today he would be under no compulsion to revise his estimate of the impermanence of the American home. If the New England houses he looked at on his way to Worcester were "slightly built," the houses of today would seem to him scarcely built at all. The number of "dwelling houses coming down hill at a good round trot" would astonish him. Because of the quantity of "good, finished, right-side-up" houses that are threatened by throughways and speedways and turnpikes and airports and other instruments of mobility, the house-moving business is enjoying a rush of prosperity. There are now more than a thousand house-moving firms in America doing over a hundred million dollars' worth of business each year. There are even "used-house lots" (like used-car lots) in Los Angeles, in which house-movers store dwellings they have bought from the government (which had to buy them from their owners) and where they can be inspected.

Developers have not changed their character or to any very great extent their methods of building or of exploitation since the 1840's when Mr. Downing complained of their laying out new villages on fifty-foot lots in which "the buyer gets nothing more than he has in town, save a little patch of back and front yard, a little peep down the street, looking one way at the river, and the other at the sky." It is true that they now cut the lumber for dozens (and sometimes hundreds) of houses at the same time, but there is nothing new about the row of identical houses or the myth of living in the country on a handkerchief of land.

Architects have long since given up the notion that houses were meant to be useful to a family or even a number of families for several generations. They now design houses not for *the* family but for *a* family, tailor-made garments that can sometimes be let out at the seams to make room for another child, but primarily spare and diaphanous sheaths that are even less concealing than the houses through which Dickens saw the sunset.

As one flies over America and looks down at the hastily conceived and jerry-built developments that despoil our countryside and devour

our rapidly vanishing resources, it sometimes seems that real-estateism may be one of the most dangerous "isms" we must face in the long run. During the 1950's America's home-building industry put up new houses at a rate of somewhat over a million a year, most of them, according to a disheartened lot of buyers, with shoddy heating systems, skimpy electrical wiring, sparse insulation and waterproofing, and ill-fitting windows. It now costs nearly 500 percent more to build a house than it did in 1890, according to A. M. Watkins in *Harper's Magazine* in 1960, or "well over twice the 22% increase in all general prices during the same period (using constant dollars)." Politicians who preach the patriotism of home-ownership (politicians like to have people stay put or settle in their precincts) are very likely to overlook in public utterances the embarrassing fact that as guardians of antiquated building codes and as the champions of equally antiquated building-trades unions, they extensively inhibit the construction of decent homes for people to buy.

People, however, buy them anyway. If, as I have tried to suggest, there has been a constant contest between the forces of mobility and the morality of those who believed that the future of America depended on its settling down, the outcome is not what anyone could have expected. America is more mobile than it has ever been and mobile in more respects. The divorce rate is far higher than it was in the last century, so that the family is far more likely to split apart, not once, but several times. But that is a drop in the sloshing bucket. The pattern for a married couple is to start life in a small apartment, move to a small house in the suburbs when the children are young, and often to a larger one as they prosper and the children get older. When the children marry and move away, they give up the larger house, which is no longer necessary or economical. Sometimes they may move back into the city; sometimes they may buy a smaller house. When the husband retires, the chances are that they will move to a different part of the country where the climate is more moderate, and ultimately they may wind up, not as the aged once did in the houses of their children, but in a colony of "senior citizens" or in a "home" or institution. The pattern, of course, varies considerably. Many young couples are now shunted about from city to city by the corporations for which the husbands work; others move, as they have always moved for a century, because they are the victims of business failures or of automation or of the relocation of industries; but in spite of this, in spite of the speed and ease of transportation, of planes and speedways and house-trailers, the percentage of Americans who own their homes steadily increases.

At the turn of the century and for forty years after that about 47 percent of Americans who lived in houses owned their own homes. By 1950 the percentage had risen to about 55 percent. According to the census of 1960, sixty-two out of every one hundred householders owned his home—thirty-three million of them.

What we have achieved is home-ownership without even remotely fulfilling the hopes of those who for so long encouraged us to buy or build. The figures on home-ownership are misleading. There are a great many Americans who own their own houses but who would prefer not to. They are caught by the housing shortage that was made so acute by the Second World War; they buy because they are unable to rent. To many an American the ideal house is a disposable house like the log cabin—warm and comfortable while he is in it, but easily got rid of when opportunity or whim or tragedy beckons him to move on.

The American's restlessness and his love of hearth, his "get-up-and-go" and his vision of domestic peace and security, have never been reconciled. But he has tried to reconcile them, to make the best of both possible worlds, the large world on which he opens the door and the small private world on which he closes his door and locks it. Sometimes, as in the houses of the frontier, the door had no key at all.

CHAPTER III

A Far Cry from Architecture

Log houses are frequently occupied, for years
together, by well-educated, active, energetic
men, who are the pioneers of civilization in
the thinly-inhabited districts in which they
take up their abode. . . .
Calvert Vaux, *Villas and Cottages*, 1857

I

"I had sometimes thought," wrote Sir Charles Lyell of America, "that the national motto should be 'All work and no play.'" Lyell's geological expeditions in the 1840's had taken him far and wide in America, and he had seen families living under all sorts of circumstances and in every condition. Though he was a man of driving energy himself, he was surprised at what he considered the typical inability of Americans to enjoy the fruits of their labors. On board a river boat on his way from Mobile to New Orleans he fell in with "one of those resolute pioneers of the wilderness" who embodied for him the ambition, energy, and above all restlessness that he encountered wherever he went. The pioneer was one of those men who "after building a log house, clearing the forest, and improving some hundreds of acres of wild ground by years of labor, sells the farm, and migrates again to another part of the uncleared forest, repeating this operation three or four times in the course of his life, and though constantly richer, never disposed to take his ease."

It was a far, uncomfortable cry from the clapboard houses in which well-mannered New England farmers lived by their tidy fields to the log houses of the frontier. But it was the same breed of men and women who lived in them, the sons and daughters of the East who followed, as though it were a star, their conviction that they would

21

find "a rich reward when they arrived in 'the land of Canaan' " beyond the Alleghenies and, for many, beyond the Mississippi. Some of them made the long trek in wagons with pots and kettles jangling underneath, and with cheese roasters, bread toasters, and Dutch ovens clattering above the squeaking wheels. They walled up the sides of their wagons with bedsteads and piled the children on bundles of bedding. Hoe handles and brooms stuck out the back, and an upended washtub served the driver of the oxen for a seat. Usually they managed to meet up with other emigrants and traveled in company, especially over the mountains, so that they could help to haul each other's wagons out of the mire. It was a twenty-five- or thirty-day trip from Philadelphia to Pittsburgh for the regular four-horse stage-wagons that transported hardware and dry goods for merchants. It was a far slower and tougher trip for the emigrants with their oxen or nags, and many wished they had never set out at all. One traveler tells of meeting a woman crouched on a log "which served the double purpose of a seat and a fire." It had taken the woman and her husband thirty-two days to get from New Jersey to Bedford, Pennsylvania; about two-thirds of the way across the state their wagon had broken down, and the husband was at the blacksmith's getting it fixed. The woman had been sitting all night on the log. "Ah! Sir," she said, "I wish to God we had never left home."

By no means all of those who sought their fortunes in the West made the trip by wagon. Once the Erie Canal had opened, many families loaded their household goods on barges, and a couple of decades later in the 1840's many of the settlers traveled west by river boats and railroads and loaded their chattels into wagons only at the edges of the forests or the prairies. Once they had found (with the aid of an agent called a land looker) the place where they intended to stop "for good," their first problem was a roof over their heads. Usually that roof was logs.

The log cabin, which has the questionable distinction of being the only kind of domestic architecture to have had the slightest political significance in America, was not, as many people have assumed, an American invention or, indeed, the kind of shelter that the first settlers on this continent built for themselves. Furthermore, it has not by any means always been the rough home for the struggling pioneer or, in more recent times, the plaything of the amateur woodsman. It achieved, at its best, a degree of comfort and luxury that many city dwellers in their brick houses would have envied.

The first settlers in Plymouth, in Jamestown, in New Amsterdam, and in Salem lived in either much more primitive or much more sophisticated buildings than the minimal log cabin. The passengers of the *Mayflower* slept on their ship and the fifty-three men went ashore each day to construct a storehouse, evidently of square-hewn logs, about twenty feet square. The snow was already flying when they arrived, and during the first winter they managed, once the storehouse was finished, to put up seven "cottages," a meeting house, and two additional storehouses, for a company of one hundred and two people, nearly half of whom died during the first winter. The cottages were built, it is believed, like frame houses, the frames being made of hewn planks or squared-off logs and covered either by wide boards, put together like the sides of a packing box, or with narrower, overlapping clapboards. The settlers in New Amsterdam, on the other hand, just dug themselves in. They started out in square pits dug in the ground like the excavations for houses today. These pits, sometimes six or seven feet deep and sometimes only three or four, were floored with planks and their sides were kept from caving in by timbers and a lining of bark walls, which in the shallow excavations stood above the ground. The roof was made of poles on which was piled more bark and sometimes sod as well, a kind of construction not, as we shall see, ideal for keeping out the rain. These dugouts were often big enough for several families and were divided by partitions to keep the families from getting too mixed up. The first miserable settlers in Jamestown (and they were miserable indeed), when they didn't live in holes in the ground, built flimsy cabins made of stakes driven into the earth with wattles of willow or hazel woven into them and then daubed with clay. In Salem the first houses were a kind of wigwam made of a frame of slender poles, the bases of which were stuck in the ground and the tops of which were bent together and lashed to make a roof. The whole building, if you can call it that, was covered with thatch.

The log cabin which has become the symbol of the pioneer, with its logs left round and with the bark often still on them, was first used in America by Swedes who settled in Delaware thirty years after the arrival of the settlers at Jamestown. It was the Scotch-Irish, however, who spread it across Maine and New Hampshire, west beyond the mountains, and south into Virginia and North Carolina.

The obvious reasons for the spread and popularity of the log cabin, and its even more simple-minded cousin the log shanty, were the availability (indeed the oppression) of trees and the fact that the cabin could be quickly built without nails (which were handmade, expensive, and heavy to carry) and with a single tool. All a man had to have was a stand of timber, an ax, and the skill to use it. If he also had an auger to make dowel holes, a drawing knife, a broadax, a crosscut saw, and the help of neighbors, so much the better and quicker, though not necessarily the snugger. The dexterity with which a pioneer used his ax was considered remarkable by visitors to the back country, but to him it was the all-purpose key to comfort and security. He used it to clear the land for his cabin and his corn, to cut his fuel, to build his house, to make his fences, and even to till his land; he was as accurate with its blade as a sharpshooter with his rifle. With it he could build himself and his family a cabin ten or twelve feet square, as a starter, in a couple of days, while his wife and children slept in the wagon or in a tent. He cut to length his six-inch logs (the lighter, the easier to set in place), put curved notches in them top and bottom about a foot from either end so that they fitted fairly snugly, and then chinked them with oak chips or moss or clay. He made the roof in much the same way and covered it with bark until such a time as he might render it tighter and more permanent with wide flat pieces of wood two or three feet long called "shakes" that he split from ash or oak. In time he might replace the shakes with clapboards. The floor, when it was not dirt, was made of puncheons, which were logs split and finished on one side with a broadax and then doweled into place.

Neither the basic cabin nor the shanty, which was built of split logs with the flat surface on the inside and whose roof was not peaked but shed-like, had windows. Only the more sophisticated cabins had them, and it was common to cover them with paper, greased to make it waterproof and translucent. The door, such as it was, usually swung out, in order that it take up no room inside, and it hung on wooden hinges or strips of leather. The rudest cabins and shanties were without fireplaces; a backlog was put against the side-wall with the fire built in front of it. The smoke went out through a hole in the roof, which also served to let in light, and through the open chinks in the walls. "In consequence of this manner of building the fire," wrote a Connecticut doctor who was exploring Ohio in the 1820's, "some of the logs were entirely burnt in two, and many much injured by the fire." During warm weather the cooking was done out of doors. In most cabins, however, the fireplace was built with care and ingenuity, not of stone, except in the fancier ones, but of logs carefully chinked and plastered with clay to make them fireproof, and the smoke was carried away by a long chimney that was also lined with clay. "The house seems to be built against the chimney . . . ," wrote an Englishman who visited Kansas in the 1850's, "if one may judge by its size and prominence, as the most important feature."

How bearable life in a cabin might be depended partly on how well it was built in the first place, partly on whether its occupants were constantly at it to make it behave. During the summer there were advantages in not having the chinking too tight, for, since there were no windows, what light and coolness there were came in through the walls—a welcome kind of air-conditioning for a house of one room with a fire constantly on the hearth. No one, least of all the man and woman who lived in an isolated cabin and had no near neighbor from whom to borrow hot coals, ever let the fire go out if he could help it. The "Lucifer match" was invented in the 1820's, but at first it was considered a toy, and though some families had tinderboxes and some kept "a kind of punk which would give off a spark when struck with steel or a knife," most families kept the fire on their hearthstones going year in and year out. The last chore at night was to "bury the fire" and the first chore in the morning was "to search through the grey ashes for living coals which might be coaxed into demonstration by pine shavings or tips of resinous boughs."

In the winter, however, the conscientious pioneer replaced his chinking lest the snows and winds blow through the crevices unmercifully; if he had skins he hung them on his walls to catch the drafts he couldn't stop with moss or clay. But no matter how careful he might be, a heavy rain had a nasty way of washing clay and dirt from the bark roof down into the cabin, dripping muddy water onto his food and bedding. A Louisville newspaperman reporting on life in Illinois in 1836 got caught in a downpour and ducked into such a cabin. He reported that "the water began to trickle in little rivulets" on his shoulders, and he found it expedient to sit indoors huddled under his own umbrella.

All life went on in the cabin's single room. At its most primitive it was furnished with stumps for chairs and tables, but families that could lay their hands on barrels converted them into easy-chairs and washstands. Spring beds were contrived by laying rows of saplings across two logs, and if they weren't precisely luxurious, they were certainly softer than the floor, where the men of the family were accustomed to sleep with their feet to the fire. Some ingenious cabin wives made a sort of settee by covering a box with muslin in which they stuffed hay. Barley straw was recommended by Mrs. Lydia Child, author of *The American Frugal Housewife,* in 1838, as the best stuffing for beds; dry corn husks slit into shreds, she suggested, were "far better" than hay. Many families brought furniture with them from the East along with their pots and kettles, plates and spoons and forks, wooden bowls, trenchers, and noggins, but they had a way of becoming victims of wear and tear. Broken-nosed teapots, pots without handles, old razors set in wood, and dried hard-shell squash became standard tableware, along with pewter plates and cracked china. There was usually just enough furniture for the family, and a visitor either displaced a member of the household from his usual perch or found himself sitting on the edge of the bed or on the floor.

By the fireplace, pots and kettles hung in rows in a recess at one side, and rashers of bacon, dried beef, and hams were strung from the cabin ceiling when the family was prospering. "Hog and hominy" was the standard diet of "proverbial celebrity," as William W. Fowler said in 1878 in *Woman on the Frontier,* "Johnny cake or pone was at the outset . . . the only form of bread in use for breakfast or dinner; at supper milk and mush was the standard dish; when milk was scarce the hominy supplied its place, and mush was frequently eaten with sweetened water, molasses, bear's oil, or the gravy of fried meat." Not many pioneer farmers had much use for kitchen gardens, but they kept a swill barrel for their hogs in a corner of the cabin. The alternate for "hog and hominy" was "bacon and greens."

The "Western border-man" relished his diet and boasted of the gusts that blew in through "the broad gaping chinks betwixt log and log," and he looked down his nose on those who lived sealed from the elements in "the pitiable habitations of 'city-raised Easterners.' " To the effete Easterner, and even more particularly to the visiting Englishman, the confusion, crowding, and stink of a cabin were disgusting. "The filth upon the floor," wrote T. H. Gladstone, a kinsman of the British statesman, "the smoke which fills the air, the blending of diverse odors arising from the cooking of hog-flesh in the room, the intermingling of pig and poultry, parent and child, within the same few yards square, the strange decking of sides and roof with household stores and buffalo skins, rifles, hatchets and powder-horns, all these things seem to be elements of charmed life to the true-born Western man."

Many cabins had a sort of loft or attic reached by a ladder and there the children often slept. A modicum of privacy was afforded by hanging up blankets or cotton sheets to make partitions behind which visitors might undress, but at best, as the Connecticut doctor Zerah Hawley was alarmed to observe, the sleeping situation was scarcely what he could consider proper. It was the general practice in almost every cabin, he noted, for "parents and children, brothers and sisters, brothers and sisters-in-law, strangers and neighbors, married and unmarried, all ages, sexes and conditions [to] lodge in the same room, without anything to screen them from the view of each other." This he found to be the case not just among the poorest families but "among the richest and most respectable . . . even in houses where there are apartments sufficient to accommodate each sex separately." It was "promiscuous sleeping," he declared. "Adult brothers and sisters, and young men and women, no ways related sleep in the same bed chamber." He found the whole business "indelicate" and of an "immoral tendency." "Of its immoral effects I could mention some instances," he wrote, though modesty restrained him. He insisted this was no matter of hearsay; he had seen it with his own eyes.

The small cabin in which the family first set up its housekeeping in the forest or on the edge of the prairie was in many instances merely the nucleus of a home. In time another cabin was built next to it, and still another, and with the outbuildings—corn cribs, shelters for horses and cattle, meat houses, privies—many farms grew to look like small villages. It was not unusual to build two identical cabins about twelve feet apart and to make a single house of them by carrying the roof across the intervening space, which became a "breezeway" or "dog-trot." The family ate there in good weather and there, too, they sat in the evening, cool and sheltered. One of the cabins was used for sleeping, the other for cooking, and such houses often had a "rude gallery" along one or both sides of it to shelter it from the sun in summer and the wind and snow in winter.

The best of the log houses were built of squared-off logs, absolutely tight against the elements, with glazed windows, their ash floors

scrubbed white by immaculate housekeepers who furnished them
with upholstered sofas and chairs and a piano, with a range to take
the place of the open hearth for cooking, and the walls covered with
wallpaper. In such cabins there were proper beds, and often a large
one with a trundle bed that slipped out from under it for a child.
When there was a visitor, he was given the big bed and the man and
woman of the house slept, if there were no other beds, on the floor
by the fireplace.

When William Dean Howells was a boy, his father decided to
move the family into such a cabin near Xenia, Ohio. It was by no
means a primitive sort of log house. Its timbers had been squared
in a sawmill and the crevices between them were not chinked but
securely sealed with mortar. The chimney and fireplace was no rude
structure of sticks and clay but was laid in courses of stone. "It was
all that could be asked for by the most romantic of pioneer families,"
Howells wrote. "It was six feet wide and a yard deep, its cavernous
maw would easily swallow a back-log eighteen inches through, and
we could pile in front sticks of hickory cordwood as high as we liked.
We made a perfect trial of it when we came out to put the cabin
in readiness for the family, and when the hickory had dropped into
a mass of tinkling, snapping, bristling embers, we laid our rashers of
bacon and our slices of steak upon them and tasted with the appetite
of tired youth the flavors of the camp and the wildwood in the
captured juices."

Howells' father was determined to have the inside of the cabin
papered, but his determination to be sensible was not altogether
sensibly affected by his profession as a newspaper editor. "He had
used a barrel of papers," Howells said, "bought at the nearest post-
office, where they had been refused by persons to whom they had
been sent by the publisher, and the whole first page was taken up
by a story, which broke off in the middle of a sentence at the foot of
the last column, and tantalized us forever with fruitless conjecture
as to the fate of the hero and heroine. I really suppose that a cheap
wall-paper could have been got for the same money, though it might
not have seemed so economical. . . . I cannot remember that it
excited any comment in the neighbors, who were frank with their
opinions about everything else we did. But it did not greatly matter;
the newspapers hid the walls and the stains with which our old
Virginia predecessor, who had the habit of chewing tobacco in bed,

had ineffaceably streaked the plastering near the head of his couch."

The Howells family experimented briefly with the traditional manner of sleeping by the fire, but only until proper beds could be fetched. They laid their mattresses on the "sweet new oak plank of the floor," and one night Howells woke to find his father sitting up.

"What are you doing?" Howells asked.

"Oh, resting!" his father replied, and he laughed.

By Eastern standards there was little cause for laughter in most families who lived in log cabins. Life held few amusements, much drudgery, and often great loneliness, especially for the young women who had left their friends in the East behind them for the "long, solitary, wordless day" of the pioneer wife. It may have been less lonely for those who had been brought up on the frontier and to whom the convention of solitude and heavy manual labor was taken for granted as the lot of the young woman who went as a bride with her husband to clear a new farm and rear a family far from neighbors. It may be that, as writers who have tried to romanticize the pioneer life insist, she asked "no greater happiness than preparing [the evening meal] by the help of such materials and utensils as would be looked at with utter contempt in the comfortable kitchens of the East." But she could not have enjoyed having no shoes on her feet and none for her children because her husband could not barter for leather and had no money with which to buy it. She could not have enjoyed looking like an old woman when she was still in her early thirties. She was, to use the language of her time, "maid-of-all-work, chamber-maid, cook, dairy-woman, laundress, and children's nurse." The chances were that she would bear ten or a dozen children, and sometimes even as many as twenty, half of whom she would see buried under the land her husband had cleared, for there were no doctors and little medicine. She had been taught, if she was reared in a rural family, to knit stockings and to weave when she was a young girl; she made her own clothes and those for her children and her "old man." Her lot was harder if she had come from the refinements of the East and from the kind of frivolous education to which so many young women were subjected. "I have often met," de Tocqueville wrote, "even on the verge of the wilderness, with young women who, after having been brought up amidst all the comforts of the large towns of New England, had passed, almost without any intermediate stage, from the wealthy abode of their parents to a comfortless hovel in a forest. Fever, solitude, and a tedious life had not broken the springs of their courage. Their features were impaired and faded, but their looks were firm; they appeared to be at once sad and resolute." If their housewifely skills had not been developed, their courage had. "I do not doubt," de Tocqueville continued, "that these young American women had amassed, in the education of their early years, that inward strength which they displayed under these circumstances."

There was the other side of the coin—the rosy, romantic, moralistic view of the woman of the frontier, the challenge thrown in the pretty faces of the refined young ladies of the East. "Here we see woman in her true glory," William Fowler wrote, "not a doll to carry silks and jewels, not a puppet to be dandled by fops, an idol of profane adoration reverenced today, discarded tomorrow, admired but not respected, desired but not esteemed, ruling by passion not affection, imparting her weakness not her constance, to the sex she should exalt—the source and marrow of vanity. We see her as a wife partaking of the cares and guiding the labors of her husband and by domestic diligence spreading cheerfulness all around for his sake; sharing the decent refinements of civilization without being injured by them; placing all her joy, all her happiness in the merited approbation of the man she loves."

If the man she loved prospered, she might see his stump-filled clearing turn into open fertile acres waving with corn, her little cabin become an insignificant wing on a fine frame house with columns on its front surrounded by fruit trees and gardens, white fences, a carriage house, tall barns, and flower beds filled with blossoms for her formal parlor—" . . . with figured carpet, red velvet draped on shuttered windows, an ebony-wood, upright Baldwin piano, cherry wood tables with marble tops, chairs and sofas upholstered in horse hair, a bookcase and a what-not." The odds were against it.

But there was always, or nearly always, hope. "The lowly occupants of log cabins," wrote one of their eulogizers, "were often among the most happy of mankind. Exercise and excitement gave them health, they were practically equal; common danger made them mutually dependent; brilliant hopes of future wealth and distinction led them on. . . . There was little room for that envy, jealousy, and hatred which constitutes a large portion of human miseries in older societies." They danced on their puncheon or dirt floors to the tunes of the fiddle, the fife, and the mouth-organ, and they drank heartily of whisky which, as it was easier to convert grain into spirits than transport it to distant markets, cost only about twenty cents a gallon. "Everybody indulged," wrote William Warren Sweet, "men, women, and children, preachers and church members as well as the ungodly." The per capita consumption of liquor in America a century ago makes ours today look namby-pamby by comparison.

II

"Now, a prairie is undoubtedly worth seeing," said Mr. Dickens, who looked at one for the better part of a day, "but more that one may say one has seen it than for any sublimity it possesses in itself." To the settler who decided to pit his strength and his luck against the wind-blown prairies of Illinois and Iowa and the territories to the west, the least of his worries was whether an English novelist thought they were sublime or not. It was how tough and unforgiving they were that mattered to him. His problems were very different from those of the settler in the wooded country. He didn't have to hack a home out of a forest; he had to dig one out of the earth. It was a toss-up as to which was meaner. Each made its own demands and each produced its own kind of life and kinds of houses to live it in.

Such wood as a family might find on the prairies would have been discarded as useless by the pioneers whose houses were built of logs, whose fires crackled with hardwoods and resinous boughs, and to whom a tree was both an enemy and an indispensable natural resource. The endless product of the prairie was grass, and the prairie settler who carried his chattels west into the "land of the long horizons" made the grass work for him, not just for the grazing of his cattle, but to build his house and to feed his fire.

The prairie counterpart of the shanty and the log cabin was the dugout and the sod house. Since the settler's first problem was simply to get his family out of the wind and the rain, and a dugout was more quickly built than a sod house, he found a hillside or a ravine and, using his spade the way the woodsman used his ax, went to work. First he dug a room about nine by twelve feet, using the hill to make the back and side walls of his house. Then he cut a series of furrows where he could find the thickest and firmest sod, and with his spade he shaped the sod into "bricks" about three feet long, and, if his furrows had been carefully spaced, of uniform width. With these bricks of sod he built the front wall of his house, laying them in courses like ordinary bricks and making a doorframe out of rails or posts. Windows were the least of his worries: the less chance the wind had to get in the better. He made his roof of poles that rested on the sod wall in front and sloped back to the side of the hill. He covered the poles with grass, on which he then put a layer of dirt, and it was not long before his roof was a prairie itself, with fresh green grass on it and a crop of sunflowers.

The floor of the dugout was earth or clay and its furnishings were likely to consist of a small iron stove, a nail keg for a seat, and a packing box for a table. Families of six slept in such little dugouts, the smallest children sleeping on the table and the adults on grass-stuffed ticks on the floor. During the day the ticks were taken outdoors so that there was room to move about in the house. It was not uncommon to have cattle or a traveler in a wagon amble over the grassy roof at night. Down came dirt into the hair and eyes of sleepers inside. When it rained furiously, which it frequently did, muddy water seeped through the sod of the roof and collected in puddles on the floor. After a really serious storm, it was often necessary for the family to dig a ditch to drain the cabin and its muddy dooryard.

There were, of course, many variants on the basic dugout, depending on their uses and locations. They served all sorts of purposes—as post offices and blacksmith shops, as cattle sheds, and even as houses for transients, and they were built with varying degrees of ingenuity, and their structure varied from place to place. The dugout I have described was typical of Nebraska and the Northern prairies. In a letter written in 1960, Mrs. John S. Fischer of Amarillo, Texas, described for me the dugout into which she and her family moved around the turn of the century in the Texas panhandle. "We were housed in dugouts," she wrote, "until lumber could be hauled from the nearest town [Childress], which was sixty miles away. A dugout was just *that* and was a comfortable place to live temporarily. They were built by digging about five feet in the turf and building walls (of turf) on top high enough to use half-windows all around for light and ventilation. They use lumber for covering, and that is topped with sod and gravel rounded enough to drain properly. Partitions and curtains were used for separating the rooms—or preferably, other dugouts were made near by. They were heated with wood stoves, and the scarcity of wood was supplemented with 'cow-chips' picked up on the prairies."

A long step up from the sod dugout was the free-standing sod house, which was built, as one pioneer said, "without mortar, square, plumb, or greenbacks." According to Everett Dick, the author of *The Sod-House Frontier* (1937), the sod house came in three types: "laid up rough," "plastered," and "hewed off smooth." The sod houses were usually built with more care than the dugouts, as they were not a step toward something else, but an end in themselves, even though their average life was only six or seven years. To make them relatively sturdy, walnut stakes were often driven down through the sod walls as reinforcement. They had windows, usually covered with buffalo robes or blankets, and were partitioned into rooms with rag carpets or quilts. The roof was held up by forked posts at either end of the building, which supported a ridge pole. The rafters were made of poles and the roof itself was brush over which was placed a layer of prairie grass and then a sheathing of cut sod. One early settler in Kansas recorded that when he laid out his sod house, he had drawn the line for the wall at night so that he could use the North Star as his guide.

The occupant of the log house could match hardships with the log-cabin dweller any time. There was an insistent and unremitting quality about the weather on the prairie that not only got into the hair and eyes, but under the skin to the roots of the nerves. The wind blew day in and day out, driving dust into the houses, filling women's hair and men's beards with grime, covering windows, seeping into cupboards and bed ticks and feather beds. The water from prairie wells was hard and nothing would soften it, and when women put out tubs and dishpans and bowls to catch the soft rainwater from the eaves, the winds had a way of making the vessels fly. There was no netting at the windows, and the houses buzzed with flies. They drowned in the gravy; they woke the children at dawn and kept after them all day. During meals one member of the family stood by with a fan made of newspapers cut into strips and tacked to a stick and waved it at the flies while the rest of the family ate. Dirt and straw dropped from the roof, and when it rained the dirt became muddy water, and the woman of the house covered the floor with pots and pans to catch the dripping and then stood at her stove making pancakes while some other member of the family held an umbrella over her. The north wind blew rain through the north wall, the west wind through the west wall, and to heat the house and to have a fire for cooking were problems as unremitting as the winds.

To all intents and purposes there was no firewood, and what there was was likely to be cottonwood that burned almost as fast as grass. Families gathered cow chips from the prairies the way European women used to gather fagots; they devised machines for twisting dried prairie grass into imitations of logs, and invented stoves into which they fed them like cartridges. But the hay-burning stove was a hungry maw, and there was always the danger when it was opened to receive more fuel that sparks would fly from it and set the fuel pile on fire. What was cooked on the sod-house stoves was mainly corn—corn cake, corn-meal mush, corn on the cob, hominy, samp, maize gruel, hasty pudding, corn dumplings, and corn muffins. A dollar's worth of corn, according to an article in the *Nebraska Farmer* in 1862, had as much nourishment in it as $2.50 worth of wheat or $4 worth of potatoes, and it listed thirty-three ways of cooking corn for the family. "Coffee" was sometimes made from coffee, but it was also brewed from "parched barley, rye, wheat, okra seeds, dried carrots," from mixtures made of "pumpkin or squash . . . baked very dark brown," or from "corn meal and molasses fried together until they were powdered." Housewives made preserves out of wild plums, and they dried fruits and vegetables —apples and peaches, corn and beans, rhubarb and pumpkin. Rhubarb was dried by cutting it into slices an inch thick, stringing it on a thread, and hanging it in the sun, and a similar method was used for pumpkin. Tomatoes were preserved in brine. Sorghum molasses and honey took the place of sugar in coffee, in desserts, in preserves, and in pickled cabbage, and in the summer the wild plants of the prairie—buffalo peas and sheep sorrel—varied, but did not much improve, the family diet. Scurvy, from lack of vitamins, and scrofulous sores plagued the children of many families.

In the middle of the last century 90 percent of the settlers in the prairies lived in sod houses or dugouts, and according to Dick "As late as 1860 a frame house was enough to cause the neighbors to call the occupants 'high toned.'" But as the century progressed, more and more families paid the cost of hauling boards from towns that had sawmills. The houses were simple, foursquare, weatherboard boxes, often with a kitchen in the cellar and another kitchen on the parlor floor, and a front porch where mother and daughters sat and sewed in good weather. The porch opened into the living room with its big fireplace, and the "sleeping rooms" were on the second floor. With the arrival of more substantial houses and the growth of villages came a more self-conscious and mannerly way of living, and to the chores that children were taught were added lessons in social behavior. Grandmother Brown, who lived in an Iowa village in the 1840's, not only had pieced a patchwork quilt by the time she was six years old, but she had learned to knit her own garters and stockings and, furthermore, was "taught good manners at Grandma Foster's school." "At recess," she reported in *Grandmother Brown's Hundred Years*, "the little girls used to play under the apple tree, while the boys would romp in the street. I remember one day, when I had been laughing boisterously, Grandma called me to her and said mildly —she always corrected us very quietly—'My child, if something amuses you, laugh, but not so loud.' When school was dismissed, it wasn't just open the door and go out, but first the girls filed past Grandma making a deep obeisance, and then the little boys marched by, cap in hand." The delicate arm of gentility had reached out from the Eastern seaboard into the prairie.

Country manners contrasted strongly with city manners. In the cities, where a semblance of European class structure persisted, an overlay of French and English etiquette acted less to restrain rudeness of behavior than to emphasize the difference between the proper and the so-called ill-bred. Etiquette tended to make finicky ceremonies of what in the country was casual and neighborly intercourse. It developed and cherished all sorts of rules for paying calls, for introductions, for whom one should ignore on the street and whom one should not—a kind of protective coloration meant to make one not invisible but inviolable, to set one apart as a "gentleman" or a "lady." While proper urban manners became immersed in formulas and formalities, proper rural manners continued to be essentially the expression of hospitality and mutual respect.

Urban manners tended to be exclusive, whereas rural manners were inclusive. The etiquette of cities emphasized the importance of bringing men and women together in social interchange but of keeping at arm's length anyone who might be considered socially unacceptable. Rural manners, by contrast, made little effort to break down the social barriers between men and women (indeed, this is still true) but emphasized equality among neighbors. To put it another way, urban manners sought to establish a society of several layers of equals, whereas country manners perpetuated a society of equality. (Small-town manners had some elements of both.) Each was protective in its own way. City society protected its privacy; rural society protected the essential relationships of a community in which everyone in moments of need was dependent on the good will of everyone else.

In general, Easterners found Western manners "very rude and uncultivated." The key to the manners of the back-country frontier was isolation and loneliness. Unlike the city dweller who cherishes his privacy and cultivates all sorts of forms of social etiquette to make it possible for him to be polite without having to give himself away, the men and women on the frontier fought with open curiosity and frankness the privacy that was forced on them by isolation. Their cabins and log houses, little arks of civilization, as de Tocqueville called them, were far apart, and only when they gathered for a wedding or to help a family in need of manpower at a "logrolling" or a "house-raising" were they likely to see anyone but a rare passerby and the members of their immediate families. They expected everyone else's business to be their business. Their first question to any stranger who happened along was "Where are you going?" Their next, "What are you going there for?" or "What's your name?" Not to answer such a question was considered affront enough to start a fight; to answer was to be taken in and showered with hospitality and advice. It was a "free country," wasn't it? And in their terms a free country meant a place where nobody had any secrets from anybody else, everybody was equal, and formalities that divided man from man were looked on with dark suspicion.

The new arrivals from the East brought with them their Eastern manners, but, as one traveler to the West observed: "The children of these immigrants, who came into the country, with their parents, partake, in some degree of their progenitors; although gentility of behavior is much adumbrated. The grand children, for want of example and instruction which their parents enjoyed, are degenerated still more, so much so, that politeness, ease of manners, and every kind of grace, is almost entirely lost or obliterated." Men and boys when visiting kept their hats on in the house, and they had a way of staring about them as they stood without a word of greeting in the doorway, sizing up the furnishings of the cabin item by item, and if they saw something unfamiliar, they would open conversation with "What do you call that?" When Anthony Trollope, the novelist son of Mrs. Frances Trollope, spent a day exploring cabins on the upper Mississippi in 1861, he was pleased to note of a woodcutter's family that "There was no stiffness or uneasiness in their manners, nor was there anything approaching to that republican roughness [he had encountered it in Western cities] which so often operates upon a poor, well-intending Englishman like a slap on the cheek." The influence of Eastern fashion, however, was not missing: the "very pretty, pale young woman," the wife of the family, who was cooking when he saw her, could, he noted, "have circulated round her stove more conveniently had her crinoline been of less dimensions."

Where fashions penetrate (it took about ten years for a fashion to get from Boston to the Mississippi in those days) one would also expect to find the penetration of social amenities, but the frontier had its own influence on the manners of America, which was a great deal stronger than that of all the preachments of all the writers of manners books who have tried to civilize American behavior. As the century progressed and more and more farms became established homesteads, as villages grew and schools spread, the manners of the Middle West changed and acquired a character quite distinct from the manners of the Eastern seaboard—easier, more openly friendly, polite but without airs and graces. Bonhomie, backslapping, the use of first names at first sight, the immediate acceptance of any stranger at face value, open curiosity about other people's business as a gesture of friendship—all of these came not from the parlors of Boston and Philadelphia but from the cabins and sod houses of the frontier, and so, indeed, did the idea that a man who cherishes his privacy is somehow suspect. These are now the dominant conventions of American behavior.

But the influence of the cabin and sod house on American life was more than just a matter of manners; one needs only to look at a ranch house on Long Island or in Illinois or in California to see the architectural progeny of the cabin, though such houses have put on so many airs and graces that they would not be likely to admit their humble origins. The log cabin is, of course, still being built today for sportsmen in our little remaining wilderness, for ski resorts, for roadside restaurants, for dude ranches and other nostalgic tourist "attractions" that cater to our sentimental notions of pioneer life. Unquestionably, part of the persistent attraction of the log cabin (now steam-heated and air-conditioned) stems from the mistaken notion that it was the first kind of dwelling built by America's first intrepid settlers. The chances are, however, that its disappearance would have been considered good riddance if it had not been for a monumental political blunder in the presidential campaign of 1840.

In that year President Van Buren, Democrat, was running against General William Henry Harrison, a Whig and the hero of Tippecanoe. It was the Baltimore *Republican* that inadvertently upset the Democratic applecart. ". . . upon condition of his receiving a pension of $2,000 and a barrel of cider," said the paper, "General Harrison would no doubt consent to withdraw his pretensions, and spend his days in a log cabin on the banks of the Ohio." The Whigs leaped on the remark with glee that approached abandon. "The battle is now joined between the log cabins and the palaces, between hard cider and champagne," thundered Henry Clay, and Daniel Webster found it politically expedient to apologize publicly for not having been born in a log cabin, an honor, he said, that had been the happy lot of his older brothers and sisters. The Whigs plastered the country with log-cabin placards and emblems; they built floats carrying cabins with their latchstrings out and furnished with barrels of cider and ornamented with coonskins, and they paraded them down Main Streets. The White House became the "Palace" where Van Buren was pictured as an extravagant aristocrat, drinking champagne and dining with gold spoons, and the log cabin became once and for all the symbol of homespun virtue, courage, and democratic, rugged, homely Americanism.

The Whigs at their convention had offered no "platform," but their exploitation of the virtues of logs had a permanent effect that no amount of "planks" could have possibly had. The national motto, as Sir Charles Lyell had suggested, very nearly became in the last century "All work and no play," and the manners and the dwellings of "these resolute pioneers of the wilderness" whom he had met on his way from Mobile to New Orleans have very nearly become the accepted casual etiquette and mass-produced homes of our own times.

CHAPTER IV

Home Away from Home

"No man," said Herbert Hoover, "ever fought
for his boarding house."
Building with Assurance, catalogue of the
Morgan Woodwork Organization, 1923

"The other day," wrote Mrs. James Parton in 1868, "I read in the paper, 'Wanted—board for a young couple.' What a pity, I thought, that they should begin life in so unnatural and artificial a manner."

Unnatural and artificial it may have been, but it was certainly not in the least uncommon. Thousands upon thousands of young brides in Mrs. Parton's day started their married life in boarding houses.

"What a pity," Mrs. Parton continued, "that in the sacredness of a home of their own, they should not consecrate their lifelong promise to walk hand in hand, for joy or for sorrow! What a pity that the sweet home cares that sit so gracefully on the young wife and house-keeper, should be waved aside for the stiff etiquette of a public table or drawing room! What a pity that the husband should not have a 'home' to return to when his day's toil is over, instead of a 'room,' as in his lonely bachelor days."

Young couples were by no means the only or even the principal occupants of such substitutes for home. During the nineteenth century it was estimated that more than 70 percent of the population had lived in boarding houses at some time in their lives, and they were everywhere—in small towns and large cities, in new communities and old, on fashionable boulevards and on unpaved back streets. They existed in every degree of luxury and of sordidness and in the genteel middle ground of middle-class decency and respectability. In the expensive establishments the guests dined on canvasback duck and terrapin, drank the best claret, and were served by waiters in white gloves; in the cheap ones the boarders scarcely knew when they were eating and when they were merely breathing, for the smell of cabbage hung perpetually in the air. The fashionable boarding houses were the converted mansions of the hitherto rich, and they were commonly presided over by "gentlewomen" who had been widowed and left with a luxurious establishment and a pittance. Turkey-red carpets ran up polished stairs and covered the parquet floors of the parlors and dining room. The "apartments" (often just a single but spacious room) were furnished with elegant canopied beds and chaise longues and papier-mâché tables inset with romantic scenes in mother-of-pearl; there were lambrequins and satin damask draperies at the windows. At the other end of the scale slovenly widows, who contended that they had seen better days (and undoubtedly some of them had), presided over down-at-the-heel, flyblown, scarcely weather-tight old houses and lashed their tenants with viperous tongues. It was in this kind of boarding house that you could "tell when there is a new maid by the color of the hairs in the biscuit."

If the boarding house had been an exception to the rule, an oddity in a land entirely of homes, we could skip lightly over it here and get on with the business of the house. But it was more than a by-blow of domesticity and a target of pious admonition, high-handed satire, and uneasy humor; it was, for a great many people, a way of life. There is no way around the boarding house on the route by which Americans were domesticated; too many of them stopped there and too many of them thought it almost ideal. It was a home for the restless, for those who were unwilling to put down roots or to let themselves be committed for the future lest something better come along. It was ideal for those who liked to pull up stakes and move on with the fewest encumbrances and with the least embarrassment. It was the home of those who were waiting: the bachelor waiting to be married, the bride and groom waiting for the windfall that would make it possible for them to live in a style to which they hoped to be accustomed, the widow waiting for the perfect servants, the aged waiting to die. It was both springboard and safety net, a place from which to leap into the future and to fall back into the past.

The boarding house, over which tears of anger were shed, on which ridicule was heaped, and at which vituperation was leveled, was a nineteenth-century phenomenon. There was nothing new then about taking in boarders, of course; country families had long had bachelor clergymen, schoolteachers, and the feeble-minded boarding in their houses. In Manhattan and in Boston as early as the 1650's there were rooming houses in which meals were also served, though, for the most part, roomers ate in nearby eating houses or victualing shops. But the sudden explosion of the boarding house to the stature of a solution to a common domestic problem, on the one hand, and a social menace on the other, was as characteristically nineteenth century as the Opening of the West, the Rise of the Common Man, the Expansion of Industry, and the Growth of Cities. Indeed, it takes all of these plus the spirit of speculation and the delicate hand of gentility to explain the ubiquity of the boarding house. It was a consequence of boom and bustle.

Those who were closest to them—those who lived in them and those who scolded the people who did—regarded the causes for their existence not as symptoms of an expanding economy but as shortcomings in the American character and failures of democratic ideals. They saw only the problems that were immediately under their noses, and since it is their lives that concern us, let us look at the problems as they saw them.

It was the servant problem that unquestionably, so they thought, was at the root of the spread of the boarding house. In the early part of the century they blamed it on the shortage of servants; a few decades later they blamed it on their inefficiency and cussedness. "Boarding house life has been rendered compulsory by the scarcity of labor," Harriet Martineau, a London journalist, observed, "—the difficulty of obtaining domestic service." Thirty years later in the 1860's the tune had changed. It was "Bridget's incompetency" that had forced the boarding house on Americans; it was she who was "responsible for one of the worst evils in American life—an evil which is not only corrupting but fast extinguishing the chief source of personal and national virtue—domestic existence." Actually, of course, it was the rapidly expanding economy, the growth of factories, and the development of the West that were drawing off those who might have become in a stagnant economy and a less democratic society a servant class.

But there was another and in some respects more cogent reason for the spread of the boarding house; it was the simple matter of economy. A great many city families found that it was much cheaper to live in a boarding house than in a house of one's own. It was for reasons of economy that so many young couples embarking on marriage spent their first years eating at the common table, conversing in the common parlor, standing in line for the common bathroom, and sleeping in small bedrooms. House rents in most cities were extremely high and so was the cost of servants—if you could find them. There were few city houses small enough for young couples of moderate means, and no proud and genteel bride was content, in any case, to get along with fewer than two servants. It was considered practical to spend a quarter of one's income on rent, though it rarely turned out to be as small a fraction as that; one could live in a "genteel" if not a fashionable boarding house and be fed and served for about what it cost in rent alone in equally respectable surroundings. The reason for the high rents is obvious; the population of cities was growing at a far faster rate than proper housing to absorb those who wanted to live in them, a state of affairs as true of Cincinnati and Chicago, the small cities, as it was of Boston and New York. The boarding house gave people the illusion that they were living beyond their means at no extra cost, or, to put it another way, they seemed to be living a genteel life at less than genteel prices.

If the availability of houses was a problem, the number and kinds of boarding houses does not seem to have been, though it was true that there was often a waiting list for boarding houses "of the better sort." Only a shortage of widows, which was highly improbable, was likely to cause a shortage of boarding houses. The spirit of speculation that made quick fortunes also made destitute widows, and it was by such women that most boarding houses were owned and run. "An American lady whose husband dies without making a provision for her," one observer of the oddities of American society noted, "or who is suddenly reduced to poverty by reverse of fortune, finds a ready expedient in keeping . . . a boarding house to extricate herself from the most urgent embarrassment." This observation which was made in the 1830's might have been made a century before or nearly a century later. It was widows who had run the lodging houses of the eighteenth century and it was still widows who were running boarding houses in this century. There was, however, still another way in which the supply of boarding houses was continually replenished, and it, like widowhood, left the wife of the overexpanded husband in a business which, though it was considered respectable for "ladies," was one which most ladies would have been happy to avoid.

Men who had suddenly prospered through a fortunate speculation were inclined to rent houses that, they often discovered, were beyond their means to support. In order to raise a little money toward the rent, they would let a room to a roomer. This was the beginning of the downward path, and soon they found themselves with several roomers, "single gentlemen or married couples 'without encumbrances.'" The next step was to let the roomers eat at the family table; by that time "the domestic circle is broken, the privacy of the house is invaded, and the house degenerates into a boarding house." It was a common pattern. "From taking in lodgers as a makeshift, to keeping boarders as a business," wrote James Richardson in the *Century* in 1874, "the blotting out of independent home-life is rapid and inevitable. The children are spoiled, the wife becomes a drudge, or worse, a schemer. . . ."

The opening of the West and the expansion of industries produced still other species of boarding houses. In some cases the workers prospered because of the system; in others they were fleeced.

Early in the century men who had left home to work on the canals and turnpikes to the West and who were paid a pittance for backbreaking work (they got from sixty-two and a half cents a day to eighty-seven and a half cents) were required to part with $1.50 to $2 a week for their board and lodging, which left them nothing to send back to their families in the East. On the other hand, in the 1830's trained mechanics who made as much as $3 a day could find comfortable boarding houses at $3 a week in the cities of the Eastern seaboard and put away (or live riotously on) the rest. In Lowell, Massachusetts, one of the industrial phenomena of the 1830's, the owners of the cotton mills organized and supervised their own boarding houses for the girls who came from New England farms by the thousands to work for them. The girls, nearly all of whom were between seventeen and twenty-four, made from $2.78 a week for the least skilled to $4 a week for experts at warping and sizing. They were required to live in the company boarding houses, which cost them $1.50 a week, but, as an astonished visitor from France observed, not only were their wages phenomenally high compared with European wages, they could put away a tidy little dowry of $250 or $300 in three or four years. Their life while they were at the mills, however, was not exactly stimulating. They worked a six-day week, twelve hours a day. The matrons who presided over the boarding houses in which they lived saw to it that the girls abided by a code of behavior set down in writing by the mill owners. It provided that the girls "must on all occasions . . . show that they are penetrated by a laudable love of temperance and animated by a sense of their moral and social obligations." This meant lights out at ten o'clock, no playing of cards at any time (though a little music was not frowned upon), required attendance at church on Sunday, and the strict observance of the laws governing the Sabbath, which all but limited the activities of their one day off to inner contemplation and walks in the countryside. Few young women stayed at the Lowell factories for more than a few years; it was merely a stepping stone to matrimony, but the airiness of the factories and the enlightened policies of the mill owners were considered one of the phenomena of the times.

There was, of course, a great variety of ways in which factory workers were housed and fed. Company towns completely under the thumb of the factory and mill owners were notorious. Workers were required to live in company houses and to trade at company stores, and most of them became inextricably bound to their jobs by debt. But there were other systems that did better by the workers, such as the "boarding-boss system" that was common for itinerant steel-workers at the turn of the century. Under this system the laborers paid the "boss" $2.50 or $3 a month for lodging and for cooking and laundry. At the end of the month the cost of food was divided equally among the boarders. It came to about $12 a month, or roughly a third of the worker's earnings. It was a good arrangement for the itinerant workers and a profitable one for the "boss" and his wife who, according to David Brody, the author of *Steelworkers in America, the Non-union Era,* increased their income by more than half of what they were paid by the steel mills. Furthermore, it was one of the very rare instances in which running a boarding house ever contributed to the status of the boarding-house keeper. A "boarding boss" was very likely to be made a foreman.

The boarding house was the easy solution to complex social and economic problems. But life in a boarding house was something quite else again, something entirely inexplicable by statistics or economic necessities, something as unyielding to graphs and charts as the American temperament itself.

Clergymen, writers on the domestic virtues, advocates of home-ownership, promoters of the arts of housewifery, and their various constituencies looked upon the boarding house as one of the great social evils of the nineteenth century. It exposed children to the overheard scandalmongering and gossip of their elders, and those it did not spoil with overindulgence it drove into their shells, too frightened to eat properly in the crowded dining rooms, too shy to be themselves in the finicky parlors. It put young men and women in the way of temptation and invited them to accept habits of slovenli-ness and laziness that could, it was believed, permanently corrupt their ambitions to set up proper homes of their own. Thousands of families, it was contended, lived constricted lives of aimless self-in-dulgence in boarding houses that were nothing more than refuges from domestic responsibility. They put down shallow roots that went no deeper than the pile of the Brussels carpet, and when they grew weary of one boarding house, they would move their trunks, their children, their gossip, and their discontent to another.

The very institution of the family itself seemed to be threatened by the boarding house. It was one thing (more or less taken for granted) that young men seeking their fortunes and striving to rise in their professions should live in boarding houses where their few de-mands for the necessities of living might be economically met. But it was quite another matter for young brides to find themselves pampered and tended and rendered useless. "I can hardly imagine," said Mrs. Trollope, "a contrivance more effectual for ensuring the insignificance of a woman, than marrying her at seventeen, and placing her in a boarding house. Nor can I imagine a life of more uniform dullness for the lady herself. . . . I have heard many ladies declare that it is 'just quite the perfection of comfort to have nothing to fix for one-self.'" Time hung heavy on the hands of the young ladies, and they reminded Mrs. Barbara Bodichon, the author of *Women & Work* (1859), "of certain women I have seen in Seraglios, whose whole time was taken up with dressing and painting their faces; with this difference, the ladies of the East spend their days in adorning them-selves to please one lord and master—the ladies of the West to please all the lords of creation." When they weren't dressing and painting their faces, they plied their needles. "I have always observed that ladies who boarded wore more elaborately worked collars and petticoats than anyone else," said Mrs. Trollope.

Other observers were less scornful and more shocked. "There seems to be an essential indelicacy in exposing to the public light the first blushes of modest connubiality," wrote the anonymous author of the *Bazar Book of the Household* in 1874. "A girl just married will not require many days of the promiscuous friction of the hotel or boarding house to lose the last remnant of maiden bloom . . . the most timid woman will soon be able to stand any fire without wincing . . . fatal to modesty and dangerous to morality." Eighteen years later a clergyman in a report of the Committee on Marriage and Divorce took a slightly different, but no less concerned view. "The commercial traveller," he wrote, "marrying and after a few weeks leaving his young wife to the temptations of a boarding house while he runs off for months on the road to be both tempted and a tempter in other boarding houses; the opportunities for that which tends towards licentiousness afforded by the employment of multitudes of young women, far from their parents . . . the rapid increase of apartment house and hotel life." The situation did not improve. Twenty-three years later in 1916, it was the same story. "Perhaps the greatest danger to the integrity of the family and the purity of the young is found in the low moral plane tolerated in so many rooming houses," wrote Walter Krumwilde in the *American Lutheran Survey*. "It takes a really superior character not to close the eyes at immoral practices among regular guests or to refuse the offer of several dollars for the use of the room for one night for immoral purposes." And he added: "The twin sister of the rooming house is the modern boarding house which professes to cater to families. . . . This institution paves the way for many social evils. It destroys in one blow the very basis of a home—i.e. privacy . . . too great familiarity grows up among the different ages, parental authority is weakened and held in contempt . . . and by the indiscriminate association of the sexes of all ages undue familiarity and immodesty pave the way for subsequent [im]morality."

In the last century the spiritual price of gentility came high in boarding houses. It was a life that matched laxness with a certain amount of discipline ("She must rise exactly in time to reach the boarding table at the appointed time for breakfast [eight o'clock], or she will get a stiff bow from the lady president, cold coffee, and no egg"), a life with rigidly observed conventions ("It is generally about two o'clock that the boarding gentlemen meet the boarding ladies at dinner. Little is spoken, except a whisper between married pairs"), and a good deal of time was got through somehow in gossip, jockeying other boarders out of their share of tea cake, and dressing for show. It was no life for a man ("I remarked that the gentlemen were generally obliged to be out every evening on business") and it was even more difficult for children, who could not escape to their counting rooms or meet their friends for a drink. "There is no place in which children appear to greater disadvantage," Miss Eliza Leslie wrote in her *Behavior Book* in 1853 "or are less [*sic*] ungovernable than at hotels or boarding houses." It was regrettable that such an upbringing, she contended, should "have an unfavorable effect in forming the characters of future men and women," but it was a trial to everyone else in the boarding house to have them "scampering and shouting" about and "lying on the sofas" in the public parlor "in the interval between their tea and their bed-time." But the genteel Miss Leslie found a practice even less to her taste than roughhouse. "Still worse," she wrote, "is the practice that prevails in some boarding houses, of the mothers sending the nursemaid with the babies, to sit in the drawing-room among the ladies; who are thus liable to have a vulgar and obtrusive servant-girl, most probably 'from the old country,' boldly taking her seat in the midst of them . . . listening eagerly to the conversation around her, and, perhaps, repeating it invidiously as soon as she gets an opportunity." And she concluded: ". . . no children, either boys or girls, can live in a public house without hearing and seeing much that it is best that they should not know."

Mrs. Sarah J. Hale, the editor of *Godey's Lady's Book,* was sufficiently incensed at the havoc that was being wrought by the boarding house to write a short novel called *"Boarding Out," a Tale of Domestic Life.* In it she told the ominous tale of a fashionable woman with four children who bullied her amiable husband into giving up their home ("This convenient house, with its finely warmed apartments; the bathing apparatus; the library, with its shelves so laden with books to amuse, to instruct and divert you; the convenience of good closet room, and those spare chambers . . . the commodious yard, the fine prospect of the country . . .") for the confinement of a genteel boarding house. And all because the lady found housekeeping a bore and a burden.

Nothing so characterized life in a boarding house as its meals and the boarders' behavior at the table. Tens of thousands of words were devoted to it in the books of travelers who regarded it as one of the stranger sights in this country, and chapters were devoted to it in books of manners. Meals were a pell-mell, speedy, silent affair, anything but relaxed, refreshing, and restful. Mountains of food were reduced in a few minutes to bones and scraps as knives and forks clicking against plates were the only sounds in the dining rooms. Dickens described such a table d'hôte (or "ordinary," as it was called) in a New York boarding house in *Martin Chuzzlewit*:

> It was a numerous company—eighteen or twenty, perhaps. Of these some five or six were ladies, who sat wedged together, in a little phalanx by themselves. All the knives and forks were working away at a rate that was quite alarming; very few words were spoken; and everybody seemed to eat his utmost in self-defence, as if a famine were expected to set in before breakfast-time to-morrow morning, and it had become high time to assert the first law of nature. The poultry, which may perhaps be considered to have formed the staple of the entertainment—for there was a turkey at the top, and a pair of ducks at the bottom, and two fowls in the middle—disappeared as rapidly as if every bird had had the use of its wings, and had flown in desperation down a human throat. The oysters, stewed and pickled, leaped from their capacious reservoirs, and slid by scores into the mouths of the assembly. The sharpest pickles vanished, whole cucumbers at once, like sugar-plums, and no man winked his eye. Great heaps of indigestible matter melted away as ice before the sun. It was a solemn and awful thing to see. Dyspeptic individuals bolted their food in wedges; feeding, not themselves, but broods of nightmares, who were continually standing at livery within them. Spare men, with lank and rigid cheeks, came out unsatisfied from the destruction of heavy dishes, and glared with watchful eyes upon the pastry. What Mrs. Pawkins [the landlady] felt each day at dinner time is hidden from all human knowledge. But she had one comfort. It was soon over.

This sort of description of American life infuriated those who read it; it was all too accurate. "Dickens in that anti-American novel," wrote George W. Curtis in 1852, ". . . has yet described, only too well, an American ordinary."

The boarding houses in which Mrs. Trollope and Miss Martineau, Miss Leslie and Mr. Dickens observed the behavior of Americans

were a far cry from the cheap boarding houses fixed in our language
by the phrase "boarding-house reach," where "the bread was scant,
the butter powerful—the tea, 'on the contrary,' quite the reverse."
It was to the patrons of such places that the anonymous author of *The
American Chesterfield* in the 1820's addressed himself when he cautioned: "Another violation of decorum, confined chiefly to tavern and
boarding houses of an ordinary class, is that of reaching across the table,
or across three or four persons. . . . This is not only vulgar, but inconvenient. It is a sure sign of having been accustomed to low company,
and should be avoided by everyone who is ambitious of being thought
a gentleman." It was of such places that a New York newspaperman,
Mortimer Thomson, who called himself Q. K. Philander Doesticks,
wrote when he described an all night fight "with an odoriferous band
of determined cannibal insects—armed only with a fire-shovel," and
to which he bid good-bye after trying his fortunes in a number of
boarding houses: "Farewell all scrawny landladies, ye snuffy bel-
dames, with your wooden smiles, farewell, ye viviparous bedsteads,
ye emancipated feather beds, and ye attenuated bolsters; a long
good-bye to scant blankets and mattresses stuffed with shavings;
farewell to hirsute butter and to ancient bread . . . farewell ye empty
grates and rusty coal-scuttles; farewell ye cracked mirrors . . . ye
fractured teacups, ye broken forks, and knives with handsaw edges;
farewell in fact, all ye lodging houses. . . ."

If boarding-house life had all been as dismal, unsatisfying, and
uncomfortable as so many descriptions have made it appear, it would
not have flourished as it did nor attracted so many adherents. Nor
indeed would it have lasted as long as it has, for it still exists today
under somewhat different guises from its nineteenth-century forebears. The decline of the boarding house was well under way by the
time of the First World War. Nostalgic articles on its passing begin
to appear in magazines then, though it was still a prime source of
material for humorous stories and satires. The landlady was a stock
comic character, imperious, ubiquitous, complaining, and abusive.
"When the roomer enters the house, she is in the hall. When he
emerges from his room, there she is. When he visits a fellow prisoner,
the landlady is nearby as he knocks at the door, and she is passing in
the shadows when he says good night. It is true that each and every
boarder imagines that the landlady is watching him in particular of

all others, and that she suspects him of something sinister." It wasn't the landlady's claim that she had seen better days that bothered her roomers; it was her claim that she had kept better boarding houses, for she thereby insinuated "that she had provided for better guests."

Privacy in a boarding house was, if not openly frowned upon, at least difficult to come by; to many boarders privacy was a state of being from which they sought to escape. ("Privacy? Oh, no, indeed," said a boarding-house keeper in a "monologue" in *Harper's Magazine*. "You needn't worry about that—we're just like one family— everyone knows about everyone else. Why Mrs. Mudd ain't had her fourth griddle-cake before we all know what time Mr. Pratt came in the night before.") Boarding houses suited those who wanted to avoid loneliness at all costs. "If you want real home life, you've got to board," said a habitué to a reporter from the *Ladies' Home Journal* in the waning days of the boarding house. "Then you have real people sitting around you at dinner—your own kind who are there for much your sort of reason. You feel that bond. They've had things happen to them. The man at your right eating his corned beef, was a millionaire yesterday. The fat lady, who trails the long fringed shawl, was once a great prima-donna. Opposite you may sit a future moving-picture star, a young novelist . . . miners, cowboys, brokers, artists, genteel army widows, motherly old maids—you get glimpses into these lives more tragic, more comic than any novel could supply. And you learn to laugh by boarding. . . ."

But there were other things that those who had lived in pleasant boarding houses missed—the jingling keys of the landlady, who "swished" as she walked about in her black satin apron; the mail scattered on the marble top of the hall table; the coffee always near the fire; bacon and eggs always available; and the minor hardships as well— the days the furnace wasn't lighted because the landlady had forgotten to order coal, the times of helping when the cook walked out without notice or the maid left, and even the wry jokes about the bedbugs that seemed to reappear with the first warm days of spring. There was a kind of camaraderie about the boarding house, a sharing of minor annoyances, an easy give and take that many confirmed boarders were sad to see depart. Even men and women who had substantial homes and closely knit families knew about boarding houses from their own experience, for the summer boarding houses in which families spent their vacations were part of a widely accepted social routine. They ranged all the way from the most fashionable and expensive to the smallest and most casual, from those in which ladies competed with each other at spas in the most expensive wardrobes to those which were simple farmhouses opened for guests in the summer, from those in which ambitious mothers hoped to trap suitable husbands for their daughters to those which were merely a modest refuge from the heat of the city streets.

The heir to the boarding house, the apartment hotel, was thought to be "worse than its parent." It made its appearance in all of the larger cities of America at about the turn of the century, and by 1910 it was very much the fashion. "Everybody who can afford it, and most of those who cannot, live in 'hotels,'" *Harper's Weekly* reported in 1910. "Those who don't dare live in them yet because of the increased expense want to."

The apartment hotel because of its size lacked much of the intimacy and some of the limitations of the boarding house and it did away with the communal table and, consequently, with the principal social glue which bound boarders together. But hotel dwellers shared certain hardships, all the same. Their complaints were no longer against the landlady, but against the desk clerk, whose genius for indifference and rudeness was legendary (and still is). The elevator had a way of breaking down after breakfast, leaving the ladies stranded in the public parlors while their husbands went off to business. If a couple wanted to get its regular table in the dining room, the husband had to keep producing two-dollar bills for the headwaiter, and as one writer noted, "People who live in family apartment hotels eat stopper chains."

About fifteen thousand married people in New York lived in apartment hotels in 1910, according to Katherine G. Busbey, author of *Home Life in America,* and comparable numbers in other cities. The reasons for their existence were much the same as those for the boarding house—the shortage of servants, the desire of young couples to achieve an ostentatious way of living without the trouble and expense of running a household, and maintenance of the social façade. Most apartment hotels, like most apartments that are being built today, were essentially flimsy structures with a minimum of architectural distinction and a maximum of flummery and pretentiousness. The entrance halls were as gorgeous as marble and mirrors, mountainous Elizabethan furniture (made in Grand Rapids), and lace curtains and damask draperies could make them. In expensive hotels the apartments were suites of three, four, and five rooms; in less expensive establishments with an average of about seventy-five apartments to a building, the usual arrangement was a suite of two rooms and a bath, for which the tenant was expected to supply his own furniture. Only in the most luxurious apartment hotels was it possible to have meals served in the private suites.

The attacks that were leveled at apartment hotels were almost precisely those that had bombarded the boarding house for so many years. The voices of those who looked upon them as destroyers of the American home, pamperers of young wives, and spoilers of children echoed the voices of those like Miss Leslie and Miss Martineau who decried the boarding house many decades before. But in our time those voices appear to have died out, possibly because no one seems to take the apartment hotel seriously as a threat to the institution of the American home and partly because of a shift in domestic morality that no longer equates permanent roots with family stability. "Why Exist in a House When You Can Live It Up in a Hotel?" was the headline on a feature story in a New York newspaper in July 1961; it reported that more than a third of New York's 389 hotels were "either totally or partly residential." More than fifty thousand people in New York live (until they go north or abroad in the summer and south in the winter) in apartment hotels and the majority of them are what we now call "senior citizens." To the old reasons for boarding (the servant shortage and the bother of housekeeping) are now added two new ones: telephone service ("You want something, you pick up the phone. And they take messages while you're out . . .") and security ("You're never alone in a hotel. Someone always looks in on you during the day, someone to guard you at night . . .").

The boarding house itself has not entirely vanished from the American domestic scene. It still exists in San Francisco, for example, under the name of "guest house," and there are a dozen or more in that city that cater especially to young men and women who have come to the city to take jobs and to look for mates. One of these, called Baker Acres, provides its newly arrived "guests" with a descriptive folder which says, among other things, that the average young man who stays there is twenty-eight years old and lives at the guest house about eleven months before going on his way. The age of the average woman is twenty-four and she only stays six months. Some of the guest houses follow the old patterns: they are established in elegant and aged mansions with marble floors, paneled walls, ornate ceilings, and reflect the lost elegance of the Edwardian era. Once you get beyond the first-floor elegance, a San Franciscan friend has told me, "You get to the shabby functional part of guest houses. They all seem to run to worn Loden green carpeting in their mazes of upstairs hallways. Remodeling and plumbing additions to the upper stories look to have been totally unpremeditated."

Life in guest houses like these is intended to have something of a club atmosphere about it—ping-pong tables, Saturday-night get-togethers, bridge parties—and, it would also seem, of the cruise boat, for they are breeders of romance and matrimony. The manager of one guest house reported to my friend that in her four years of running The Lodge there had been ten weddings of co-guests, five of which had happened under her very roof. As the evenings are long, there is time in guest houses for friendships to flower. Dinner at The Lodge is served from six to seven.

The theatrical boarding house still exists in cities like Los Angeles where there are a great many hopeful young and aging actors waiting for jobs, but it has more or less disappeared elsewhere. In the days when vaudeville troupes, stock companies, and tent shows traveled everywhere in America the theatrical boarding house was a common appurtenance of almost every community of any size. Now the traveling companies of Broadway shows stay in hotels and the few remaining tent-show companies that still play in the Middle West travel by car and live in trailers.

To all intents and purposes the boarding house which contributed so much and so oddly to the domestic felicity and problems of America is gone. The permanently rootless find other ways of putting roofs over their heads. Construction workers live with their families in trailers. Many of those who in an earlier age would have spent their summers in boarding houses now attach a house to the backs of their automobiles and head for the beaches, the woods, and the lakes. The aged, who used to be scattered through boarding houses, now congregate in homes and institutions and even in communities established for their own special problems, and each week brings new plans for establishing new kinds of facilities for their care. "Old-age ghettos," they are now being called, in many respects healthier and more sanitary than the boarding house, but in many respects far less human and humane.

The boarding house, as I suggested at the beginning of this chapter, was the home of the waiting. It was the product of an age in which security, as we now think of it, was not taken for granted as every man's right and reasonable expectancy. It was characteristic of a time when nearly everybody seemed to be living on the verge of something better or something worse, when the swings of the public and personal economic pendulum were violent and unpredictable, and the shifts from one social class to another came more rapidly than they do today.

By comparison the nature of our society has hardened into a less flexible pattern. The distinctions between the rich and the poor are, for the most part, far less extreme, and for all the nonsense that is preached today about "gracious living," it is more sensible than the "genteel living" of the nineteenth century. There are those who contend that we have settled into a gray and self-satisfied mediocrity, a smug concern with gadgets and entirely conventional status symbols in place of rambunctiousness and adventurous and freewheeling ostentation. We do not wait, ready to spring at opportunity, but rather plod cautiously up the corporate ladder to safer and safer plateaus on which to nurse our fear and frustration. We have, in other words, been tamed, housebroken, domesticated. It is no wonder that the boarding house, where every man was a law unto himself and a state of perpetual warfare existed between the boarding-house keeper and her roomers, has disappeared into the catalogue of minor American myths. But for all the moralizing at its expense, all the fears that it evoked among the protectors of the American home, it seems unlikely that it contributed as much to the delinquency of children and their parents as have the housing developments of our own time or the dreary sameness of our mass-produced, single-class suburban wastelands.

CHAPTER V

The Domesticators

Let it be our task to surround them with such
refining influences as will render them better
fitted for the higher and nobler life, and will
smooth for them the upward path. Let us, in
short, give them *homes* which may refine and
elevate as well as shelter.
Henry Hudson Holly, *Country Seats,* 1863

A scene bursting with as much energy, optimism, and contradiction
as the one on which this book opens inevitably invited the
skeptical, the pious, the practical, the sentimental, and the hopeful
who were also articulate to make pronouncements and to give advice.
On the one hand there were those who thought that gentility was an
evil that threatened to undermine the good sense and good health of
American women; on the other there were those who believed that
until gentility became universal, America would be a nation of boors
and roughnecks. There were those who thought the American house
was either artless or pretentious and in either case an unsuitable
dwelling for Americans. (What, they wanted to know, did farmers
and merchants think they were doing living in imitations of Greek
temples?) There were others who thought that the attitude of American women toward their households was shockingly uninformed,
wasteful, and a threat to the well-being of their children and, hence,
to the future of the race. Still others, whose primary concern was
with the human soul, looked upon the family and the household with
a view only to its piety.

The old aristocratic traditions, which had set the standards of behavior of those who dominated politics and wealth during the early

years of the Republic, were shaking loose from their long-established moorings, and a new sense of equality among men began to express itself in manners that made the ladies of Boston and Baltimore wonder what America was coming to. The election to the presidency in 1828 of Andrew Jackson, the hero of the Battle of New Orleans, an Indian fighter, tall, rawboned, uneducated, but canny and scrupulously honest, ushered in what has been called "The First Age of the Common Man." Jackson represented to the men of the frontier and to farmers and laborers in cities and towns the antithesis of Washington, Jefferson, John Adams, Madison, and Monroe, and the very opposite of a rising class of privileged families who, they feared, did not have the common man's best interests at heart. At the party after Jackson's inauguration a "band of ruffians," in backwoods clothes and boots, climbed through the windows of the White House to turn the reception into a brawl. "It was the people's day, the people's President, and the people would rule." They stood on the furniture, threw up on the carpets, smashed china and glass, and very nearly suffocated the President himself against a wall. The spectacle sent shudders down genteel spines, of course, but it was both more and less than a rude occasion. The antics of a few, drunken celebrants were of no consequence, but the fact, as James Truslow Adams put it, that "the election had been a victory not merely for a section, but for a class," was of great consequence. A new wave of egalitarianism spread through the country and had far-reaching effects that were not only political but social, that changed not only the nature of the Houses of Congress but the nature of individual houses and individual manners.

One result of this new wave was a flood of manuals, magazines, and columns of advice in newspapers which in the last century and a quarter has shown not the slightest signs of abating. A few of the men and women who have written them have had a very considerable effect on the ways Americans have lived and what they have lived in, and their ideas look fresh and useful to us today. For the most part, however, they were journeyman scriveners who did the best they could with other people's ideas (which they frequently stole without permission or credit) and are instructive now only as an indication of what people would put up with reading in order to "improve" themselves.

It surely was not the intention of Dr. Timothy Dwight, the eminent divine and president of Yale College, to provide a text for hundreds of manuals on the house and how it should be lived in, but he sounded a note that fell upon eager ears. In his *Travels in New England and New York* in 1821 he wrote: "Uncouth, mean, ragged, dirty houses, constituting the body of any town, will regularly be accompanied by coarse, grovelling manners. The dress, the furniture, the mode of living and the manners, will all correspond with the appearance of the buildings, and will universally be, in every such case, of a vulgar and debased nature. . . . The very fact, that men see good houses built around them, will, more than almost anything else, awaken in them a sense of superiority in those by whom such houses are inhabited."

HOW TO KEEP HOUSE

The first of the household manuals appeared just a few years after Dr. Dwight had made this pronouncement. It was *The American Frugal Housewife* by Lydia Maria Frances Child, the daughter of a baker in Medford, Massachusetts, a spirited young woman who had written two novels and started a magazine for children by the time she was twenty-five. She was twenty-seven when the initial version of her book appeared in 1829, and it was the first attempt by any American writer to provide the housewife not merely with a list of recipes and home cures for the ills of the flesh but with some "principles" of household management. As the title of her book implies, Mrs. Child had her mind on the pennies. "Begin humbly," she cautioned her readers. "As riches increase, it is easy and pleasant to increase in hospitality and splendor; but it is always painful and inconvenient to decrease." The book went into many editions and in 1838 Mrs. Child proclaimed that it was "the extravagance of all classes" that worried her. "Men with fixed incomes spend every cent of their incomes," she wrote. "Men who rush into enterprise and speculation, keep their credit up by splendor. . . . 'I know we are extravagant,' said one of my acquaintance, the other day; 'but how can I help it? My husband does not like to see his wife and daughters dress more meanly than these with whom they associate.'" She was shocked by the fact that "mechanics . . . will indulge their daughters in dressing like the wealthiest; and a domestic would certainly leave you, should you dare to advise her to lay up one cent of her wages."

Not only common sense but moral duty inspired Mrs. Child's book. "Let women do their share towards reformation," she wrote.

"Let them prove, by the execution of ingenuity and economy, that neatness, good taste, and gentility, are attainable without great expense." Children, she believed, should be taught the value of economy and work at the tenderest possible age. "In this country," she said, "we are apt to let children romp away their existence, till they get to be thirteen or fourteen." This, she insisted, was not only wasteful but bad for the character. "A child of six can be made useful," she insisted. Children could knit garters, suspenders, and stockings; they could make patchwork and braid straw mats for the table and the floor. They could weed the garden and pick berries and carry them to the market. "It is a great deal better," she said, "for the boys and girls on a farm to be picking blackberries at six cents a quart than to be wearing out their clothes in useless play. They enjoy themselves just as well. . . ."

Mrs. Child set the fashion for exhortation in *The American Frugal Housewife*. She was bent not merely on helping the housewife, but on reforming her; she was interested not only in telling her how to keep meat fresh in summer ("The moment it is brought into the house, it should be carefully covered from the flies, and put in the coldest place in the cellar"), but in making her justify each passing hour ("Time is money") and keep her sense of proportion ("It is really melancholy to see how this fever of extravagance rages, and how it is sapping the strength of our happy country"). Household manuals ever since have been moral treatises in one guise or another—pious, practical, or humorous.

In the next few decades there was a multitude of books for the housekeeper to choose from if she felt the need of advice. Dr. William A. Alcott, the cousin of the famous transcendentalist Bronson Alcott, was dissatisfied with the books on the household which were "little more than large bundles of recipes for fashionable cookery" and produced *The Young Housekeepers*. "It is high time that this noble profession (housewifery)," he wrote, "lying as it does, like agriculture and horticulture, at the very foundation of human happiness, were disabused. It is high time that the miserable notion that it is vulgar or mean were discountenanced. . . . If every housekeeper knew her own dignity, and would live up to it, impurity and licentiousness would soon cease." There seemed to be nothing that proper housekeeping couldn't fix, and few moral problems that it could not solve.

Catharine Maria Sedgwick, who was a friend of Nathaniel Hawthorne and William Cullen Bryant and of the actress Fanny Kemble, not only wrote novels but felt impelled to enter the arena of household reform. In a number of books of essays, *Home* (1835), *Live and Let Live; or Domestic Service Illustrated* (1837), and *Means and Ends* (1839), with a grace that is uncommon in such writing, she exhorted young women to learn the skills of housekeeping and assured them that there was nothing vulgar or demeaning in knowing how to perform such duties. "Ladies" were not exempt from such knowledge. "Women in the highest stations," she said, "are made unhappy by the want of it. They are dependent on ill-trained domestics, their houses are ill-kept, their husbands are displeased, and their children uncomfortable. . . ." It was the "gentility" bug that had bitten so deep that even farm families were infected. "Girls of our farmers' and mechanics' wives, are generally well educated in domestic affairs," she wrote, "but occasionally, from imbecility in the mother, but far more often from mistaken views, there are lamentable exceptions." Still another literary lady, Eliza Leslie, the daughter of a Philadelphia watchmaker who was a friend of Franklin and Jefferson and a member of the American Philosophical Society, produced a contribution to household literature in 1840 called *The House Book*, though her primary interest was in books for children, in cookbooks, and in books on how to behave. Compared with most writers on the home, Miss Leslie was lighthearted, and though she could scold ("Complaints are increasingly heard of the deterioriation of servants; but may not one source of this growing evil be traced to the deterioration of the *mistress* . . . ?"), she wrote to be read with pleasure, and the sales of her household books and stories made her a comfortable fortune. It was said that her contributions to magazines were certain to increase their circulation.

Household reformers are not notable for their wit or, usually, for the incisiveness of their intelligence, but there was one who was busy a century and more ago who still has the capacity to instruct and astonish. Catharine Esther Beecher was endowed not only with impatience, without which a reformer is impotent, but she had the kind of intelligence that confronted practical problems with a straightforwardness and imagination that still make her solutions seem remarkably up-to-date. She did far more than take the accumulated lore of the household, codify it, bathe it in pious sentiment, and use it to admonish her contemporaries. She took the house itself, examined it, found its plan inconvenient, wasteful, and unnecessarily fussy, and proceeded to offer suggestions that it took architects the better part of a century to adopt.

Miss Beecher, like so many of those who were bent on reforming the household, came from a family in which missionary fires burned brightly. Her father was the tireless Congregational preacher, crusader for temperance, and religious educator Lyman Beecher. Her younger brother, as we have noted, was Henry Ward Beecher, at whose words from the pulpit a generation of ladies swooned, and her little sister, Harriet, caused a sensation (and some said a war) with her novel *Uncle Tom's Cabin.* Catharine never attained the fame of her brother and sister, but in many respects her career was more distinguished, if less spectacular, than either of theirs.

Catharine was only sixteen when her mother, whom she described as "remarkable not only for her intelligence and culture but for a natural taste and skill in domestic handicraft," died. Harriet was a child of five and Henry was still an infant, and it was Catharine who brought them up. Her own education was largely what was given her by her parents and a brief exposure in a private school in Litchfield, Connecticut, to the "primary branches of drawing, painting and music." When she was twenty-three, her fiancé, a professor at Yale, died in a shipwreck, and the following year (1824) she founded a very successful school for girls in Hartford, Connecticut, and thus the pattern of her career was established.

Wherever Catharine looked she saw nonsense. The smattering of polite knowledge with which young ladies were plied was, she thought, not only a waste of their time but a waste of their health as well. Schoolmarms and ambitious mothers kept them poring over their books until they suffered from "incipient curvature of the spine." Girls never took any exercise; it was not considered genteel for them to perform any household chores, and outdoor exercise was frowned upon as unladylike. In winter the only fresh air they breathed was when they went sleighing, "sitting motionless in the open air, with hot bricks at their feet, and their faces in danger of being frost-bitten." Her own school (and it was the first of two that she founded and presided over) set out to correct this nonsense, and she carefully plotted its curriculum to make healthy, useful, self-sufficient women of the girls who were committed to her charge.

Miss Beecher was, one might say, a feminist in reverse. She had no patience with those of her contemporaries who were eager to see women invade what had always been assumed to be a man's world, and to her a woman's bondage to her husband was ordained by God and sanctified in heaven. She ardently disapproved of woman's suffrage and rallied others to oppose it. Her crusade, and she was an extremely energetic and single-minded crusader, was to free women from their own silliness, so that they might make the most out of being women. Why, she wanted to know, should not women be trained for their profession of housewives and mothers with the same intelligent care as men were for their professions? She deplored the fact that women with few financial resources slaved that their children might go to school and learn a lot of useless chatter. She deplored the stays and corsets that deformed women's bodies, the pastries with which they stuffed themselves, and the fact that they led their lives "more by lamps and gas than by sunlight." She deplored the low opinion women held of domestic service.

A Treatise on Domestic Economy, Catharine Beecher's first book, appeared in 1842, and in various forms under various titles and with many modifications it continued to appear until more than thirty years later. Her advice ranged from the importance of cleanliness and the virtues of early rising, to the importance of manners ("Good manners are the expressions of benevolence in personal intercourse, by which we endeavor to promote the comfort and enjoyment of others, and to avoid all that gives needless uneasiness"), the care of the sick, the "preservation of a good temper," and "the care of domestics." There were chapters (forty of them in all) devoted to laundry, to garden vegetables, to the care of the parlor, to sewing, indeed to every facet of housekeeping. But more important than any of these sensible homilies was Miss Beecher's attack on the problem of the construction and planning of the house itself. "There are five particulars, to which attention should be given, in building a house," she wrote, "namely, economy of labor, economy of money, economy of health, economy of comfort, and good taste." She believed that most American houses were too large for their purpose and therefore wasteful of time, money, and labor. She deplored the fact that ". . . the kitchen will be in one story, a sitting-room in another, and the nursery in a third. Nothing is more injurious to a feeble woman, than going up and down stairs, and yet in order to gain two large parlors, to show to a few friends, or to strangers, immense sacrifices of health, comfort, and money, are made." She concerned herself with the convenient location of the cistern and the pump, the placement of fireplaces ("Where the fireplace is in an outer wall, one third of the heat passes out of doors, which would be retained in the house, if the chimney were within the rooms").

What she had to say about the planning of a house in her first book was, though sensible, by no means as sophisticated or as imaginative as the chapter on the house which appeared in *The American Woman's Home* in 1869, a volume in which her sister Harriet collaborated. Miss Beecher's "Christian House," as she called it, was prophetic in its simplicity, in its organization, and in the use of mechanical devices. She understood that mechanization was a means of simplifying the chores of the house, and to this end she devised a storage wall on rollers which served not only the purpose of closets and cupboards but could be easily moved into place to make one bedroom into two. She designed what we now call a central utilities unit at the core of the house, so that fireplaces and kitchen stoves were back to back, and the stoves could be divided by sliding-panels from the rest of the kitchen, which she had planned as carefully as any modern kitchen engineer for storage, dishwashing, and disposal. She recommended beds that fitted one under another and became a couch in the daytime. The stove that she suggested included a rotating broiler.

Catharine Beecher put into practice the crusade that she preached. She was obliged to give up her school in Hartford when her father was made president of the Lane Theological Seminary in Cincinnati in 1832, as he needed her to keep house for him. But she established another school there, the Western Female Institute. It throve for five years until the Panic of 1837 caught up with the speculators and consequently with nearly everyone else. Few families had money to spend on education, and more particularly on the education of young women. Catharine's health, in spite of her preaching to others, was not good, and she abandoned the idea of a school of her own and devoted herself to organizing colleges for women where they could find, as she said, "the professional advantages of education for my sex equal to those bestowed upon men." She helped to found colleges in Burlington, Iowa, in Quincy, Illinois, and in Milwaukee, and she was responsible for getting her curriculum of domestic science accepted, for better or worse, as a part of higher education.

Miss Beecher was seventy-eight when she died in the spring of 1878. She bore, it is said, a strong physical resemblance to her brother

Henry Ward Beecher, and she was known not only for the considerable force of her character and the strength of her personality but for
her charm and her social wit. She never gave up her crusade. In the
last edition of her book, which was published in 1871 and by then
was called *Principles of Domestic Science* (a textbook), she included
a lecture addressed to "Female Teachers." In concluding she says:

> We are now entering upon a great and hazardous experiment, on which
> the prosperity and even the existence of our country depends. The
> nations of Europe and Asia have but begun that immense flood of emi-
> gration that is coming by millions; a large portion enter our kitchens and
> schools. And the housekeepers and school-teachers of our country are to
> become missionaries, not to foreign lands, but to the heathen thronging
> to our homes and our schools. Oh! what a glorious and yet fearful re-
> sponsibility rests on all of our profession!

Few of the reformers of the household had Miss Beecher's intellectual bite. Mrs. Sarah J. Hale, who was forced by widowhood to
support herself with her pen and became the famous editor of *Godey's
Lady's Book,* was indefatigable and clever and through the publication
of all sorts of advice on the niceties of the house, on manners, and on
house-planning preached gentility to families everywhere in America.
She was more polite journalist than headlong crusader, and she lacked
Miss Beecher's forthrightness and passion. She wrote a number of
short novels chiding her contemporaries for their handling of servants
and, as we have seen, for trying to escape their domestic duties by
living in boarding houses, and she contributed her own slim volume
on etiquette. Miss Beecher's sister Harriet, writing under the name
of "Christopher Crowfield" for the *Atlantic Monthly,* produced a
series of essays on the house written as narratives and treating
with humor the problems that her sister treated with solemnity. The
essays were collected under the title *House and Home Papers* and
published in 1865. Mrs. Sara Payson Willis Parton, the wife of the
widely known biographer James Parton, made a considerable reputation for herself under the pseudonym of "Fanny Fern." She had
been a pupil in Miss Beecher's school in Hartford, where she was
known by the nickname "Sal-Volatile." She was a facile newspaper
and magazine columnist with a sharp tongue; her quarry was pretentiousness, cant, and snobbery and she extolled the virtues of home,
garden, family life, and children, and contributed amusing if not very
surprising advice on household matters and on manners.

Since Miss Beecher's day there have been, of course, a great many
dedicated women trying to convince other women of their domestic
responsibilities. Some of them have been compilers of cookbooks, and
it was common a century ago to include along with recipes for roasts
and pies and puddings, instructions for how to make concoctions that
would, among other things, cure the dropsy, take stains out of woolens,
remove freckles, catch flies, and starch clothes. There have been crusaders like Ellen H. Richards, who was involved in an experiment
called "The New England Kitchen," which was intended to "prepare
good, nutritious food to be carried home by people working during the
day and neglecting the provision of the right diet for their families."
Mrs. Richards believed that "such a step would have great value,
through dietary improvements, in reducing drunkenness among working people." The workers were not interested in being saved, however,
and the "kitchen" failed. "I'd ruther eat what I'd ruther," one worker is
reported to have said. "I don't want to eat what's good for me."

The invention of the term "home economics," coined at a conference
in Lake Placid, New York, in September 1899, seems in some ways to
have taken the freewheeling excitement of the old reformers and
reduced it to a sort of plodding academic discipline. This is adequately
demonstrated, it seems to me, by the title page of a book called *Housewifery* published in 1919. The author is given as "Lydia May Balderston, A.M., Instructor in Housewifery and Laundering, Teachers
College, Columbia University." Miss Beecher, I am sure, would have
been pleased by this academic recognition of the washtubs.

MINDS OVER MANNERS

If one were to judge the behavior of Americans in Miss Beecher's
day by the number of books on etiquette that poured from the presses
then, manners were in an even more alarming state than the household. From 1830, for the next three decades, books devoted to seemly
behavior and etiquette appeared at a rate of more than three a year.
Twenty-eight were published in the thirties, thirty-six in the forties,
and thirty-eight in the fifties, and many of them went into many
editions and found their ways to hundreds of thousands of parlors
and kitchens and ladies' chambers. Obviously, de Tocqueville and
other visitors from Europe were not alone in finding the manners of
democracy "prejudicial."

Some of the same people who wrote books on the household also wrote books on manners. Miss Leslie's *House Book* was followed by her *Behavior Book* (1853). Dr. William Alcott, who in spite of his fragile health seems to have been indefatigable in his drive to cast light into the dark corners of youth, produced *The Young Man's Guide* (1832), *The Young Woman's Guide* (1836), *The Young Mother* (1836), *The Young Wife* (1837), *The Young Husband* (1838), and *The Boy's Guide* (1844). Miss Beecher, though she did not write a "manners" book, included chapters on etiquette and polite behavior in each edition of her books. Miss Sedgwick, the novelist, dwelt at some length on manners in her books of essays on the home. "The most striking and prevailing defect in the manners of America is, I believe, a want of courtesy," she wrote. "This has probably arisen from the general spirit of rights, condition, and education."

But by no means all, or nearly all, of the books on manners were written by the forerunners of "domestic science." They were written by novelists like Lydia H. Sigourney, by the biographer of Lafayette, Mrs. John Farrar, by T. S. Arthur, the author of *Ten Nights in a Barroom*, by pious gentlemen like George W. Hervey. Polite behavior was only a minor part of their concern, and the manners books of the early part of the last century are scarcely kin to the books of etiquette that are published today. They were concerned, one might say, with the "whole personality," and not merely with the techniques of the dinner table and the parlor, with the customs of calling cards, with invitations, and with the demands and limitations of polite conversation. A young gentleman or lady who sought instruction in a manners book of the 1830's could find advice on how to get in and out of a parlor, of course, and on how to hold a knife and fork, but he would also find advice on almost every aspect of his character. In *The American Lady* (1836) by Charles Butler, a woman would, for example, find exhortations on the "Importance of the Female Character," on "Industry," on "Economy," and on "The Employment of Time," along with chapters on beauty, health, dancing, reading, "considerations antecedent to marriage," and a dozen other matters, including "emulation." In *The American Gentleman* published in the same year and written by the same author, a man could find advice on "supporting the dignity of the commercial character," on "the influence of fashion," and on "chastity a valuable virtue in a man." Like the household books, manners books were to a very considerable extent moral tracts.

Mrs. Farrar's *The Young Lady's Friend* (1838), which is one of the liveliest, most sensible, and quite justly one of the best remembered of the early manners books, devotes a great many of its four hundred and thirty pages to such matters as "the improvement of time," "behavior to the sick," "dress," and how to treat one's parents and friends.

American manners have evolved in a climate in many ways very different from those of the civilizations to which most Americans owe their heritage. In most European countries manners have evolved as fences, and conventions of public behavior have been devised to protect one's "place." The shopkeeper had one set of manners toward his customers and another toward his employees, as the butler did toward his "master" and toward the servants, and the squire toward his gamekeeper and his mother-in-law. The idea that manners should be an expression of general regard for one's fellow man is the product of a society that hoped to be classless, and though it has often fallen far short of its intentions, our conventions are the very opposite of those designed to protect one class from another. What we have tried to do in America is to perpetuate a set of conventions that give the impression of not being conventions at all but attitudes which, we hope, indicate that one of us is as good as another, as deserving of consideration, and as responsible for maintaining a state of good will. Almost as far back as one can go in the literature (if it can be called that) of American etiquette, one finds that manners are referred to as "minor morals." They are not, in other words, considered as conventions but as part of one's humane duty to one's fellow man, and even when they are merely poses they take the form of egalitarianism rather than of polite gestures for setting man apart from man.

Those who were devoting themselves to the improvement of manners were faced with a problem that seemed to embrace everyone. The new republican spirit played hob with the old aristocratic notions that the lower classes owed an attitude of deference to "their betters." On the other hand, even in an egalitarian society in which every man was as good as every other in the eyes of God and presumably the law, it seemed to be essential that a man's position be respected. Miss Beecher had said that "All the proprieties and courtesies which depend on the recognition of the relative duties of superior and subordinate have been warred upon [in the name of republicanism]; and thus we see, to an increasing extent, disrespectful treatment of parents by children; of teachers by pupils; of employers by domestics; and of the aged by the young. In all classes and circles there is a gradual decay in courtesy of address." The republican spirit and respectful manners were not inimical, though they sometimes seemed to be. James Fenimore Cooper was especially impatient of the obtuseness, as he saw it, of republican manners. "He is the purest democrat," he wrote in 1838 in *The American Democrat*, "who best maintains his rights, and no right can be dearer to a man of cultivation, than exemption from unseasonable invasions of his time, by the coarse-minded and ignorant." It was not only the rapid rise of some families from relative poverty to relative wealth (and in some cases from real poverty to real wealth) that sent the young and their parents to the pages of manners books to discover how they should behave in their new circumstances. In growing cities as far west as the Ohio and the Mississippi there were efforts to establish at least the appearance of a cultured society with manners and tastes appropriate to an ambitious urban community—a sophistication and ease that were a sharp contrast to the bustle and business that made the new cities grow at such a rate.

Most of the books of etiquette were directed to women and were called by such names as *The Lady's Vase* or *Letters to Young Ladies* or *The American Lady*, though there were books for men as well, most especially those which were done-over versions of Lord Chesterfield's letters to his son, shortened for American consumption, with chapters appended which applied to American customs and the special fumblings of American men. It can be said with some accuracy that the writers of manners books had no great hopes of ever making men into suave and debonair creatures with graceful manners; the most they hoped for was that they might restrain them from being oafs and boors who kept their hats on in the parlor, spoiled the wallpaper by leaning their chairs against it, wiped their mouths on their sleeves, or spat at the table. Indeed, it was so taken for granted that men kept low company that one manners book cautioned that when a man got married he should drop all of his bachelor friends and should introduce none of them to his bride unless specifically asked by her to do so.

Of all the social sins committed by men none was so repulsive to those who wrote on manners or so nearly universal as spitting. Tobacco juice splattered the nation. In 1827 the anonymous author of *The American Chesterfield* (he called himself merely "a member of the Philadelphia bar") wrote: "The practice of chewing, leads to that most ungentlemanly and abominable habit, of spitting on the floor, and into the fire. No floor in the United States, however clean; no carpet however beautiful and costly; no fire-grate however bright, —nor even our places of divine worship,—are free from this odious pollution." It was "an outrage against the decencies of polished life," he said, and he added: "When in a house a person has occasion to spit, he should use his pocket-handkerchief; but should never spit upon the floor, or into the fire." He did not exaggerate. An English journalist who visited here in the 1830's observed: "If the floors of boarding-houses, and the decks of steam boats, and the carpets in the Capitol, do not sicken the Americans into reform . . . what remains to be said?" The brightly polished brass spitoon continued to be a parlor commonplace almost until the end of the century.

The manners of women posed quite different problems. The social sins that they committed were not, in many respects, shortcomings, they were overdoings. In the name of being "ladies" they became imperious, rude (especially to domestics and shop clerks and men in public conveyances), and so consumed with the outward forms of gentility that they scorned their husbands' gaucheries at the same time that they bedeviled them for money to purchase the expensive symbols of refinement. In general the manners of women came in for a good deal more censure than those of men, probably because men were expected to be headstrong in going their own ways regardless of conventions. Men had more important things to worry about than manners, namely money and politics. Women, however, were scolded for talking too much, too loud, and about too little. They had a great deal to say; they read a great deal, but what they said was of little consequence. They were thoughtless of the convenience of others, and their manners, especially in public and especially toward men, were considered appalling, not only by the many foreign visitors who wrote accounts of America in the last century, but by the writers of manners books as well. Again and again travelers' accounts of America describe with acrimony how women accepted all sorts of courtesies from men whom they ignored entirely, taking their seats in carriages without so much as a nod of acknowledgment. "American ladies occupy, from mere courtesy," wrote one uneasy visitor, "a rank in society which is not only opposed to that which they hold in private life and in their own families, but which is actually incompatible with the exercise of discretion on the part of gentlemen. 'The ladies must be waited upon;' 'the ladies must be helped. . . .' On every occasion they are treated as poor helpless creatures who rather excite the pity than the admiration of men. . . ." The docile lady at home turned into a tigress in public, and though she was scolded for such behavior by women who wrote books on manners, she seemed determined not to learn. Not even the satirical approach seemed to do any good, though Mrs. Parton tried it:

When you enter a crowded lecture room, and a gentleman rises politely, —as American gentlemen always do,—and offers to give up his seat,— which he came an hour ago to secure for himself,—take it, as a matter of course; and don't trouble to thank him, even with a nod of your head. As to feeling uneasy about accepting it, that is ridiculous! because, if he doesn't fancy standing during the service, he is at liberty to go home; it is a free country.

It is difficult for us today to understand the conflict imposed by the idea of "gentility." On the one hand it was regarded as a most desirable goal and attainment by writers on manners because it was, at its best, the mark of "good breeding." On the other hand it was the extravagant forms that gentility took, the over-ladylikeness, the affectations, the snobbery, and the fashions that threatened woman's education and health against which writers on manners inveighed. In many respects gentility went hand in hand with prudery, which was not thought of as prudery at all but as delicacy. Nothing was regarded with greater disapprobation in a woman than indelicate behavior, and the lengths to which delicacy went were no better demonstrated than by the polite attitude toward childbirth. While marriages and deaths were reported in the newspapers, the births of children were not. "No lady allows herself to be seen publicly while she is visibly enceinte," wrote Thomas Grafton in his *Civilized America* in 1859. "A rigid confinement to her house, and even to her chamber is observed for a considerable time preceding her confinement. . . . It has frequently happened to me to miss ladies from . . . parties . . . and on enquiring . . . be told that they were 'in the country' or 'visiting' and on meeting them, in probably a year or more, to find them [with a new child]." It was indelicate for a daughter to mention her pregnancy to her mother, though they might well sit together and sew on baby clothes, which they then stored away without the slightest mention of what they were doing.

Where delicacy was such a delicate matter it is not surprising to find a writer like Miss Leslie inveighing against ungenteel language in her *Behavior Book*. "When a load of wood or coal is put down at your door," she counseled, "say not that it is dumped." Like the words *slump* and *slumped*, dump had "too coarse a sound to be used by a lady." She also cautioned against the word *muss*, as "when a young lady says 'her scarf is mussed.'" She advised that the "English synonym 'mess' has a rather better sound," that one should never say "snooze" for "nap" or that a "man in faded clothes" looked "seedy." "Even if you are a provincial New Yorker," she said, "give up calling the doorstep or porch by the ancient Dutch name of 'stoop,' (stoep), and do not talk of going out on the stoop." *Stoop* like *dump* sounded ungenteel to Miss Leslie. They were signs of ill-breeding.

Miss Sedgwick in a chapter on manners in *Means and Ends* (1839) lists the signs of ill-breeding, and the first that she mentions is "illiterate and vulgar language," but there were others that she thought just as important: ". . . for young persons not to offer their seats to their parents or to other persons older than themselves"; ". . . to eat too fast, to take up your food dripping with gravy, to stuff your mouth full . . ."; ". . . to walk heavily, to slam doors, to talk in a loud tone, and to shout in laughing, especially in the streets." Her list is a long one, of which these examples are only a few. Elsewhere in the same book Miss Sedgwick said what in essence all of the manners books of the Age of Jackson were driving at: "I have never seen better models of manners, (the essentials of manner, 'spontaneous modesty, self-denial, and respect for others,') than in the home of a New England farmer, where the parents, respected and self-respecting, were fountains of kindness to their household; where the children blended in their manners to their parents filial reverence with social equality; where the strong bond of love between brothers and sisters was manifest in reciprocal devotion graced with courtesy, and where the guest was received with a manner that no code nor instructor could have produced, because it expressed conscious dignity, independence, and pains-taking benevolence."

This was the ideal of republican (or as we now say, democratic) manners. It was in this code that de Tocqueville saw hope for the manners of democracy, and it was this attitude that lay behind the manners books of Alcott and Mrs. Sigourney and Mrs. Farrar, and that permeated the chapters on manners in Miss Beecher's books. As the century progressed, however, manners books became more strictly books of etiquette. The intricacies of teas and receptions, of balls and "kettle-drums" and calls, of giving dinner parties, and especially of dropping cards became so elaborate that almost nobody could steer a course through them without a pilot.

One gets a hint of the complexities of entertaining from such statements as this one from a book called *Sensible Etiquette* published in 1878: "A Washington authority says, 'Do not be persuaded to exceed ten courses [at dinner].' This is good advice." And from this: "The custom of passing two kinds of soup, and two kinds of fish, greatly retards the speedy serving of the dinner when the number of guests is large." Etiquette books devoted entire chapters to the technique of using calling cards and the proper forms for invitations, in much the same way that books of etiquette today do. They were filled with advice about what wine to serve with what food, about when one should and shouldn't take off one's gloves in the dining room, and a thousand other details of delicate behavior. Now that the country was grown up, men were no longer let off as easily as they had been. In a book called *A Manual of Etiquette* written in 1868 by a woman who called herself "Daisy Eyebright," the author fires this opening salvo: "Men often speak of good manners as *an accomplishment*. I speak of them as *a duty*. . . . There are a great many men who feel that good manners are effeminate. They have a feeling that rude bluntness is a great deal more manly than good manners. It is a great deal more beastly." And then she rings the familiar moral changes on her theme: "Not only is the violation of good manners inexcusable on ordinary grounds, but it is sinful. . . . Every man is bound to observe the laws of politeness. It is the expression of good-will and kindness. . . . It is a religious duty, and should be part of religious training."

It is very nearly impossible to say how many books of etiquette have been published in the last century and a half. I have a shelf of about seventy of them and Arthur Schlesinger, Sr., lists a great many more in his delightful study of manners books, *Learning How to Behave*. They were produced as premiums by soap companies and given away free by soft-drink bottlers. They appeared bound in paper for a quarter and as parts of sets of books in which one could find little volumes on culture, morality, parlor games, and etiquette all put up neatly in a box. They were given away like Christmas calendars by rural grocery stores. Many of the slim paper-bound ones stole whole chapters without permission or acknowledgment from more sturdy hard-bound ones that had titles such as *The Charm of Fine*

Manners, The Gentle Art of Pleasing, and *The Complete Bachelor.* There were textbooks for school use such as *Lessons on Manners* that included blackboard exercises. In addition to manners books, there were a great many manuals on how to write letters, which were, in essence, books of epistolary etiquette, far more important then than in the later days of the telephone. (To invite a friend for dinner by telephone was, indeed, considered improper for years after the telephone was in common use. Etiquette acknowledged no substitute for the handwritten note or the engraved invitation.) There were also fat tomes like Thomas E. Hill's *Manual of Social and Business Forms* that began to appear in the 1870's; they were an education in themselves and a reference library to boot. The title page of one of them, published in 1881 in Boston, offers the reader this rich menu:

> Gaskells' Compendium of Forms, Educational, Social, Legal and Commercial, embracing a complete course in penmanship and bookkeeping, and aid to English composition, together with the laws and by-laws of social etiquette and business law and commercial forms, a manual of agriculture, mechanics and mining, and a complete guide to parliamentary practice, the whole forming a complete encyclopaedia of reference, elegantly illustrated.

Another devotes somewhat more of its nearly seven hundred pages to manners:

> Golden Manual or the Royal Road to Success, showing what to do and how to do it, containing the rules of etiquette for all occasions; how to speak and write the English language correctly; etiquette of conversation; correspondence; dress and polite society; weddings; parties; receptions; calls; etc. Embracing courtship, marriage and domestic life; words of wisdom for young people; directions for the right choice of husband or wife; home occupations; games and amusements, with full directions for athletic exercises, the cultivation of the mind and body. . . . Etc. etc.

This volume is "superbly illustrated" with engravings such as "School of the Vestal Virgins" and portraits of famous men and women with comments about what sorts of husbands and wives they were. It also contains a chapter on "House Building, or How to Obtain a Home," illustrated with drawings of façades and floor plans, and the houses, though modest, are up-to-date. They ranged in price from $1,000 to $2,800 to build.

It is not easy to draw a sharp line between the nineteenth-century fashion in manners books and the kinds of books of etiquette which sell so well in our time. In some respects Emily Post owed a good deal to Mrs. M. E. W. Sherwood, Robert Sherwood's grandmother, who wrote a book called *Manners and Social Usages,* which was first published in 1884. "There is no country," Mrs. Sherwood wrote in her preface, "where there are so many people asking what is 'proper to do,' or indeed where there are so many anxious to do the proper thing, as in the vast conglomerate which we call the United States of America. The newness of our country is perpetually renewed by the sudden making of fortunes, and by the absence of a hereditary reigning class. There is no aristocracy here which has the right and title to set the fashions. . . . If we are to live together in unity we must make society a pleasant thing, we must obey certain formal rules, and these rules must conform to the fashion of the period."

Mrs. Sherwood was quite confident that her advice was the best possible compilation of American and European ways of doing the correct thing. She knew "everybody who was anybody" on both sides of the Atlantic, and she was a snob of a sort that America, in the days when it was fashionable for young American women to marry titled Europeans, produced in a highly distilled version.

Emily Post's *Etiquette: The Blue Book of Social Usage* appeared in the summer of 1922 and was an immediate and spectacular success. Mrs. Post was, to use an expression that was common in her day but which is rarely heard now, "to the manner born." Her father was a prominent architect and she spent her summers in Tuxedo Park and Bar Harbor, was educated in private schools, and married the scion of a fashionable Long Island family. Like Miss Leslie and Mrs. Sigourney and Miss Sedgwick, she was a writer of fiction (her first book, *Flight of a Moth,* was published in 1904), and like those earlier writers on manners she had humor and good sense. The year that *Etiquette* was published it led the nonfiction list of best sellers, and Mrs. Post's name became, to all intents and purposes, the name for her book: "Look it up in Emily Post." There was nothing stuffy about either Mrs. Post's attitude or her prose style, but she spoke with authority. She was quite aware that attitudes toward such prickly matters as chaperonage were changing and that decorum was not the rigid thing it once had been, and she put her emphasis, in discussing such matters, on the good sense of her readers. Following the rules of etiquette was to

Mrs. Post no substitute for behaving with dignity, and if young ladies got into trouble because they were improperly chaperoned it usually had nothing to do with violating established customs but with violating their own sense of what was right. "Ethically," Mrs. Post wrote, "the only chaperon is the young girl's own sense of dignity and pride; she who has the right attributes of character needs no chaperon—ever. If she is wanting in decency and proper pride, not even Argus could watch over her. But apart from ethics, there are the conventions to think of and the conventions of propriety demand that every young woman must be protected by a chaperon, because otherwise she will be misjudged."

Mrs. Post's attitude toward chaperons changed and mellowed as customs changed, and the chaperon disappeared from the last editions of her book. She was, of course, in favor of observing the amenities; to do so made it so much easier for everyone, and etiquette was designed, she believed, to make life pleasanter, not more difficult. "Etiquette," she said, "is the science of living. It embraces everything. It is the code of sportsmanship and of honor. It is ethics." Her basic rule of etiquette was to make the other person comfortable. She was impatient with pretentiousness; she disliked hostesses who served themselves first, and she could not abide dirty silver, but she was not prissy. Her *Etiquette* is filled with anecdote and situations and she gave her characters names such as Mrs. Worldly, Mrs. Stranger, Mrs. Younger, Mrs. Kindheart, Mrs. Oldname, and Mrs. Toplofty. Up to the time of Mrs. Post's death in 1960 her book had gone through eighty-nine printings and almost constant revisions. It had sold somewhat over a million copies. She also wrote a column on manners that was syndicated in two hundred newspapers, and in 1946 she established the Emily Post Institute, for the purpose, according to her family, "of continuing the tradition of gracious living by making available through its publications the most current information on correct social usage."

Emily Post's name is still synonymous with what is socially correct. Once when she was puzzled by a complicated table setting, she went to Tiffany's for advice. The clerk reached under the counter and came up with Mrs. Post's book to find the answer. On another occasion she found herself in a taxi with a stranger (it was during the Second World War, when sharing a cab in New York was not uncommon), and when the other woman was about to get out and discovered that she only had a dime and a five-dollar bill, she said, "I wonder what Emily Post would do in a situation like this."

"She would do exactly what I shall do," said Mrs. Post, "it is my taxi and I shall pay for it."

"Do you really think so?" the woman asked.

"Yes," said Mrs. Post, "I do."

Mrs. Post's book has been superseded by Amy Vanderbilt's *Complete Book of Etiquette, a Guide to Gracious Living*, which was first published in 1952 and has long since passed the million mark in sales and is available in a shortened edition as well as in its seven hundred pages of minute details about almost every sort of social situation. It owes a great deal to Mrs. Post, of course, in both detail and in tone of voice, but it is far more encyclopedic. Its opening sentence is: "Who needs a book of etiquette?" and the answer is "Everyone does."

"It is easy to deride the copying of rules of politeness by those who had nothing to do with setting them," wrote Arthur Schlesinger, Sr., in the conclusion of *Learning How to Behave*, "but in America the willingness to imitate has in the long run had the effect of lessening class distinctions." It has also, of course, met in some degree the demands of a highly mobile society in which ladders have played and continue to play such an important part. Americans are always climbing ladders—social ladders, business ladders, academic ladders, ladders of success; and it has mattered to them, for good reasons and bad ones, that they should behave according to the customs of the rungs that they have achieved. They have wanted to avoid embarrassment, both their own and that of the people into whose circle they have moved. During the Second World War, for example, when a great many young women found themselves suddenly the wives of "officers and gentlemen," books on how to be a navy wife or an army wife, and all that implied about how to entertain the colonel or the commander, whom to call by what title, and when and when not to speak up, sold handsomely, and Emily Post's sales took a sudden leap. Now that corporations look twice at the wives of promising young executives before moving them up the ladder, a new market for manners books has been created. Furthermore no one can remember everything that one has to do to plan a wedding, not even a caterer, and there are millions of people who believe that it is better to follow a set of rules than to offend some aged aunt or to give a snobbish acquaintance a chance to raise an eyebrow.

The total effect of books of manners on the behavior of Americans, compared with the effect of our quarrels with the intransigence of the wilderness, our inability to settle down and establish homesteads of enduring stability, our continually renewed belief in the rags-to-riches phenomenon, and our abiding sense of the equality of man, has been slight. As a reflection of our struggle to become domesticated, books of etiquette, however, bear some relation to the truth. They are a mirror—not the morning mirror in which one sees oneself as one is, but the evening mirror in which one sees oneself got up, turned out, and hopefully ready to face the agreeable, promising, and almost but not quite forbidden world of pleasure and sophistication.

BUILDING BY THE BOOK

The most durable evidence of the family reformers of the Age of Jackson and the decades preceding the Civil War is, of course, the handiwork of architects and builders. The household books and manners manuals are now lost or hidden away in libraries, but a good many of the houses in which they were first read are still filled with the sounds of children and the smells of cooking. They are there for anyone who is interested in looking at them, as a reminder of the continuing search for the good life. We are, to be sure, careless about preserving them once their usefulness has diminished to the point where they are too expensive to maintain, and we tear them down if they happen to be in the way of a thoroughfare or a redevelopment project or a supermarket. But a great many of them have survived in spite of this, not out of sentiment or because of any historical conscience (though a few famous houses have been preserved for such reasons), but because they continue to be livable.

The profession of architecture was almost unknown to most Americans in the 1830's. A Frenchman trained in the profession, James Gallier, arrived in New York in the spring of 1832 and was dismayed to discover that "the majority of people could with difficulty be made to understand what was meant by a professional architect." Carpenters and bricklayers, he found, called themselves architects, and it was to them that gentlemen who wanted houses went for their designs. Since precisely the right degree of gentility and opulence meant more than originality or convenience to these newly prosperous gentlemen, they usually looked about them until they found houses that they thought suitable to their social aspirations. They then "bargained with a builder to erect for them such another, or alterations upon the mode that they might point out." Having agreed more or less on what was wanted, the French architect wrote, "the builder hired some poor draughtsman . . . to make plans, paying him a mere trifle for his services." In some cases (Gallier could scarcely believe it) "proprietors built without having any regular plan" at all.

Happily the carpenter-builders were frequently men of judgment and sensibility, and they had the wit to make generous use of the "house manuals," which were, to all intents and purposes, the cookbooks of their trade. In elaborately illustrated volumes like Asher Benjamin's *The Practical House Carpenter* and Minard Lafever's *Beauties of Modern Architecture,* and in a quantity of other manuals which were also avidly read by their clients, they could find every detail of what was needed to produce a house in the most stylish manner. They could find pilasters, full Greek cornices, balustrades, pillars, indeed everything that they could want in constructing the internal and external ornaments that so gladdened republican hearts.

In the 1840's a new kind of house manual began to appear. It was not the sort of carpenter's handbook that was so widely used in the early part of the century, but a book of pictures and plans of houses, from the simplest cottages to rich villas, accompanied by homilies on the importance of beauty, location, sound planning, the use of proper (and appropriate) materials, and suitable colors. Andrew Jackson Downing, the son of a nurseryman in Newburgh, New York, who became one of the most influential tastemakers of the last century, was largely responsible for the new kind of manual. He was the author of a number of books on horticulture (which won for him when he was still in his thirties an international reputation) and on the building and style of houses, and he was the editor of *The Horticulturist.* In 1847 he edited an edition of an English book, *Hints to Young Architects* by George Wightwick, and appended an extensive chapter of his own filled with practical information such as "notes and hints to persons about building in the country." From then on house-plan books, mostly written by architects, appeared in profusion with such titles as *Modern House Builder from the Cottage to the Log Cabin to the Mansion* (1857), *The American Cottage Builder, a series of designs, plans, and specifications from $200 to $20,000 for homes for the people* (1854), and *The Economic Cottage Builder, or Cottages* *for Men of Small Means* (1856). There were dozens of them, some appealing to gaudy tastes, some, like Downing's *The Architecture of Country Houses* (1850), counseling moderation, restraint, and economy. There was no reason, he believed, why the mechanic and the farmer should not live in houses as tastefully designed as those of the rich landowner and the banker. It was not money that made the difference between the authentic and the tawdry; it was a sense of the appropriate and a regard for beauty.

"No one," wrote Downing in his magazine, "can accuse the Americans with apathy or want of interest in architecture, at the present moment. Within ten years past, the attention of great numbers has been turned to the improvement and embellishment of public and private edifices; many foreign architects have settled in the Union; numerous works—especially upon domestic architecture—have been issued from the press, and the whole community, in town and country, seem at the present moment to be afflicted with the building mania." That was not to say that all was well. He added: ". . . we are in the midst of what might be called the experimental stage of architectural taste. With the passion for novelty, and the feeling of independence that belong to this country, our people seem determined to *try everything*."

Downing's principles and preachments were echoed again and again in house manuals by other architect-writers. His protégé, Calvert Vaux, whom he had brought here from England as his assistant and who later became one of the architects of Central Park in New York, wrote *Villas and Cottages* (1857) and produced articles on the house for *Harper's Magazine*. There were Gervase Wheeler's *Rural Homes* and George Woodward's *Suburban and Country Homes* (1873) and dozens of others. The plans for many of the houses in such books were for sale. The usual price for a design that was "selected from the artist's portfolio" in the 1840's was $25. If, however, one wanted a special design, one could get it "without superintendence or working drawings" at a somewhat higher price. A design for a cottage that cost $1,000 to build could be had for $50, for a $10,000 house for $100, and for a $20,000 mansion for $150. A design for a simple farmhouse fetched $30 and for "a church of moderate size" $100. If all one wanted was a nice design for the "front elevation only of a house," it cost a mere $15.

Most house manuals were not intended as the final word on what a family should build and live in. In *Villas and Cottages* Vaux explained what many of the house-manual writers had in mind: "The accompanying designs . . . are not brought before the public as model designs, to lessen the necessity for the exercise of individual taste, but as far as possible, to increase its activity. Such books are needed as stepping-stones; for no general popular progress can be made in any art without ample and cheap opportunities for comparison and criticism. . . ."

But there were moral reasons as well as aesthetic ones. "Were our country residences more generally decked with simplicity and taste," wrote John Bullock in *The American Cottage Builder* (1854), "we imagine that the number of our young men who wander from the patrimonial estate, and precipitate themselves into the dissipated and vitiated follies of a city life, could be very materially lessened." And O. S. Fowler, who believed everyone should live in an octagonal house and wrote a little book called *A Home for All* to prove it, moved directly into the matter of domestic bliss and wrote: "How much fretfulness and ill temper, as well as exhaustion and sickness, an unhandy house occasions. Nor does the evil end here. It often, generally, by perpetually irritating others, sours the temper of their children, even *before birth,* thus rendering the whole family bad-dispositioned *by nature,* whereas a convenient one would have rendered them constitutionally amiable and good."

The kinds of houses that the writers of books on domestic architecture have recommended as the most suitable and most modern have, of course, changed continually in style since the time of Downing and his immediate followers; the tone of voice of the authors, however, has changed hardly at all. They have exhorted their readers to be sensible, to avoid both financial and artistic extravagance, to give thought to the future as well as to the present, to respect the demands of beauty as well as of practicality, and above all to acknowledge the skill and taste of architects. Many of the books have incorporated the latest information on the mechanisms of the house, on the practical problems of plumbing and ventilation and heating, as well as the latest tastes in window seats and porte-cocheres and hallways. There have been books on *The Healthful House, The Convenient House, The House in Good Taste, The House Beautiful, The Livable House, The House of Individuality,* and in recent years *The Modern House in America* and *Tomorrow's House.*

Through such books runs a somewhat defensive and proud theme. The relationship between the architect and the client seems to have been in continual need of shoring up, and the authors of books on the house have long felt impelled to convince their prospective clients that they have something to offer that the builder does not. They have emphasized the economy of employing an architect who could get the client more for his money (more convenience, more beauty, better construction) than the contractor-builder could. It was, they said, the business of the architect not only to protect his client's interests but to anticipate them. As an expert in the design of houses the architect knew better than his client what the client really wanted and, furthermore, knew how to get it at the most reasonable cost and with the best aesthetic effect. The architect was aware that his position and his calling were anomalous ones—he was the embodiment of practicality and of artistic sensibility at one and the same time, a combination that the nineteenth-century American had little reason to believe existed at all. The architect's defensiveness, which has by no means entirely disappeared in our own day, was strongest in the middle of the last century, when he was endeavoring to establish himself as a professional as dignified and as essential to the community as the physician or the lawyer. It was an uphill fight.

It was the semisophisticated and the pretentious who made the most difficult clients for the architect. "The two greatest trials of the architect of taste," Downing wrote in his *Rural Essays* in 1851, "are to be found in that class of travelled smatterers in *virtu,* who have picked up here and there, in the tour from Liverpool to Rome, certain ill-assorted notions of art, which they will combine in one sublime whole, in the shape of their own domicile; and that larger class, who ambitiously imitate in a small cottage, all that belongs to palaces, castles, and buildings of princely dimensions." The architect's conviction that he knew better than his client what was good for him gave him a reputation for arrogance which clients took especial delight in puncturing. If anything went wrong with a house, if the roof leaked or the flue failed to draw, or if the spring thaw flooded the cellar, it was "that damn aesthete" who was to blame. A contractor-builder was less vulnerable because his pretentions were less lofty.

"No other artist comes into such direct personal contact with his patrons," wrote Mrs. Schuyler Van Rensselaer in an article called "Architecture as a Profession" in the *Chautauqua Magazine* in 1887. "None other has such a need to understand what *they* want, as well as what he wants himself. No other is so dependent for a chance to do his best, upon his powers to influence their judgment, to control their wishes, to fall in with and yet guide and elevate their tastes. *Tact*—which means a keen insight into other minds and a perfect control of one's own mind and tongue—is desirable in every relationship of life, but absolutely essential if one would succeed in architecture."

But tact has not been enough to protect the architect from the assault of clients or from the wariness that keeps potential clients away from him. He is blamed not merely for his seeming arrogance and concern with aesthetic values; he is accused of extravagance, of "running up the costs" for the sake of fussy (to the client) details, and of refusing to cut corners where doing so would reduce his building to something lower than his professional standards allow. As Robert Woods Kennedy explains in his admirable book *The House* (1953), the architect is expected to be three men at once—artist, structural expert, and businessman. An architect equally proficient at all three of these functions, he suggests, is likely to be not distinguished in any one of them, so that the work he produces is mediocre but unobjectionable, a quality that most clients unfortunately find satisfactory. Mr. Kennedy is of the persuasion, as many talented architects who have tried to explain their function to the public are, that "it is the norm rather than the exception among artists to feel that the world misunderstands them." He does not insist, however, as would seem to be the logical conclusion to this statement, that talented architects who are artists are likely to get lost in the commercial struggle. The impression that the books on domestic architecture give the layman is that the architect is a romanticist at the drawing board and a realist in the drawing room, a dreamer with his pencil and a pragmatist with his client. It is his function to conjure up the ideal setting for the good life, state it in both artistic and practical terms, and convince his client that it is, indeed, the way he wishes to live.

Like the writer on the household and the author of books on manners, the architect has been a reformer concerned with improving the domestic happiness and civilized behavior and surroundings of his clients. One cannot but feel, in looking back at the books that architects have produced, that their contributions to creature comfort have been greater than their contributions to aesthetic delight. The house books for the most part have not been written by architects who have contributed to aesthetic advances; they have been the products of popularizers of styles that were defined by someone else. In the process of inviting the public to accept new ideas about architecture, they have watered the ideas down with clichés until the original intention of their creators has been scarcely recognizable. If much has been lost aesthetically in this process, much has been gained in other respects. Through house manuals and through magazines and newspaper columns devoted to the evolution of the house, many ideas of comfort and convenience have found their way into houses that by any standards of aesthetics are abominable.

The fact is that an architect, good or bad, is a luxury that only a very small percentage of families can afford or ever have been able to afford in America. Fewer than 12 percent of the houses built today are designed by architects for specific families, and while an architect can make a little money on a $100,000 house, he loses money on a $25,000 one. For all their dismay at the kinds of houses that contractor-builders erect in such large numbers, architects would rather design hotels and office buildings and supermarkets than houses for clients who can afford only modest dwellings. As a result, the only access that most Americans have to the ideas of architects is through the so-called shelter magazines (*House Beautiful, Better Homes and Gardens,* and the like), through the homes sections of magazines like *Look, McCall's,* and the *Ladies' Home Journal,* and through the numerous picture and plan books of houses that are still published every year. There is essentially little difference between the way architectural ideas spread today and the way they were transmitted in the days of Downing and *Godey's Lady's Book.*

If Miss Beecher, Mr. Downing, and Mrs. Farrar were to meet today to discuss what has happened to the household, the architecture, and the manners of America since they undertook to advise about them in the 1840's, each would find much to praise and much to regret.

Miss Beecher would look upon the modern kitchen and take some satisfaction at how closely in its efficient planning it resembles the kitchen she designed for the book she wrote with her sister Harriet, *The American Woman's Home.* She would be pleased to see girls and women getting so much vigorous outdoor exercise, and she would be relieved that their clothes were a great deal more sensible than in the days of stays and the fourteen-inch waist. She might, on the other hand, be dismayed at the way women have invaded the world she believed properly belonged to men, that they dabbled in politics, usually on the fringes or doing menial work, and deserted their homes to take jobs that in many cases they did not need. She would be amused to find the storage wall that she conceived for her "Christian Home" now commonly in use as a partition, though she might wonder why it was not movable, as she designed it to be.

Mr. Downing would probably not think ill of the simplicity of many of the ranch houses that are being built, but he would despair at the manner in which the landscape has been despoiled by contractor-builders who seem to have learned almost nothing in one hundred and twenty-five years. He would, I think, enjoy the modern house which incorporates the outdoors in its plan, for he loved trees and shrubs and considered them an essential part of a dwelling. He would like the "honesty" of much modern design and the use of new materials. He would, on the other hand, regret that architects have not managed in a century and a quarter to gain the confidence of most Americans but are still looked upon as a rich man's luxury.

Mrs. Farrar would be relieved that "gentility" was no longer such a preoccupation with women, but she would suspect that "gracious living" as a concept was not much of an improvement. She did not like pretension in any form. She would think that the manner in which children treat their parents has, if anything, deteriorated, but she might be pleased that the treatment of domestics has taken a turn for the better mainly because there are fewer of them and therefore those who have them go to more trouble to treat them like human beings. She would be surprised to discover that no one eats with his knife any more. She had seen nothing wrong with it, but the three- and four-tined fork was scarce in her day, and peas slipped through a two-tined fork.

On one aspect of the American household Miss Beecher, Mr. Downing, and Mrs. Farrar would, I believe, be as one in their surprise if not in their approval. No one in the early part of the last century could have guessed the gyrations through which the American house would evolve from a temple into a box, the extravagances through which it would pass, or the heights and depths (both physical and aesthetic) that it would achieve. Nor could they have guessed what the accumulation of these flights of fantasy and achievements of technology would do to the looks and character of the American landscape.

MAY-DAY IN THE CITY.

America on the Move

The streets of New York used to be in an uproar every May (moving) Day. The scene above is 1859, but with different conveyances and costumes it might have been 1939. The houses on the train below were for railroad construction gangs in the 1870's. Today the trailer is the home of such nomads, who now take their families with them.

Home Is Where You Find It

Foreign visitors a century ago were astonished to see houses being moved by oxen. Now house moving is a big industry and the secondhand house dealer collects used houses in lots like "car lots." The houses above are being moved to such a lot in California. The trailer camp below in Sandusky, Ohio, in the 1940's is a twentieth-century version of a gathering of covered wagons on the plains in the 1840's.

POLITICAL BARBECUE OF 1840.

Home on the Frontier

Skillful axmen could build a log cabin in a few hours that would last for years. Sod houses (below) took longer and lasted a few years at best—even if the horses stayed off the roof! The log cabin (left) is the only American architecture that ever did anyone a political favor.

The Redoubtable Domesticator

Catharine Beecher believed that women should be womanly and know how to manage women's affairs. Her most famous book on how to do practically everything in the household was written with her more famous sister, the author of *Uncle Tom's Cabin,* and published in 1869. Her ingenuity is demonstrated by her invention, the movable storage wall (lower left) and the deceptively simple plan (with a central "utilities unit") for a country house. She called it "The Christian House."

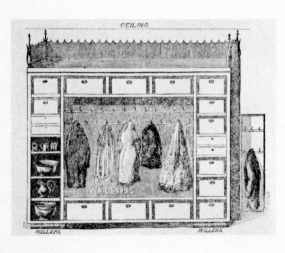

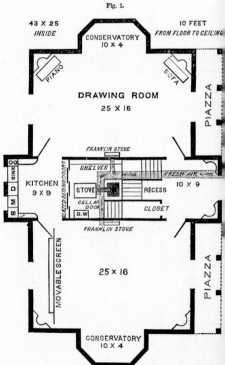

Fig. 1.

THE DOMESTIC SCIENCE LABORATORY—INSTRUCTION IN LAUNDRY-WORK.

How to Do It

Schools to teach young women how to be good housewives resulted from Miss Beecher's long crusade. Above, laundry is being taught as a "science" in 1890. Manners, never very scientific, have filled hundreds of different etiquette books in the last century and a half. The genteel illustration below is from *Correct Social Usage*, 1906.

HOW A MAN CALLS

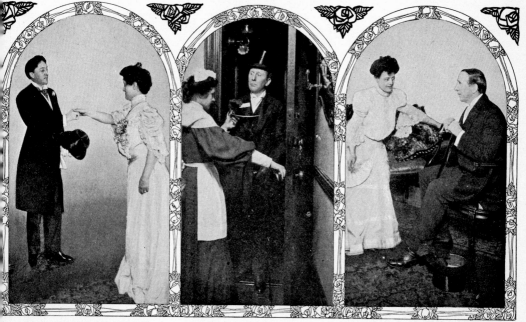

THE CORRECT HANDSHAKE   PRESENTING CARDS   DISPOSITION OF HAT, GLOVES, ETC

Mind Your Manners

Hill's Manual of Social and Business Forms was firm about the difference between bad and good table manners in 1882, as the pictures (left and below) indicate. It is hard to think of a gaucherie not shown in one or an attitude of gentility in the other.

Push-button Bridget

A cartoonist in *Puck* in the 1890's had the right idea about mechanized housecleaning, but he should have had the lady of the house—not the maid—pushing the buttons.

The Tyranny of Service

America has always had a servant problem. *Harper's Bazar* in 1887 printed the cartoon above to show the transition of an immigrant girl from "perfect treasure" to uppity "French cook" in six months. Below are the servants of the Stevens family of Hoboken, N. J., in 1895. They were professionals who coped with a forty-six-room mansion.

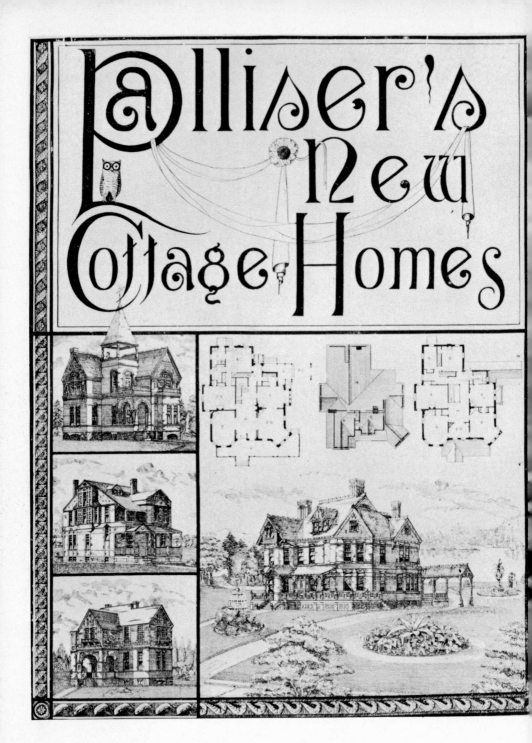

You Name It, We Design It

Many thousands of American families have found their dream houses in plan books like this one, published by a firm of architects, Palliser, Palliser & Co., in 1887. Why bother with an architect when you could order complete plans and specifications for five or ten dollars?

CHAPTER VI

The Hatrack

Any place I hang my hat is home sweet home
to me.
                              An American Saying

If the American is characteristically restless about where he hangs
his hat and unwilling or unable to put down roots deep enough to
satisfy the believers in family tradition, he has been equally fickle
about what sort of house he has wanted to live in. No sooner has he
made up his mind what the proper house should be than it has been
suggested to him by architects, and other shepherds of sense and
sensibility for the home, that he was quite wrong. As a believer in
progress both material and cultural he has hesitated to lag behind the
advice that was given him. So he has been partly the victim and partly
the purveyor of the notion that to make up one's mind about the dimensions and accouterments of the good life is "bad for business," that
change and growth are synonymous, and that as a consumer it is part
of his duty not to know his own mind. He has not had this idea put
over on him; he invented it. He has seen it make the economy of his
country grow; he has applauded the conveniences and creature comforts that it has added to his home, and for the most part he has looked
the other way when it has been suggested to him that inability to make
up his mind about what was important to him might, in the along run,
make life unlivable. But the wasting of natural resources is always
somebody else's problem to worry about; "they" (whoever they are)
will take care of that. His problem is to get the most out of life and,
for our purposes, the most out of his house. He has been no better able
to decide what that house should be than where, if anywhere, he
wanted to settle down in it.

If you were to ask almost anyone, even a child, to make a picture of a typical American house, the chances are that he would draw a more or less square, two-story house, with a front door in the center flanked by a couple of windows on either side, and with a steeply pitched roof and a chimney at one end, or possibly with one in the middle. He would, in other words, draw something like a Cape Cod cottage or a New England "salt box." He would not be likely to draw a Greek Revival house with columns, or a Gothic cottage, or a Tuscan villa, or a house with a mansard roof, or a "Queen Anne" house with a wide porch, a corner tower, and second-floor balconies, or a little château, or a half-timbered cottage, or a Spanish mission house, or a bungalow, or a flat-roofed "modern," or even a ranch house. He would not draw a brownstone city house or a Renaissance palace or a twenty-story brick box pierced with windows and hung with balconies. He would, in other words, skip the last hundred and fifty years of American houses and go back to a simple concept of the house that remains the standard idea, if not ideal, of family shelter. But the American house is not this (though we have moments of reviving it, as we did in the 1920's and again briefly after the Second World War before the ranch house took command); it is a confusion of styles, of romantic notions, of avenues of escape, and of hopes for utopia.

Many whose hearts are in the past believe that architecturally we have regressed from the sublime (the Greek Revival) to the ridiculous (whatever version of the current modern house they happen to dislike most). The truth of the matter is that by any standards of common sense we have picked our way from one kind of ridiculous to another, with occasional sublime examples, usually just far enough off the main road so that few people were aware of them. For all the pragmatism which the American likes to think guides his attitude toward life, common sense has never been the controlling factor in the kind of homes in which he has wanted to live. When driven to find shelter in the forest or on the prairie, he was sensible enough (the log cabin and the sod house were the essence of practicality considering their surroundings and the tools and materials at hand), but whenever reasons beyond those of mere shelter have been concerned, the guiding spirit has been romantic, not pragmatic, and the sensible has again and again been sacrificed to the sentimental, the sensual, or the sensational.

Americans have steadfastly believed that the house that is merely sensible is barely fit to live in. Shelter is the minimum function of the house, and comfort is only a step above shelter. One can, after all, be comfortable in a hayloft. The minimum requirement of the American home is, and has been for a long time, luxury, or at least the illusion of luxury, which is comfort plus the effect of extravagance. It has been the pursuit of luxury that has guided the curious evolution of the American house from the time of the Greek Revival, so much in vogue when Mrs. Trollope and Dickens were here, through a cavalcade of styles to our age of the glass box, the ranch house, and the pink-and-baby-blue house trailer tinseled with chromium.

By a curious paradox we have achieved luxury more often than not at the sacrifice of comfort. We have put up with the inconveniences of steep narrow staircases in order to have elegant, wide, and high-ceilinged entrance halls. For the sake of having not just one parlor but two in our city houses we have put the kitchen in the basement and the servants' rooms under the eaves in the attic. We have, in other words, put our concepts of proper manners, our regard for social forms, and our symbols of gentility ahead of our convenience, and we have bent the twig of the house to the winds of fashion. Our houses in many cases have been attempts to create illusions, Never-Never Lands a long way from hustle and busyness, from the market place and the factory, illusions of being above and beyond all that, illusions of culture and history and refined sensibilities. We have built houses with a storybook unreality about them. We have lived in replicas of Greek temples, in facsimiles of medieval gate houses, in scaled-down copies of Elizabethan country houses, and villas that overlooked the Florentine landscape, in little Louvres and little Versailles and little wooden echoes of Rhine castles. We have mistaken fanciness for tastefulness and tastefulness for culture, and we have sought to create the illusion of a past and a history where we had none. We have tried to live in two worlds at the same time. On the one hand it has been the world that a German visitor to America in the 1830's, Francis Grund, observed: "It is as if all America were but one gigantic workshop, over the entrance of which there is a blazing inscription, '*No admission here except on business.*'" On the other it is the world of parlors smelling of pomander and potpourri, of twelve-course dinners, of liveried servants and formal calls, of elaborate devices for converting the pleasures of leisure into social amenities of crushing boredom. The wonder is that so many American houses, in spite of the pigheaded devotion to gentility that for so many years dictated so many of their aspects, were such pleasant places in which to live. In some respects their nonsense was the most sensible thing about them.

By comparison with the nineteenth-century house and the house of the first three or four decades of this century, the ones that we are building today seem, on the surface, at least, a good deal more practical. They seem to suit our informality, our lack of servants, our heating and cooling gadgets, our precooked meals, our rapid means of transportation, our conventions of hospitality. In other words, they suit our cherished illusions about ourselves, which is probably all that can be expected of any house. But in fact they suit them as well as the houses that Mr. Dickens saw from the train window on his way from Boston to Worcester suited his contemporaries.

THE GREEK REVIVAL

It was in country houses that most Americans in the 1840's were ushered into the world by midwives, sought the satisfactions of displaying their worldly success, and died in springless beds. In those days only about one American out of ten lived in a city. The line between rural America and urban America was far sharper than it became thirty years later, and if it is so blurred as to be indistinguishable in our time, the edges of the cities then divided the population into two distinct classes of people. Good rural folk were shocked by the extravagance and profligacy of city folk, and those who lived within the city's rim laughed condescendingly at the country folk and their unsophisticated manners.

There was, however, no such thing as a typical country house in those days, any more than there is a typical country house today. They varied all the way from the sod-roofed dugouts, with their average life of about six years, to the mansions of the planters on the James River in Virginia, from the log cabins, whose chinking had to be constantly replaced, to sea captain's homes, built with the care of a clipper ship's hull, in coastal New England villages. If there was a typical style for homes in the 1830's and 1840's equivalent to today's ranch house, it was the ubiquitous temple, a sort of domesticated house of the gods, in a style that we now call Greek Revival.

Little Parthenons were everywhere. They dotted the hillsides of New England ("our templed hills") and looked down on the Hudson, the Ohio, and even the Mississippi. They sat cheek by jowl in the newly built towns of upper New York State and nestled among the older brick and clapboard houses of long-established villages in Virginia and Maryland. They came in all sizes, many shapes, and a great variety of degrees of elegance, just as the ranch house does now. White columns, sometimes round and sometimes square, sometimes fluted and sometimes plain, held up pediments on all manner of houses and, of course, on banks and stores and college buildings and hotels. The Greek style was considered universally appropriate. It was equally suitable for the plantation house of the South and for row houses in big cities. It suited the modest farmer on his carefully nurtured acres, the prosperous merchant on his tree-lined village street, and the landed gentleman with his tidily landscaped lawns and carriages drawn by Morgans.

Presumably no kind of architecture should have a more permanent look than a temple, for none is so associated with the concept of enduring values. But there was a look about the temples that Americans built by the thousands between 1820 and 1860 that had a here-today-gone-tomorrow quality. It was this look of unreality that had disconcerted Dickens and Mrs. Trollope, and if such houses have an air of serenity about them today, it is a calm and dignity with which the kindness of time has endowed them; it certainly does not come from the mood in which they were built. They were the product of an age in which everybody seemed to hope that elegant and stylish surroundings would lend some degree of exterior composure to their busy and inelegant drive to make their fortunes and assure their positions in the community.

"I felt becomingly classical," Captain Marryat wrote on a visit to upstate New York, "whilst sitting on the precise birth place of Jupiter [Mount Ida], attended by Pomona, with Troy at my feet, and Mount Olympus in the distance." The Greek War for Independence had set off a "Greek mania" in America; one result was the shower of Greek names that settled on the map of America, and another was the notion that temples made suitable houses for the citizens of a republic. Lord Byron symbolized to a great many Americans the romantic struggle of the Greeks for their freedom. Marryat was surprised to discover, for instance, in the frontier settlement of Sault Sainte Marie, a community of about fifty log cabins, still surrounded by a palisade against unfriendly Indians, two complete editions of Byron's works.

The Greek war was by no means the only impetus that caused the landscape to erupt with columns and pediments, with colonnades and porticoes. Some historians of our architecture call the Greek mania merely a stylistic fad that was essentially a revolt against English taste, a patriotic reaction to casting off the British yoke and against the unpleasantness of 1812. But there are more practical explanations that seem to come closer to the nature of the expansive American temperament. Oliver W. Larkin suggests several in his admirable *Art and Life in America*: one, that builders "worked for patrons who wished a maximum of impressiveness with a minimum of cost"; another, that "what the average builder needed was a vocabulary simple enough to be spoken by the unlearned, flexible enough to take a character from the local dialect, and, above all, translatable into wood"; and, third, that "perhaps the strength of the temple style derived from just this ability to mean one thing to a banker, another to a sugar planter, and still another to a Boston transcendentalist." Asher Benjamin, one of the most influential of the men who wrote manuals on how to build the domestic temple, claimed that it was popular because its details, designed to impress the impressionable, were bold, highly visible, and above all cheap to execute.

Not everyone, of course, lived in a temple, but it is safe to say that almost anyone, at least in the East, who could raise money to build a new house had his heart set on one with columns. In this respect the taste of that time was even more conformist than our taste today; not all of our contemporaries covet a split-level, and even split-level tastes come in styles that cater to split-nostalgias—mixtures of ranch and colonial, of Cape Cod and "functional." But then, as now, a very small portion of the families that could afford to buy or build houses consulted architects.

Carpenter-builders were kept busy fixing up the old and building the new. Sometimes they applied the details that they found in the manuals, like three-dimensional decalcomanias, to already built houses —even log cabins were occasionally sheathed with boards and touched up with Greek details. More often, houses that were essentially nothing more than foursquare wooden boxes pierced with little windows donned columns and entablatures. (They are easy to spot in almost any New England village today.) When a carpenter-builder started from scratch, he would often take any old and familiar plan of a house, adjust it a little to the family and site, and put on a Greek slip-cover, no matter how dismal and damp the two-story columned porch might make the rooms it overshadowed. If, however, he were to catch the prevailing spirit and had a client who wanted to go the whole hog, he would, especially if he worked in the northeastern part of the country, build what was called a "story-and-a-half" house. It was by all odds the most popular design, and while it sacrificed something of common sense to fashionable notions of sensibility, it also offered the family some new comforts and conveniences that it had not enjoyed before.

Farmers and villagers who first saw a story-and-a-half house going up in their community must have thought that the builder had parted with his senses. Compared with the houses that they were used to, it was lopsided. Somehow the front door, which had always belonged in the middle, had got itself off to one end of a tall-columned porch that ran the full width of the house. Furthermore, instead of letting you into a central hall that ran straight through the house with all the ground-floor rooms opening into it, this front door let you into a little side hall out of which a steep, narrow staircase climbed like Jacob's ladder to the second floor. There was a good reason for the side hall. It was a new scheme to avoid the inevitable draftiness of a through hall that whisked cold air into every room in winter and made it necessary to keep the fires in all the grates going at full blast. The ceilings on the first floor were a good deal higher than in the old houses, which made the rooms cooler in summer but harder to heat in winter, and all of the principal parlors, the dining room, and the master's "chambers" were on the first story. (The kitchen might also be there, or it might be in an extension on the rear or, not infrequently, in the basement.) Where there was more than one parlor, the rooms often opened into one another with Ionic columns between them, and in larger and more splendid houses the rooms were ornamented with a Greek entablature, a kind of wide formal molding at the tops of the walls. In the center of the parlor ceilings chandeliers hung like frozen cascades from plaster rosettes.

The story-and-a-half house had annoying faults as well as virtues, a common characteristic of houses that are built to suit a fashion. The plan was a good deal more flexible than the old one in which there were usually four rooms on the first floor opening into a central hall, with a somewhat similar arrangement on the second floor. But the story-and-a-half house was scarcely ideal for the climate in which it was most frequently built. The rooms on the second floor crouched under low ceilings; their windows were small, and the roof above them was of a very shallow pitch, too shallow to be shingled. Consequently the roof was usually covered with tin that turned the rooms into ovens in the summer and often sagged and leaked under the heavy weight of snow in the winter. It was a price that many families were willing to pay to be modern, possibly because if anyone in the family suffered it was likely to be the children and the help.

By no means all, or even the majority, of Greek Revival houses were of the story-and-a-half variety. Many, and among them the most elegant, were symmetrical temples on an ample scale, and the symmetrical plan often played hob with the flexibility of the house. It resulted in two of everything, one on either side of the center front door and hall —two parlors, two "French rooms," two identical bedrooms, with the kitchen pantry, dining room, and servants' rooms fitted jigsaw fashion in the back of the house.

Initially the interior of the Greek Revival house was rather chaste in its decoration: wallpapers were out of fashion and painted walls in gentle colors were in. Furniture had an Empire and horsehair simplicity and formality about it; mantels were frequently white marble with relatively simple moldings, above which were mirrors in gilt frames which, in more pretentious houses, were imported from France. But as the next few decades passed and furniture and carpets began to be turned out in factories rather than in cabinetmakers' shops and on hand looms, twisted rosewood chairs, carved with fruits and flowers, and brightly patterned Brussels and ingrain carpets cluttered once sparsely furnished parlors. Whatnots laden with shells and figurines and bits of rare minerals turned up in corners, and wax flowers and stuffed birds under bell jars ornamented the mantelpieces. Francis Grund has been pleased to note in the 1830's that "No ostentatious attempt is ever made to display either fortune or riches; but on the contrary, everything avoided which, being contrary to republican plainness, might offend or unnecessarily attract the attention of the people. . . . Whatever political reason there may exist for the prevalence of this taste; it . . . impresses a peculiar character of simplicity on the domestic life of Americans."

Grund seems to have been trying hard to put the best possible light on what he hoped was the republican spirit among the rich. It must have struck him that the typical rich plantation house that he saw in the South with its "large covered piazza, resting on wooden or stone pillars, extending the whole front of the building" and with its plenti-

ful complement of slaves attending to every luxurious comfort, was
not unlikely to attract the attention of the people. If he had seen
Andalusia, the templed mansion that Nicholas Biddle with the help of
the architect Thomas U. Walter designed for himself by the Schuyl-
kill River near Philadelphia in 1833 (and which was said to have cost
only $15,000), he could not have been unmoved by its pretension.
"The two great truths of the world," Biddle, who was the president of
the Second Bank of the United States, had proclaimed, "are the Bible
and Grecian architecture." His contemporaries did not all think he was
particularly godly (there were unpleasant rumors about his ethics as
a banker), but nobody could deny his passion for the Greek. As it was
not considered proper for a gentleman to gamble within the sacred
walls of his home, Mr. Biddle built a separate and much smaller
temple near the river, where he could game with his friends. His mag-
nificent house still stands, as imposing a temple as ever housed an
American financier—or all but a few classical deities.

It is splendid mansions like Andalusia and the great plantation
houses of the South like Oak Valley in Louisiana, with its dignified
and graceful two-story columns and wide porches and balconies, that
have made the Greek Revival house seem to us like the pleasantest of
our native pleasure palaces. But there were few houses of such elegance and style, and fewer Americans who cared about style for style's
sake. It was fashion that mattered—the easiest of all skin-deep com-
modities to come by. When fashion reflects a basically sound style, the
general effect is likely to be not only agreeable but reasonably durable,
and while we scarcely notice the many Greek Revival houses that still
remain on village streets, we do not find them offensive as we do so
many gimcrack houses built later in their century and in ours.

The Greek mania was by no means restricted to the farm and the
village. Its characteristic devices and ornaments were applied to the
city house as well, though instead of being permitted to spread, they
were, of course, constructed into vertical shapes. Columns stood at the
sides of front doors, sometimes Doric, sometimes Corinthian. Anthony
Trollope found them "Vicious bit[s] of white timber plastered on the
fronts . . . of red brick houses," but to the Americans who put them
there they were essential accouterments of taste.

The style of Greek Revival houses varied somewhat in detail from
city to city. The high stoop was *de rigueur* in New York, for example
(it was both architecturally and etymologically a contribution of the

Dutch who settled Manhattan), while white marble steps were considered essential in Philadelphia and Baltimore. Philadelphians were more modest about the size of their houses than either Bostonians or New Yorkers, but they made up for their lack of commodious "apartments" with a passion for cleanliness, and looked down on New Yorkers, whose streets were filthy and whose doorsteps were covered with grime.

But wherever it was, the characteristic city house then was one of a row of houses, deeper than it was wide, with two or three stories and a basement. The front door, set usually at one side, opened into a long narrow hall on what was called the parlor floor, for the very good reason that it often had not just one but two adjoining parlors separated by the inevitable columns. Occasionally the dining room was also on the parlor floor, and food was transported to it from a basement kitchen by dumbwaiter. In many houses, however, the dining room was in the basement, its windows barred with ornamental ironwork, the only view from them the feet, trouser bottoms, and skirt hems of passers-by on the sidewalk. On the two floors above the parlor floor were bedrooms, usually two square ones on each story, one front and one back, and two hall bedrooms, long and narrow and just wide enough for a bed and a bureau. One of these hall bedrooms was often appropriated for a sewing room.

The kitchen and the washroom, as the laundry was commonly called, opened from the basement floor into a backyard of sorts. Deliveries were made on this floor through a basement entrance that opened into a narrow dark hall which skirted the dining room and let into the kitchen. Below the kitchen was a cavernous cellar, sometimes with a dirt floor, but in better houses flagging covered the earth; in this cellar were bins for storing wood and cannel coal, vegetables and fruits, a ventilated closet for hanging meat and poultry, and a locked butter box to which the mistress of the house kept the key. (A little later in the century the cellar would also have a bin for anthracite and a hot-air furnace.) The house was, an architect writing in the *Century Magazine* said in 1874, "little else but a string of stairs, with more or less extended landings," and it enslaved housewives and their domestics alike. "Up and down, up and down, the women folk are perpetually toiling as in a treadmill," he wrote, "wasting daily in the fruitless and health-destroying labor of carrying themselves from floor to floor an amount of strength sufficient to do the whole work of a sensibly constructed house. . . ."

During the time of the Greek mania there were, of course, far grander and far simpler houses than this more or less typical sort in the city. There were granite and marble mansions sitting on patches of lawn behind iron fences, with libraries and galleries and ballrooms, with servants' dining rooms and sitting rooms, with boudoirs and retiring rooms. There were also tenements, houses not unlike the ones described above, with a family to a floor and sometimes a family to a room, respectable but poor. But slums were never far from the porticoes and marble steps of the pious and burgeoning middle class.

There has never been in America an architectural fad that equaled the Greek Revival for the universality of its appeal, the sweep of its acceptance or, in some ways, the shallowness of its meaning. That is not to say that many of the houses were not pretty, comfortable, or elegant. Indeed, the residue that they have left upon the landscape is an extremely fortunate one, one that we have come to accept as characteristically American and which we now regard as associated with the virtues of architecture that preceded the finicky, romantical, and pretentious building of the worst (by no means of the best) of what we mistakenly call in this country Victorian. But the looks of Greek Revival houses belie their motivation. They were a passing fancy, and they were a fashion in more respects than they were a genuine style.

Not everyone was taken in by it or fell victim before the mania. "The mind of this country has never been seriously applied to the subject of architecture," wrote Horatio Greenough, famous in his day as a sculptor, famous now as the most acute architectural critic of the first half of the last century. "Intently engaged on matters of more pressing importance, we have been content to receive our notions of architecture as we receive the fashion of our garments and the form of our entertainments from Europe. In our eagerness to appropriate we have neglected to adapt, to distinguish,—nay, to understand. . . . Captivated by the classic symmetry of the Athenian models, we have sought to bring the Parthenon into our streets, to make the temple of Theseus work in our towns. We have shorn them of their lateral colonnades, let them down from their dignified platform, pierced their walls for light, and instead of the storied relief and the eloquent statues which enriched the frieze, and graced the pediment, we have made our chimney tops to peer over the broken profile and tell by their rising smoke of the traffic and desecration of the interior."

The high tide of the Greek fad began to recede in the 1840's but it was several decades before it disappeared, especially in what was then called the Northwest and is now called the Middle West. It lingered on until the 1860's, though other architectural fads in the East had nudged it out of the main stream of fashion. It was the product of a society youthfully restless, enthusiastic for show and for the appearance of being adult. The Greek Revival house was a good place to hang one's hat for a while, but not for long.

There is no reason to look with the same attention at other architectural phases through which the American house has passed in the last century; the story is very much the same, though the speed with which fashions came and went was more rapid and the mannerisms that were adopted are bewildering in their variety. It is necessary for the purposes of this book, however, to have in one's eye what the American house looked like in its various manifestations, and the ways in which its plans changed and adapted themselves to the family, its needs and its aspirations, its image of itself, and what industrialization and the gradual urbanization of the country have done to alter it.

THE PICTURESQUE

At the very moment when the Greek Revival was enjoying its greatest popularity there were, as there always are about those fashions that have captured the popular taste, mutterings of dissent among the custodians of the public's sensibilities. Downing called them "tasteless temples," and since many people of influence in matters of taste listened to Downing and repeated his words, fashionable taste turned from temples to other kinds of romanticism. If it was not possible to change the American character or dampen its exuberance, it was possible to redirect its enthusiasms. When the temple which was revered for its ancient origins became merely "old hat," it was despised. Taste leaped from the fourth century B.C. (and before) to the fourteenth century A.D., from the age of Pericles to the Middle Ages. The proper house for an American became Gothic Revival rather than Greek Revival, and instead of living behind porticoes he now looked at his garden through leaded glass panes. At its best the Gothic Revival house (and it was at its best when it was designed by Downing's

friend and collaborator A. J. Davis) was a handsome and sparsely ornamented structure built of stone and with a plan that, compared with
either the Greek Revival or with the standard house of the colonial
days, was downright playful. The foursquare, symmetrical arrangement of the house needed to play no part in the design of the Gothic
dwelling, and the tone of voice of those who advised Americans about
how to build their houses became a great deal more sensible than it
had been.

The first cry was to get the kitchen out of the basement, where
it had often been, in country as well as in city houses: it was inhuman
to make servants work there and it was inefficient besides. Why, as
Catharine Beecher said, should a woman who heard a child cry have
to climb two sets of stairs to get from the kitchen to the nursery? More
attention was given to the adjustment of the plan of the house to its
site. The dining room, for example, should be so located that it took
advantage of the morning sun, whose warmth as well as cheer might
take the gloom off breakfast. Ceilings were high for the sake of coolness in summer, but the new houses did not make towering ceilings on
the first floor and low, cramped ones on the second floor, as the story-
and-a-half house had done. Irregularity in the shapes of rooms became
a virtue, as did the irregularity of the plan of the house itself. Parlors
and libraries swelled with bay windows, some of which were filled
with hanging plants and climbing ivy and potted ferns, some of which
had cushioned window seats. It became possible to step from one's
bedroom onto a private little balcony and look down on the lawn with
its formal flower beds of cannas and its open rustic summerhouse. The
veranda (or piazza, if you prefer) began to assume the functions of an
outdoor living room, though it did not achieve its real heyday until
later in the century. The austerity of the Greek Revival house gave
way to a more relaxed, less Puritan concern with comfort, and luxury
became identified less with space than with how much of the space
could be cluttered up with pretty "coxcomalities," as Mrs. Trollope
had called the *bibelots* on parlor tables, and busy furniture and ornaments.

By no means all Gothic Revival houses were stone. Many were made
of wood (commonly of vertical sheathing or "board and batten," as it
was also called) with vergeboards cut with a scroll saw out of wide
planks. In spite of the advice of Downing and Calvert Vaux and others
who wrote about domestic architecture, there were those who built of

wood but painted it to look like stone, and there were many who
accepted the Gothic fashion and turned it into a fad whose exuberance
and fanciness were far from what Downing and the others had in
mind.

Along with the Gothic came the Tuscan (or just plain Italian) villa,
usually with a square corner tower and always with a gently sloping,
and preferably tile, roof, the Swiss (or Switz) cottage, and before very
long houses with the "curvilinear" and the mansard roofs borrowed
from France. Brackets were under the eaves of almost all houses built
in the 1850's, and today you will find in many towns Greek Revival
houses which were brought up to date by adding brackets and vergeboards and often bay windows.

The cellars of the houses of the 1850's and 1860's did not change
greatly. The washroom stayed there, as did the "sauce" cellar (for
storing vegetables), the coalbin, and the cool closets for storing meats.
In some houses the "cold cupboard" and the "buttery" were sheds
attached to the back of the house next to the kitchen. (Indeed, it is
true of many houses still standing from Gothic Revival times that the
Gothic is all on the front and sides and that the backs are plain sheathing and run out into low sheds, made as inconspicuous as possible.)
The front hall, however, changed considerably and began to assume
an importance that later in the century revolutionized the plan of the
house. Halls became something more than mere passageways out
of which climbed straight steep stairs.

When Dickens revisited America in the 1860's he must have been
surprised not merely by the changes in the shapes of houses and how
much more substantial they looked, but by their color. Downing had
said that to paint a house white was "vulgar"; houses should be painted
in "somber hues" so that they would not be scars on the landscape but
would blend into it. Browns and dark reds and greens, stone colors and
moss colors, became the standard shades for houses (though some
farmers continued to insist that white was good enough for them) and
remained standard for the rest of the century.

With the decline of the Greek Revival came almost fifty years of
what we now think of as the characteristic nineteenth-century house
—ample in its proportions, comfortable in its many and varied rooms,
designed for privacy, for the attention of many servants, but not, on
the whole, very cheerful. Many of its parlors and living rooms and
libraries were darkened by the roofs of verandas. The mahogany and

oak of its banisters and dadoes seemed to absorb the freshness out of
the air and the warmth out of the light. Our inclination today is to
get at these halls and parlors with pots of white paint, to tear off the
verandas and the porte-cocheres and let the light in. Sunlight, however, was only an occasional friend of the nineteenth-century householder. Women kept the shutters of their parlors closed lest the sun fade
the blossoms in the flowered carpet and the damask on the dos-à-dos.
Light into stair halls was filtered through amber and ruby, cobalt and
emerald glass, and into sitting rooms through ferns and vines in front
of windows. Ladies exposed themselves to the unhealthful rays of the
sun as little as possible lest their milky skins be coarsened; verandas
permitted them to sample the fresh air without such danger. At least
part of the gloom of the nineteenth-century house was a romantic
gloom, a genteel and luxurious, rich and soulful gloom. The garish
and the gaudy had no place in proper houses. The quiet of the home
was the antithesis of the bustle of the world of commerce, and the
pious home (scarcely anyone dared admit he was not pious) exhibited
an almost ecclesiastical distaste for the uninhibited rays of the sun.

The plan of the typical city house in the East did not change greatly
from that of the Greek Revival era, though in New York a veneer of
brownstone darkened the façades and in Boston bow windows bulged
with tiresome regularity on the front of house after house. In the
newer cities of the West, however, houses were not built in blocks as
they were in the East, but were set down on individual plots of land,
with a little grass and a few trees, in a great variety of styles. Basically
they were "balloon-frame" houses built of two-by-fours. It was the
invention of the balloon frame that had made it possible for Chicago
(where the system was invented) to become a city overnight in the
1830's. It required no highly skilled carpenter to put it together; "not
mortise nor tenon nor other mysteries of carpentry interfered with the
swiftness of its growth." All that was needed was "a keg of nails, some
two-by-four studs, a few cedar posts for foundations and a lot of
clapboards, with two strong arms to wield the hammer and saw." But
the exuberance of the West in the 1860's demanded something more.
Verandas were adorned with ornate railings cut with a scroll saw;
windows were ornamented with rosettes; frostings and finials appeared
on roofs and openwork scrolls under the eaves of gables, "suggestive of
nothing so much," said the Chicago architect John Wellborn Root, "as
'nudels' in a German soup." In Chicago the great fire of 1871 did away

with most of this wooden exuberance, and it became law in most Western cities after the fire that houses within the city limits might not be built of wood. Householders and developers, their spirits undampened, built their fantasies in stone and brick with bay windows of copper, cornices and turrets of galvanized iron, and carved panels of terra cotta.

By 1870 there was such a confusion of styles from which the housebuilder might chose that it was no mean problem for him to decide whether he wanted a Romanesque villa, a crenelated Elizabethan house, an Anglo-French house, an "ornamental cottage," something in "the pointed style" (or modified Gothic), or, as was often the case, a combination of several of these, sometimes called merely "picturesque." (All of these and a good many more were recommended in a single plan book by Isaac H. Hobbs in 1876.) This was the kind of burden on taste, this free and extravagant opportunity for choice, that was bound to produce a revolt. In matters of taste most Americans prefer to be told what is good and suitable and proper. America was ripe for a new wave of conformity.

THE QUAINT AND THE ARTISTIC

In 1876 ladies in bustles and bonnets and gentlemen in top hats and Prince Alberts clasped to their bosoms a new fad in design and ornamentation of houses that very nearly matched the Greek Revival in the eagerness with which it was greeted. The Queen Anne style, as it was called, spread its mannerisms across the continent in a way that the Greek Revival could not possibly have. Much of what had been wilderness beyond the Mississippi in the 1840's was now dotted with villages and boom towns and prospering cities, and the Queen Anne house adapted itself easily to an extravagant era that wanted to let its fancy and its money run free.

The style first appeared at the Centennial Exhibition that startled the world with its mechanical wonders and exotic arts in Philadelphia in 1876. What millions of Americans saw there that changed the character of the American house for many years was a group of English "cottages," the headquarters of the English Commission to the Exposition. They were built in "half-timbered and shingle work," and they vaguely reminded Americans of the early days of the Colonies, when the shingled house with a steeply pitched roof was common. But the

English cottages had an extra ingredient of picturesqueness and romance at the same time that there was an orderliness about their appearance. "The Centennial Exposition . . . brought our people together
and showed them many truths," wrote an architect in a discussion of
the suburban house seventeen years after the show was over. "It taught
them that back of all the uses of life there could be art in everything."
The words *quaint* and *artistic* became part of the householder's vocabulary, and the forms they took are evident today in what we now refer
to in many cities as "the older parts of town." You will find the mark
of Queen Anne in nearly every American community from one coast
to the other at no matter what latitude you may cross the continent.

The Queen Anne house is typically built of wood and often
sheathed with shingles. It frequently has an octagonal or round tower
at one of its corners that face the street. Its veranda is wide and its railings are spindled. Its roof is long, sharply pitched, and pierced with
peaked dormers, and its chimneys are frequently in shapes borrowed
from Elizabethan country houses. Its several upstairs balconies are
characteristically recessed into the house and sheltered by eaves, and
it comes in all sizes, all degrees of luxury; it was the home of the millionaire and of the laborer, of the bank clerk, the physician, and the
parson. It reached peaks of exuberance in the plan books of the 1880's
and 1890's and was still being recommended by them in 1913. In the
hands of first-rate architects like H. H. Richardson and Charles
McKim the shingle style, as its variants are called, achieved great
subtlety of design and dignity. Less talented but successful architects
of the same era turned its clichés into mockeries of style, and today in
Grand Rapids and St. Louis, in Austin, Texas, and in Philadelphia
you will find that many such houses are now split up into apartments
or given over to "roomers" and are frequently the principal architecture of declining or "blighted" neighborhoods. Urban renewers can
scarcely wait to get at them and tear them down.

But the Queen Anne house, which was better suited to the age of
the bustle than it seems to be to the age of its mechanical counterpart
the tail fin, introduced some new elements into domesticity. It was
freer in its plan than the Gothic cottage of the fifties or the villa of
the sixties. It was rarely, if ever, symmetrical, and at the same time that
it hinted at what was later to become the open plan, it also achieved
for its inhabitants an increase in privacy. This is not as contradictory as
it may seem. The hall, which a generation before had been a mere

passageway from the front door to the stairs, became the center and core of the house, and in many cases larger than any other room in it. It was a "family room," in a manner of speaking, through which every member of the family passed, and not only passed but stopped. "The stairway fell away from the threshold to a less obtrusive place," wrote the architect Bruce Price in *Homes in City and Country* in 1893. "As the hall grew, the parlor, as its uses and purposes were more absorbed by the hall, became of less importance. The fireplace became a prominent feature, and placed in the hall and more elaborately treated, became an inglenook, with the mantel over it forming an imposing chimney-piece. . . . The new hall having become broad and ample, and the rendezvous and seat of the home life, took its position in the most desirable place in the advanced plan."

Not only did the Queen Anne house mark the beginning of the end of the oppressive parlor, a social discipline that held Americans in a formal strait jacket for two generations, but its porches became outdoor living rooms with swings and hammocks and grass rugs and wicker furniture. There women entertained their friends at tea, young people sang to the accompaniment of the mandolin, kisses were stolen, and troths were plighted. In the winter, sections of the porches were frequently glassed in to make solariums that served in the cold months as extra sitting rooms. On the "back galleries," as the rear porches of the houses were called, women in negligees might spend summer days sewing and entertaining their intimate friends, while on "upper galleries" the children could play on rainy days and the upstairs maid could air the bedding. To preserve the privacy of the spacious hall and of the piazza-turned-living-room, the entrance of the house was moved, whenever possible, from the front to the side, so that callers no longer approached the house in such a way as to infringe on the peace of the family. The door let into a small entryway. "The entry is for access," said Mr. Price firmly, "the hall, veranda, lawn, and the prospect beyond, belonging to the private life of the house. . . . Even Liberty Hall must have its defense."

Variations on the Queen Anne house were almost endless; there seemed to be no tricks that couldn't be played with it, no liberties that it did not allow. Its towers and balconies and porches were sometimes built of stone instead of wood. Frank Lloyd Wright in *The Natural House* said of it: "Essentially, whether of brick or wood or stone, this 'house' was a bedeviled box with a fussy lid; a complex box that had to be cut up by all kinds of holes made in it to let in light and air, with an especially ugly hole to go in and out of. The holes were all 'trimmed'; the doors and the windows themselves trimmed; the roofs trimmed; the walls trimmed. Architecture seemed to consist in what was done to these holes." It became difficult to tell where Queen Anne stopped and adaptations of other earlier styles of architecture took over, and the line between the Queen Anne house that had gone over the edge into hideousness and the one that stayed on the side of pleasure and adventurousness without license was often a fine one, as distinctions of taste frequently are. Almost no one looks at these houses today; the eye slides over them. They are not old enough to be "interesting," they are too numerous and familiar to be curious, and they are too easily discarded as being hideous. Fashion has passed them by.

PALACES, APARTMENTS, AND BUNGALOWS

While Queen Anne reigned over an era of freedom in the plan of the house and filled towns and provincial cities with spindles and galleries, a new generation of architects who had been trained at the Beaux Arts in Paris (or trained by those who had been there) were persuading the rich (and by now the rich were very rich) to live in what they called "adaptations" of Renaissance palaces, in imitations of châteaux from the Loire Valley, in Malmaisons and little Versailles and Rhine castles. Resorts like Newport and Lenox became suitable places for the ghosts of princes and duchesses and barons to prowl and, presumably, for the wives of merchants and manufacturers and financiers to entertain at balls and garden parties. The contemporary adjectives for them were "stately" and "sumptuous" and "lavish," and they were all of that. Out of their marble entrance halls, presided over by sculptured goddesses, staircases rose and gently curved to upstairs expanses of twenty or thirty bedrooms. In their picture galleries romantic landscapes in tortured gilt frames jostled each other against brocade walls. Tapestries hung in drawing rooms and Aubusson carpets covered their floors. Fireplaces big enough for roasting steers were set in carved-marble chimney pieces. Fountains set about with palms played in halls and courtyards, and hundreds of candles flickered in chandeliers that hung above the heads of forty or fifty guests dining on twelve courses and seven wines and attended by ten or twelve butlers in livery.

Houses of wondrous pretensions rose on Fifth Avenue and on Nob Hill and looked out over Lake Michigan, and the suburbs of cities sprouted with baronial estates. The demand for "adaptation" (strictly speaking it was not outright plagiarism) was first made popular by the architect Richard Morris Hunt, in the 1870's, and it is still with us. If it was good enough for the rich, it was good enough on a far smaller scale for the merely well-off, who were more than willing to sacrifice comfort and convenience to live in the little châteaux, little castles, little Elizabethan country houses with which our older suburbs up to the 1930's were filled. During the Depression and the Second World War building all but stood still, and after the war the principal sort of adaptation was, and continues to be, the variations played on the "colonial" and the Cape Cod cottage. In 1903 Harry W. Desmond and Herbert Croly, the authors of a splendidly illustrated volume on *Stately Homes in America*, remarked, "The truth is that in all intellectual and aesthetic matters, Americans are extremely conservative. While they undeniably possess the instinct to be effective as well as efficient; they want to be effective in an entirely safe way; they want to avoid being crude and ridiculous." The house that is an "adaptation" is still, in the minds of a great many Americans, the safest way to avoid the "crude and ridiculous"; it means to them respectability and gentility and it gives the effect of being "established," a part of the continuity of a conservative, sensible attitude toward progress that has little use for fads. If "adaptation" in the hands of the Vanderbilts and the Astors and the Goelets was an instrument of ostentation, today it has become the trade-mark of conservative well-being. For the factory manager, the labor leader, the lawyer, the druggist, the broker, and the salesman it is the symbol of having arrived, though arrival does not mean that there is not still someplace else to go.

During the years when Queen Anne was first popular and "adaptation" was the darling of the rich, two important changes were taking place in the nature of the community that altered the ways a great many Americans lived and what they lived in. Industrialization after the Civil War meant that many families that had been accustomed to the wide skies and fragrant earth of farms were moving into metropolitan areas on which soot fell from factory chimneys. As the cities grew more dense, the suburbs grew more popular. The suburban house changed, of course, with the shift in fashion to Queen Anne, and in a somewhat mannerly and slow-moving way the looks of suburbs became different from the days of the Gothic cottages and Tuscan villas and the mannered manors of the 1860's. But there were those who thought that suburban life was scarcely worth living, the true urbanites. The city of the 1870's was, as it is today, far more private than the country or the suburbs for those who cherished their privacy. It was the wellspring and the arena of the arts, the Olympus of the gods of finance and commerce, the Mecca for the quick-witted. It was the delight of the impatient, for whose taste flowers and grass grew too slowly, and of those who were not content to measure out their lives only in the majestic rhythm of the seasons.

Those who loved the city were fearful for its future. There were plenty of places for the poor to live in, but squalor crept inexorably into old buildings and the state of the slums grew increasingly alarming. There were also plenty of houses for the rich, who could afford to waste both space and money and who could buy the mansions built by speculators and staff them with servants. It was those with moderate incomes who were having to desert the cities, whether they wanted to or not, and nowhere was their problem as critical as it was in New York. We have discussed the fact that many families lived in boarding houses. Others rented large houses and made ends meet by renting out rooms to lodgers, and a few, but very few, lived in flats that were built for that purpose. The same kind of alarm struck those who were interested in the future prosperity of cities that strikes the city fathers today. The city was becoming the home of the rich and the poor, and the middle classes were moving out. "Thousands who would live in the city, could they find suitable homes here," wrote James Richardson in 1874, "and who would be worth millions to the city, are driven to the surrounding country to build. . . ." The answer then, of course (as it is today), was plenty of attractive middle-income housing. But of what sort?

In 1870 the apartment house was all but unknown. In the 1840's A. J. Davis had built on Fifth Avenue and 42nd Street, opposite the Croton Reservoir, a block of what were called "French flats" in the Gothic style, but they were considered somewhat eccentric and they were expensive. It was all right for the French to live in flats, if they wanted to, but it would never do for Americans. Who, in his right mind, would want to live in a hive with a family overhead and another family below and the noise of somebody else's crying children and the smell of their cooking? It was all very well for the poor to live in such a fashion if they could afford nothing better, but anything else was preferable. Just because European cities, including ancient Rome, had solved the problem of housing with flats was no reason why the Americans should fall to such depths. How could a man honor his hearth in a hive of hearths?

The apartment house was, however, the answer. It was the only way in cities that householders could avoid "living like hermit crabs in other creatures' shells, suiting their lives to dwellings that do not fit them, and themselves to a style of living agreeable neither to their taste nor their pockets." How else could the average family with an income of about $1,600 hope to achieve even "the mere decencies of life"?

There had been a few apartments built in the 1850's (most notably one by Richard M. Hunt on Wooster Street in New York) which offered "complete facilities for modest housekeeping on separate floors" in the manner of flats, but the first apartment house that can be called the progenitor of the modern apartment was built in New York in 1870 on 18th Street, the Stuyvesant Building. It was an immediate and surprising success; New Yorkers considered it "large, massive, and handsome," and thought its style "at once rich and modest." It was followed a few months later by another apartment house on 13th Street, built by the same investors. The apartments were six rooms and ten rooms, "including kitchen and servants' rooms," and were "designed for strictly independent housekeeping, in good but not extravagant style."

These first apartment houses suffered from not having elevators (though their proprietors had no trouble renting the apartments), but within a few years elevators were common and consequently apartments on upper stories, once cheaper than those on lower floors because of the climb, now became especially desirable. They were, for one thing, less likely to be robbed than those on the street floor. "The elevator," wrote Everett N. Blanks in an article called "The Cliff Dwellers of New York" in 1893, "being democratic, has done much to do away with an aristocracy of wealth in the American apartment house, by performing unwittingly for tenants the duties of a board of equalization, both in the matter of rent and of self-respect." In the twenty-three years between the building of the Stuyvesant and Mr. Blanks's article in *Cosmopolitan* some seven hundred apartment houses had been built in New York, and from walk-ups they had grown as tall as fifteen stories.

The apartment house eased many domestic difficulties that had long been taken for granted by the American family. It saved hundreds of steps a day and most importantly those on stairs. It provided in the basement a communal laundry, and in some apartment houses a communal kitchen as well, and a communal nursery on the roof. It was applauded because it gave women "leisure to cultivate the higher intelligence" and because it saved on servants' wages. There was no furnace to tend and there were no front steps to sweep.

But there were those who thought its life was false and unwholesome. "It's made for social show, not for family life at all," wrote William Dean Howells in *A Hazard of New Fortunes*. "Think of a baby in a flat! It's a contradiction in terms; the flat is the negation of motherhood. The flat means society life. It's made to give artificial people a society basis on a little money—too much money, of course, for what they get. So the cost of the building is put into marble halls and idiotic decorations of all kinds." But the pretense was no worse than the plan, so far as Howells was concerned. The typical "railroad" flat was a series of rooms strung like railroad cars along a narrow hall, and bedroom windows, when there were any, looked across narrow ventilation alleys at blank walls. "I don't object to the conveniences," Howells said, "but none of these flats has a living room. They have drawing rooms to foster social pretense, and they have dining rooms and bedrooms; but they have no room where the family can come together and feel the sweetness of being a family. The bedrooms are black holes, mostly, with a sinful waste of space in each." The tenements in which the poor lived and the kitchens that were the centers of their lives were preferable, he thought. ". . . the flat abolishes the family consciousness. It's confinement without coziness; it's cluttered without being snug. You couldn't keep a self-respecting cat in a flat; you couldn't get down cellar to get cider. No: the Anglo-Saxon home, as we know it in the Anglo-Saxon house, is simply impossible in the Franco-American flat, not because it's humble, but because it's false."

The apartment house has lost nothing in pretentiousness since Howells encountered it in New York in the 1880's, but it has lost a great deal in other ways. Its walls have become paper thin, its ceilings low, and its kitchens mere closets. It is no longer confined to cities, but has spread to the suburbs, where its inhabitants enjoy neither the benefits of a piece of their own ground to cultivate nor the entertainments of the city streets to look down upon. In some respects the most far-reaching contribution of the nineteenth century to American domesticity was the high-rise multiple dwelling, a socially acceptable swarming of families.

The luxury apartment house is the only kind of domestic palace that is still being built. Its lobby, like the entrance halls of the palaces at Newport in the 1880's, is rich with mosaic and travertine, with arrangements of plants (often, to be sure, plastic imitations of tropical trees and flowers), with mirrors and marble benches and murals, and its doorway and elevators are presided over by lackeys in livery. But such apartments are only for the rich and the nearly rich. In apartment houses for those who subsist on that undefined euphemism the "middle income," tenants are their own elevator operators. Their apartments with peepholes in the doors to protect them from thieves and muggers are scarcely larger than a few log cabins strung together and not as large as bungalows. Air-conditioners cool their low-ceilinged rooms in summer and spray water on passers-by on the streets below. The apartments are often equipped with balconies in a gesture at the spirit if not the manner of the Tuscan villa and the Queen Anne house, though one rarely sees anyone using them; they are a cliché of design rather than a contribution to private pleasure. Yet millions of Americans prefer to live in apartments in crowded cities to owning their homes in suburbs. Possibly it is because it is easier to move out of an apartment than a house, both physically and spiritually. It is a hatrack that it is not easy to give one's heart to, a semipermanent waystation with its roots not in the ground but in the air.

At the same time that the apartment house was establishing itself as the permanent answer to the problem of city housing, the progenitor of today's small suburban house was being built by the thousands in communities from California to Maine. It was the bungalow, cheap to build and cheap to live in. It was the first fad in house construction that started on the West Coast and found itself, like the ranch house today, snatched up by the Middle West and the East. Its plan was almost as open as a one-room log cabin. The front door opened directly into the living room, which in turn opened without a door into the dining room. The bungalow was a forerunner of the ranch house and more or less contemporary with the "prairie" houses built by the young

Frank Lloyd Wright in the first decade of this century.

The bungalow was usually just one story high, with a gradually pitched roof of shingles or occasionally of tiles. Its porch was typically supported by heavy, square, tapering columns of field stone with a field-stone chimney to match, though sometimes the columns were cement or brick or even wood. It never enjoyed the universal popularity of the small versions of the Queen Anne house, but it was the ranch house of the two decades before the First World War. Its principal virtue was a maximum amount of space at a minimum cost with a minimum of maintenance. It was a frontier kind of house that settled perfectly comfortably into a village or a suburb, and it went far in breaking down the notion that a house to be a house at all and not just a cabin had to have a second story. It can be said, I believe, that the bungalow had more to do with how suburban Americans live today than any other building that has gone even remotely by the name of architecture in our history.

JUST YESTERDAY

A great deal has happened to the American house since the days of the bungalow fad, some of it good, some of it ingenious, and some of it regrettable. During the 1920's our suburbs were filled with storybook houses whose architectural heritage seemed to come from *Grimm's Fairy Tales,* houses that looked as though they were made of ginger cake with raisins for windows, houses out of which Mother Hubbard might be expected to pop. There were little pink Spanish missions next to little half-timbered English taverns with leaded glass windows. There were Dutch and Norman and, of course, colonial houses, all of them tightly surrounded by little blue spruces and yews and snuggled against little garages with weather vanes on their ridge poles. In the suburb in which I lived in the twenties, Englewood, New Jersey, there was a contractor who made an excellent thing of converting Queen Anne houses into half-timbered English houses merely by taking off the porches, nailing irregular timbers to the outsides, and filling in the interstices with stucco. It was also in the twenties when men and women first spent their weekends prowling through barns looking for "early American" furniture; cobblers' benches and spinning wheels turned up in living rooms and cherry beds and bureaus were the *sine qua non* of the bedroom.

The 1930's and the Depression put a damper on building of all sorts, and the war brought it to a virtual standstill. Rents were frozen and houses that were fit only for destruction were patched up and made the best of. In some cities "emergency housing" was built to give shelter to war workers, and in the vicinity of Washington, for example, developments designed in the Williamsburg manner, brick colonial villages, popped up like dollhouses, paper-thin with "quaintness" appliquéd on their façades. They were uninsulated and when the temperature fell into the twenties their pipes had a nasty way of bursting.

Immediately after the war there was a flurry of domestic building and a host of ingenious suggestions for meeting the housing shortage. Airplane manufacturers made plans to mass-produce aluminum houses; someone in Texas invented an enormous machine for pouring entire houses of concrete at one shot, and the age of the prefabricated house seemed to be upon us. (Not, to be sure, that prefabrication was anything new. James Marston Fitch in *Architecture and the Esthetics of Plenty* says that "there are records of prefabricated house frames being made as early as 1578" and that "The Louisiana French were shipping them to the West Indies as early as 1727." "Portable houses" used primarily for summer camps were not uncommon in the late nineteenth century, and during the Depression of the 1930's prefabrication was touted as the answer to low-cost housing, but nothing much came of it.) But instead of "prefabs" we got mass-produced suburbs on the order of Levittown on Long Island, thousands of identical Cape Cod cottages, and a few years later, of course, we got the ranch house and the ubiquitous picture window. The ranch house, which at its minimum is scarcely architecture at all, came in all sizes and many degrees of luxury. In the hands of a few West Coast architects it departed from the standard elongated box and became a house of considerable charm, called a ranch house only because it was made of unpainted wood sheathing and was only one story high. The "modern" house, which during the 1930's had been flat-roofed with corner windows and "bull's-eyes" and owed its style largely to the Bauhaus in Germany, began to lose the clichés that identified it as "modern"; it became far less doctrinaire, less like the "machine for living," and at its best remarkably pleasant, convenient, and handsome. Even today, however, it is built only by the prosperous who are also adventurous.

The trek from Greek Revival to Ranch (and beyond) has been in the opinion of many people a retrogression, a retreat from civilized to catch-as-catch-can living, a turning away from a life in which the family controlled its own destiny to a life controlled by the forces of mass media, by dependence on mechanical gadgets, by immersion in giant corporations and in even larger and more anonymous communities. In the search for progress, they say, we have lost our individuality and identity and so have our homes. This is easy to say and easy to argue.

But there is another way to interpret the story of what has happened to the American and his house. The householder is far less pious than he was in the 1830's, but he is far more humane. He may not summon his servants to family prayers, but neither does he have his servants sleep in the cellar where it is damp or in the attic where it is breathless. He has, moreover, got over the notion that there is a servant class, something he never quite believed in anyway. He may crave to be ostentatious every bit as much as the rich of a century ago did, but by and large he subscribes to the restraints on him which make his extravagances not greatly different from anyone else's. The $75,000 ranch house and the $7,500 "shell" house have more in common than did the Tuscan villa and the log cabin, just as the Cadillac and the Chevrolet have more in common than the pure-bred carriage horse and the ox. The consequence of distributing the fruits of industrial democracy has been that the worker and the proprietor have moved closer together, and it has meant that those who used to tend the rich, polish their brass and dip their candles, are now tending themselves, polishing their own cars and mowing their own lawns. Some of what we have lost in elegance we have gained in self-respect. That is not all that we have lost nor all that we have gained. Thirty percent of Americans still live in substandard houses, in city slums and country slums, in peeling tenements, in shanties, in houses with their porches crumbling and their roofs leaking. We have no reason to be smug.

In some respects the search for luxury since the time of the Greek mania and the First Age of the Common Man appears to have been the exact opposite. We no longer associate luxury with space, but with convenience. We have lost a great deal of drudgery both by simplifying the plan of the house and by increasing its mechanical efficiency. We have also lost most of the chores that spread responsibility for the home over all of its members, and in so doing we have lost some of the adhesive that bound the family together. We have gained in creature comforts: our heat is automatic and we have it when we want it; our light demands no more of us than to remember to have extra bulbs on hand; our mattresses are more comfortable; our plumbing is more convenient and more plentiful, and we take hot water for granted. Our delight in ample space (if we don't have to manage it) is no less than it has ever been, but we look at it differently from our grandparents. The more space, the more there is for us to do—not for servants to do. What was once considered the luxury of space is now the onus of space. We no longer worry about making cozy-corners or inglenooks, as the owners of nineteenth-century houses did; our rooms are scarcely bigger than cozy-corners. We no longer wonder whether we should take in our aging parents to live with us; there's no place to put them.

The pursuit of luxury (or at least the illusion of luxury) led us from the time of the Greek Revival up a spiral of fanciness and extravagance to the massive palaces of the 1880's and the Queen Anne house gone wild in the 1890's. Since the turn of the century the spiral has been slowly winding downward. Little by little we have been whittling away the inconveniences of life by whittling down the size and complexity of the house. We have done this largely because we had no choice: it became more and more costly to build, at the same time that there were fewer and fewer people who were willing to help other people keep house, and more and more mechanical contraptions were invented which almost, but not quite, took their place.

As we have whittled we have cut off some of the pleasures of the house along with some of the nuisances, and we have swept out some of the gratifications of life along with the shavings. We have not, however, reduced the home merely to a hatrack in a box, though we have gone, it cannot be denied, a long, discouraging way in that direction.

PART TWO

Downstairs, Below Stairs, Upstairs

CHAPTER VII

The Kitchen

The sight of a tidy kitchen is not so very disgusting, even to men of refined tastes.
O. S. Fowler, *A Home for All,* 1854

In 1854 the phrenologist, O. S. Fowler, who was obsessed with
the notion that all right-minded people should live in octagons,
said that the kitchen was the "stomach" of the house. In 1962 James
Marston Fitch, the architectural critic, in referring to the farm
kitchen of Fowler's day, said that it was a "factory . . . merely the
center of a whole industrial complex." The kitchen has also, of
course, been called the heart of the house and its soul. Today it
might most accurately be called its laboratory.

Until fairly recently the kitchen has been a focal point of nostalgia for men, who have associated it with warmth, pleasant smells
of cooking, satisfied hunger, being waited on and fussed over while
they watched their mothers or their wives work for them. A man's
or a boy's only kitchen chore was to chop the kindling or split the
logs for the stove, to carry the filled coal scuttle from the cellar and
sometimes to empty the ashes. For women, on the other hand, the
kitchen has always been a place of toil, of heavy pots, of often
oppressive heat, of floors to be scrubbed, dishes to be washed, towels
to be boiled, flour to be sifted, oilcloth to be replaced, shelves to
be papered, candles to be dipped, and an endless chain of unremitting chores to be performed day in and day out. But in spite
of this it was also for a good many women a sort of studio in which
their domestic artistry flowered. Now, of course, men are not exempt from what was once considered women's work, and though
there are still some women who practice the magic of cookery, the

prebaked biscuit, the frozen fillet, the "mix," the bottled dressing, the all but predigested dinner have turned the function of the stove into something like the function of a Bunsen burner, and the woman from an artist into a minor technician.

Such nostalgia as sticks to the kitchen is usually associated with the country, not with the city. In a great many country houses and especially in the houses of farmers, the kitchen was also the dining room, and to all intents and purposes, the living room as well. The parlor, or the "really" room as some homesteaders called it, was almost omnipresent, but it was not a place to put the feet up and relax, to do homework, to sew, or to snooze—a word, you will remember, that Miss Leslie found "ungenteel." It was to the kitchen that the farm family came from their unheated bedrooms long before the sun was up to splash cold water from a tin basin on their faces and to wipe the sleep out of their eyes on a roller towel that was changed once a week. It was there that they sat in the evening around a table lighted by a coal-oil lamp and read the farm papers, made clothes for the children, or pieced together patchwork quilts from discarded dresses and waistcoats. The kitchen was obviously more than just the stomach or the factory of the farmhouse.

In the prosperous houses of the village, the suburb, and the city, and in the homes of "gentlemen farmers" on their well-tended acres, the kitchen was the domain of the "help," and the housewife gave it the widest possible berth. Her function was supervisory and it behooved her to know how things were done in the kitchen "even though," as the author of a cookbook published in 1887 said, "she hopes never to be obliged to do them." It is little wonder, then, that in almost all city houses and in a great many country houses the kitchen was relegated to the basement, or that on the typical plantation of the South, where service was plentiful and haulage no problem except to those who hauled, the kitchen was a separate building. But in the country and the city any means of taming the cussedness of the kitchen's demands, of making it more cooperative, more convenient, and less time-consuming, were worth trying. Those who had to do their own housework were quick, for obvious reasons, to grasp any new idea or gadget that promised to reduce their toil. Those who hired others to do their work for them found urgent motives in the ever-present "servant problem." The modernization and mechanization of the house started in the kitchen.

The Common Man had not been common for long before the reformers set out to put some sense and order into the plan of the kitchen and its location. Mr. Downing, Miss Beecher, and nearly all of the others who were concerned with the household inveighed against the common practice of putting the kitchen in the basement of country houses. Not only was it damp and therefore bad for the health of servants, but it made too many stairs to climb and put the housewife to too great inconveniences in supervising her kitchen. The most usual excuse for putting the kitchen in the basement was economy: it cost less to build a house with a kitchen under it than to add it on as a wing. To incorporate a kitchen into the first-floor plan of a rectangular house in the 1830's was a very rare thing. It was not in the least uncommon, however, to tack the kitchen on to the back, the first of a series of one-story additions that clung to the house like the tail of a kite. Even in quite formal houses on which a good deal of architectural thought and care had been lavished, the kitchen, the cold-cupboard, the buttery, and the woodshed (none of which could be seen from the road) were more like a series of large doghouses than part of the architecture of the house.

In his octagonal house O. S. Fowler located the kitchen so that, as he put it, "the wife, when she leaves the sitting-room to attend to kitchen duties—pleasures—instead of feeling that she is going way off alone out of doors, feels that she is only a step removed from the rest of the family." Miss Beecher made a similar gesture to the housewife in her "Christian House" when she made the kitchen accessible to both living room and bedroom, and a few years later Sereno E. Todd in his *Country Homes* declared that "the arrangement of the kitchen should be such that one can go out of doors, down cellar, up stairs, and in the pantry from the kitchen. Always plan your kitchen first, then make every other room in the house conform to the arrangements of the kitchen." He anticipated the modern house when he added: "If practicable, let the kitchen and the dining room be so arranged that they may be made, when necessary, as one room."

The argument about whether the kitchen should or should not be in the basement was not quickly resolved. The plan books of the 1870's were still in disagreement about it, and many suburban houses stuck to the old system, though by that time it was a well-

known fact that the resale value of a house with a first-floor kitchen
was higher than one with a kitchen in the basement. By that time,
also, technology had done a great deal to change the plans and
workings of the kitchen from its still relatively primitive state of
the 1830's. Invention crowded upon the kitchen from a dozen directions. New contraptions for cooking appeared from factories; new
ways of storing and preserving food were invented; new means of
transporting the produce of the land, of harvesting it, of fattening
cattle, and of butchering had their direct impact on the size and
shape and convenience of the kitchen, on its appearance, and, of
course, on those who operated it. By the end of the century it was
possible for Lillian W. Betts to say in *The House and Home, a
Practical Book*: "Science is her [the housewife's] handmaiden; invention a servant following her, often preceding her, to light the
path where she has not yet discovered the need of light. Science
and invention have revolutionized housekeeping. They have made
it possible for a woman to fill the office of housekeeper and yet
have the leisure to enjoy the graces of life." Science had done so
much to liberate the housewife that the problem was "whether
women will abuse the freedom" with which they were newly blessed
and become more involved than they should in activities outside
the home, "until home becomes the secondary, not the primary
object of her life."

The most important, and in some respects the most humane,
change that technology brought to the nineteenth-century kitchen
was the arrival of the cookstove. What we think of as the primitive,
stoveless kitchen was common well into the 1840's in most city and
country homes, and for several decades after that in much of the
back country. To be sure, some pioneers lugged their stoves with
them, and many children brought up in the prairies had never seen
an open fireplace. But the wide hearth from which coals could be
drawn to keep pots simmering, the brick oven, preheated with brush
and light wood for baking, the half-cylinder of sheet-iron or tin
known as a Dutch oven that sat in front of the fire for roasting, the
metal reflectors for intensifying and directing heat against meats,
the pots and kettles hung over the flames from metal brackets were
the complex tools it took to feed most families in mid-century. There
were houses in which the kitchen had two wide doors, one on either

side, so that a horse could haul in a tremendous log each morning and then be led out the other door. "It was a wonder," wrote Candace Wheeler, as she looked back at the changes in the household as the nineteenth century came to its end, "that the women who ministered as cooks before those great altars were not devoured by the flames."

Benjamin Franklin's famous iron stove for heating rooms (it met with general disapproval when it first appeared in the 1740's) was the grandparent of the cookstove. The first "indirect heat oven," as it was called, was invented by a distinguished physicist (American-born but a loyal British citizen), Count Rumford, in the last years of the eighteenth century, but it was an American missionary to the Indians and one of the founders of Oberlin College in Ohio, Philo Penfield Stewart, who patented a stove in 1834 that ultimately changed the American kitchen. He called it the "Oberlin" and made his patent rights over to Oberlin College. Housewives were delighted with it, delighted to be done with the chores of the old open hearth; they had the new gadget set into the chimney piece, which was often large enough to house both the stove and its woodbox. The mid-century was a time when it was fashionable to make the most utilitarian household objects as "artistic" as possible and when it was commonly believed that the products of science urgently needed the civilizing application of flowery ornament. As the inventors added ovens and broilers, movable grates, storage space, hot-water jackets, and ways of adapting the stoves to either wood or coal, the designers added more and more garlands and vases and scrolls to the molds in which the iron for the stoves was cast. But even if the stove grew larger and more efficient and more ornamental, it still had to be fed by hand, banked at night, emptied of its ashes several times a day, and it had a persistently unpleasant way of powdering the kitchen with dust. Like most mechanical household contraptions, it injected new kinds of snobberies into the household. In country where wood was plentiful, housewives preferred it to coal because it was less likely to fill the kitchen with grime, and besides, a Missourian of that era reported, coal was considered "poor folksy stuff, fit only for homes on the wrong side of the tracks."

The gas range made its first halting appearance in about 1850, nearly four decades after the first gaslighting company opened for business in Baltimore. It was regarded with deepest suspicion as an instrument filled with promises of explosion for nearly thirty years after it came on the market. By the 1880's it was in fairly general use, but even as late as 1899 it was still considered an extravagance and the manufacturers of the Jewell Gas Stove felt called upon to say in their catalogue that "the popular prejudice is gradually giving away." Writers of household manuals, however, had much to say in its favor, principally on the grounds of economy and comfort. It only burned fuel when it was needed and it did not keep the kitchen at miserable temperatures in the summer.

A good many other fuels were tried and one of them, kerosene, is still in use. Coal dust, tar, and sawdust were reduced under pressure into fuels that could be burned in ranges. The gasoline stove enjoyed a dubious popularity in the 1890's. It filled "newspapers of that era," said a Missouri editor in his reminiscences, "with items about death and destruction incident to explosions in kitchens in which they had been installed." The gasoline tank had a mean way of going dry while a roast or turkey was in the oven. If the housewife replaced it, and then became distracted by some other chore, there was trouble. "Getting busy with something else," one husband ruefully wrote of an experience suffered by his wife, "she forgot to touch a match to the gas until several minutes had elapsed, by which time so much had accumulated that a loud explosion followed. The oven was torn from its moorings and hurled several feet out upon the kitchen floor. Its door came open and there was a terrible mess of baked turkey, dressing and gravy over a wide expanse." The kerosene (or coal-oil) stove which came along a few years later was docile by comparison, though it was by no means foolproof and contributed its share of tragic fires. It was popular (no one thought he would be so careless as to become a victim) partly because there was no fuel to be hauled several times a day, partly because it generated enough heat to keep the kitchen warm in winter but was much cooler in summer than coal or wood, and most particularly because kerosene was so inexpensive. Its wick, however, demanded vigilance and trimming or it emitted a grimy black smoke.

Cooking with electricity was first tried experimentally in England in about 1890, more as a stunt than as a domestic promise; it was used here primarily to amuse and astonish visitors at fairs. The Columbian Exposition in Chicago in 1893 dazzled skeptical housewives with a "model electric kitchen." ("In the café of the Electric Building the cooking is done by electricity," a guidebook to the fair reported. "It bastes its meat, and is altogether an accommodating sort of fuel. With an electric plant in a kitchen one can rig it out so that it will broil a beefsteak and turn an ice cream freezer, pare potatoes, scrub, sweep, and wash clothes. It would not be a much greater expense to make a connection with the nursery and keep the baby sufficiently rocked with the same machine. One drawback to the use of electricity for such purposes is that it is an expensive fuel. . . .") Fifteen years after the fair was over in 1908 three manufacturers almost simultaneously put electric ranges on the market. They were not a bargain. They were appallingly slow: the cook had to wait from forty-five minutes to an hour for the oven to get hot enough to use, and there was nothing that the stove manufacturer could do to speed it up. The utility companies that produced electricity could not deliver the "juice" to heat elements of more than six hundred watts. The ranges were expensive to install in the first place and once installed they were filled with temperament and subject to frequent breakdowns and the almost constant ministrations of service men.

These early electric ranges looked more like the iceboxes of the same era than stoves; they were finished in "the finest grade of oak," and like iceboxes they had drain pans into which the airtight ovens exuded condensed steam through small tubes. The dials for regulating the burners and timing-devices were just a few inches off the floor, and so little electricity flowed into the stove that a cook could not use the burners on the top and the oven at the same time. As stoves had traditionally been black, the public was somewhat suspicious when white porcelain panels appeared on electric ranges in 1917, and when the first all-white model went on display in 1925 people complained that this was impractical and that the enamel easily chipped. The dials at that time moved up to a convenient level and the oven moved up above the burners, where it stayed until streamlining put it inconveniently back near the floor in the mid-30's. It has remained there ever since except in a relatively few kitchens where sensibly eccentric women prefer not to have to bend almost double each time they want to look into the oven and have insisted on having it recessed at a convenient height into the kitchen wall.

The stove, to be sure, was just one of the worries of the housewife and the cook in the kitchen in the nineteenth century. Refrigeration was a problem, so was water, so was the disposal of refuse, so was the storage of staples, and so were houseflies. The walls were a problem, and the floor, no matter what one did about it, was a backbreaking chore to keep clean. All of these aggravations in varying degrees yielded gradually to the onslaught of scientific experiment and technological invention.

Keeping food fresh and edible was a far more acute problem for the family in the first four decades of the nineteenth century than it became when icebox refrigerators came into fairly general use in the 1840's. The protection of meats was, of course, the most delicate problem of all. In the summer months beef and mutton became tainted in a day, and it was necessary to kill a chicken not more than four hours before the cook plunged it into boiling water, plucked its feathers, cleaned it, and put it in the stove. Milk turned an hour or two after it came from the cow, unless it could be chilled, which sometimes it was by lowering it in a bucket down the well. The instructions for storing foods that Robert Roberts gave in his *House Servant's Directory* in 1828 hint at the problem:

> Vegetables will keep best on a stone floor, if the air be excluded.—Meat in a cold dry place.—Sugar and sweetmeats require a dry place; so does salt.—Candles cold, but not damp.—Dried meats, hams, the same. All sorts of seeds for puddings, saloop, rice, &c. should be close covered to preserve from insects; but that will not prevent it if kept for long. . . . Straw, to lay apples on, should be quite dry to prevent musty taste. Large pears should be tied up by the stalk.

Mrs. Child in her *American Frugal Housewife* warned of meat: "If it consists of pieces, they should be spread out separate from each other, on a large dish, and covered. If you are not to cook it soon, it is well to sprinkle salt on it. . . . If you have to keep it over night, it should be looked to the last thing when you go to bed; and if there is danger it should be scalded."

The icebox removed this kind of fear, or at least this degree of hurry and suspicion. But the regular supply of ice to the city home became possible only after the harvesting of ice from ponds and lakes and rivers grew from a local crop into a mechanized industry. The ice business prospered during the nineteenth century to such an extent that ice, like cotton, became a commodity for export. The efficient farmer had his own icehouse, sometimes built mostly below ground with only its peaked roof and entrance door showing, sometimes entirely above. Sawdust was the usual insulating material. The walls of the icehouse were filled with it between the outside and inside sheathing, and the ice was buried in it. In those parts of the West where sawdust was difficult to come by, straw was used instead. Under a roof of shingles or thatch held up at its corners by poles, the ice was stacked above a floor of stamped-down straw on which planks were laid, and the walls of the icehouse were bales of straw packed six or eight feet thick. In cities and towns ice was delivered by wagon. As many of us can still remember, with his heavy tongs the iceman pulled a cake of ice a yard high, half a yard wide, and a foot thick to the back edge of his wagon, drew a line on it with his ice pick, like a glass cutter with his tool, chipped a furrow, and then split the block into chunks suitable for an icebox. Then with his tongs he slung the piece onto a leather shield on his shoulder and carried it to the house.

By the end of the 1830's the home refrigerator sat solidly in the pantries or on the back porches of most houses. Miss Leslie described them in her *House Book* in 1840:

Refrigerators—These are large wooden boxes, standing on feet, and lined with tin or zinc, being generally inter-lined with charcoal, and having at the bottom a receptacle for ice, and a drain to carry off the water that drops from it as it melts; a vessel being always set underneath to catch the droppings. They are divided into compartments . . . and furnished with moveable shelves or slats on which to set things. During the warm season they must be every day replenished with ice. They are a convenience which no family should be without.

Miss Leslie recommended that each family should have two such refrigerators—one for meats and poultry and one for butter, cream, milk, and other "dairy." (They cost from $20 to $200 in her day.) She also thought it was nice, if not necessary, for a family to have one made of mahogany in the dining room for keeping water cool and for chilling wine.

The icebox, as she described it in 1840, changed very little in any essential way in the next seventy years. Some families, of course, couldn't afford them and kept their ice wrapped in pieces of carpet in tubs. Other families built their own and used powdered charcoal or coal ashes for insulation. Architects recommended the refrigerator be so placed that it could be filled with ice without the intrusion of the iceman into the house. This was accomplished by buying a refrigerator with "an outside icing door" and by cutting a door behind it in the wall of the kitchen or pantry. "Be sure," said a writer for *House & Garden*, "to have a hydrant placed where the iceman can have no excuse for not washing the ice." It was likely to have a little sawdust still on it.

"It will be infinitely better," Maria Parloa, who wrote a regular column on the house for the *Ladies' Home Journal*, said in 1898, "to live without a refrigerator than to use one that is not in perfect condition." The icebox took constant looking after. The waste pipe through which water drained from the ice chamber had a way of getting plugged up and had to be cleaned out with a wire. If the zinc lining cracked, water soaked into the wood of the cabinet, which became musty and gave a musty taste to the food in the refrigerator. The pan underneath had to be emptied every day; if it was let go for several days it became too unmanageable to carry without spilling on the pantry floor. Some foolish families thought they could get around this by hitching the drainpipe of the icebox to the waste pipe of the house, only to find that sewer gas backed up into the refrigerator.

If the icebox changed little from the 1830's to the 1910's, the uses of refrigeration radically changed the American diet and greatly cheered up the family table. In 1842 James Laidley, a caterer in Buffalo, New York, received a shipment of oysters, carefully packed in ice and stowed in a refrigerator, from Albany. In that same year Chicago celebrated the arrival of its "first lobster." It was carried on ice from the East Coast as far as Cleveland, then boiled and sent on to Chicago. The invention in the 1860's of the refrigerated railroad car brought thousands of tons of meat into New York from the abattoirs of Chicago. Bananas were shipped from the West Coast all the way to the markets of New York in 1869, and in the following year grapes and salmon and vegetables traveled by train from California to Chicago. The first foods to travel by rail were, to be sure, delicacies for the tables of the rich, but they foretold the day when the regional eating habits of America would, if not entirely at least extensively, give way to a more or less national diet.

Refrigeration meant, of course, that foods that easily perished when they were not chilled began to cost the housewife a good deal less in the market. It also meant that she could stretch her household budget further because she could keep leftovers which once she had to get rid of lest they spoil. She could now serve her family fresh meat throughout the year, and "cold storage" poultry and eggs, though not as desirable as fresh, could be had at any time for reasonable prices. Ice cream became, according to *Godey's Lady's Book* in 1850, "one of the necessities of life. A party without it would be like breakfast without bread or dinner without a roast."

The tendency toward a national rather than a great many regional diets was further hastened by the invention of the tin can in 1839 in Boston and its extensive use during the Civil War, by shipment of food on river steamers and coastal ships, and by the invention of the Mason jar, with its glass top, its rubber ring for sealing, and its wire clamp. It first appeared in 1858, and if it did not greatly ease the housewife's chores (it surely made extra work when the time came to "put up" vegetables and fruits), it varied the family's diet during the winter months, and sometimes won her coveted prizes at the county fair.

The mechanical refrigerator, that is, the refrigerator which made its own ice, was, like the indirect-heat oven, a European invention. A Frenchman, Ferdinand Carré, constructed the first successful freezing machine (it produced ice by the ton, not by little ice cubes) and it was displayed at the London Exhibition of 1862. Neither it nor Carré's experiments with a small unit of household size had anything but an indirect effect on the family kitchen until 1916, when the first home electric refrigerator was manufactured in America by Kelvinator. It was followed the next year by a machine called Guardian (later renamed Frigidaire) and soon after by Servel. The first machines cost about $900 and obviously were only for the prosperous and for restaurants. Yet by 1923 there were twenty thousand refrigerators in the United States, according to Sigfried Giedion, the historian of modern technology, and by 1941 there were three and a half million, and it was considered "an indispensable element in the American household." The freezer, which has not only furthered the elimination of regionalism but has very nearly eliminated the seasons of the year, was Clarence Birdseye's contribution to civilization. His inspiration came when he was spending a winter in Labrador, not a place most people would want to winter, and noticed that fish and reindeer meat froze rapidly, indeed almost instantaneously, in the arctic temperatures, and were thoroughly fresh and edible six months later. He patented a process for reproducing this phenomenon in 1925, and three years later frozen foods were on the market. It was not until after the Second World War and an interval during which many families rented lockers for frozen-food storage in commercial freezing plants that the home freezer began to appear in home kitchens almost everywhere.

When Harriet Martineau examined our society in the 1830's, the family marketing was man's business, not woman's. Miss Martineau found this division of household duties "very fair." Markets in big cities were bustling, noisy, filled with brilliant colors, and swarming with sellers and buyers, with drays and carts, with the booming voices of butchers and oystermen, fishmongers and coffee venders, with the whinnying of horses, and the piping of children as hard at work as their elders. Fragrant branches and festoons of flowers decorated the butchers' stalls. Vegetable and fruit stands were piled with "turnips scarcely larger than hen's eggs and nearly as white," with spinach and water cress "all moist with dew," and strawberries "in their luscious prime . . . shaded with fresh grape leaves." There were cages of pigeons and ducks and chickens, "forests of greenhouse plants," horse-radish grinders with their "reeking machines," doughnut and root-beer and coffee sellers. Through this the shopper wandered, his sleeves plucked at by men and women in aprons, his ears assaulted by their shouts for his attention. It was a more proper place for men than for women to shop.

A great deal of the food that came into the city house did not, however, come from the markets. Peddlers moved slowly down the streets with their carts or barrows crying their wares and their produce. "Oranges—sweet oranges!" they called, and "Strawberries, any strawbe-e-erees!" Sometimes the driver of the cart was silent while his partner went from house to house, blowing a bosun's whistle as a warning signal, and then knocking at the door. Wagons filled with passenger pigeons and grouse and prairie chickens were common in the autumn and winter in the Eastern cities. "Pigeons were considered expensive if over a dollar a dozen," wrote the daughter of a clergyman of her New York childhood in the 1850's, "or prairie hens at more than seventy-five cents a brace." Milk was also bought from carts and the housewife provided her own container for it. It was frequently anything but desirable. Cities swarmed with "swill-milk" dealers who fed their cows on distillery mash and often added molasses, chalk, and plaster of Paris to the milk to make it look acceptable. (Massachusetts was the first state to enact milk-reform laws in 1856.) Peddlers sold services as well as produce and bought as well as sold. Glaziers cried "Glass put'een," and chimney sweeps "Sweepho! Sweepho!" The tinker beat a pan and cried "Pots and pans! Mend your pots and pans!" And the scavenger tribes of ped-dlers, whom wary housewives would not let beyond their doors, cried "Rags—rags, any rags?" and men whose pushcarts were strung with jangling bells cried "Bottles! Bottles!" Sometimes the cries were melodious, their syllables drawn out, breaking from a higher key to a lower, then soaring up again, and clipped off sharp at the end. Fish-mongers blew braying notes on small tin horns, one long and three short blasts. The men who ground the scissors and knives swung bells like boarding-house dinner bells, and carried their pedal-run wheels on their backs.

The country kitchen was, to a very great extent, supplied with produce from the family garden. Root vegetables were stored in the cellar, sometimes under the house but sometimes in a separate cellar dug nearby and roofed over like a sunken icehouse. Other vegetables, after the invention of the Mason jar, were, as we have seen, preserved and kept in glittering rows in a storage cupboard, which was also often in the cellar. Hams and bacon hung from cellar rafters in a meat cupboard protected from flies. Staples were bought (or, by farm-ers, more often bartered for) at the village store—rice and salt and coffee and tea, and the chemicals that were the standard basis of house-hold magic, such as gum ammoniac to make cement for repairing crock-ery, pearl ash and unslaked lime to extract oil from boards or stone, potash to make soap, camphorated spirits to discourage mosquitoes, oil of vitriol for shoe blacking, and dozens of other ingredients commonly mentioned in the cookbooks of a century ago. The cookbooks not only prescribed recipes for foods, plain and fancy, but concoctions for curing whooping cough and cancer, for making cold cream or rose water or bait for rat traps, for indelible ink, for smelling salts, and for cheap paint for the barn.

The country store, on which more nostalgic sentimentalism has been poured than it deserves, was from the point of view of visiting. Europeans far less interesting as a community center than as an astonishing phenomenon of merchandising. Harriet Martineau was delighted to discover in a little store on the edge of the wilderness in western New York State "glass and bacon, stay-laces, prints, drugs, rugs, and crockery; bombazines and tin cans, books, boots, and moist sugar." Captain Marryat, who was in the western part of the state at about the same time, remarked that in two towns on Lake Erie there were "stores better furnished and handsomer than any shops at Norwich in England." "Would you furnish a house in one of them," he said, "you will find every article of furniture—carpets, stoves, grates, marble chimney-pieces, pier glasses, pianos, lamps, candelabra, glass, China, &c, in twice the quantity, and in greater variety, than at any provincial town in England."

But as in the city, the peddler was an important part of the logistics of the house and especially of the kitchen. All sorts of peddlers rattled their ways over corduroy roads to brighten the days of farmers' wives and children with their glittering stocks of tin utensils and wooden clocks "with the Yankee spirit in them . . . they were usually too fast." Since most farm families, even those rich in produce, had little or no money, farmers' wives traded their rags, the cloth they had woven, and other goods they had made in their households for whatever they found irresistible that the peddlers brought to their doors. Miss Martineau, who thought the peddlers picturesque (but could not understand why there were no traveling glaziers to repair the broken windows which she was distressed to see everywhere she traveled in the back country), looked sadly to the day when their numbers would dwindle. "There will be fewer carts," she wrote, "nicely packed with boxes and baskets. There will be fewer youths in home-spun, with grave faces, and somewhat grim deportment, in well-laden gigs. There will be fewer horsemen, with saddlebags, and compact wooden cases. There will be fewer pedestrians, with pouches strung before and behind, an umbrella in one hand, and an open book in an-other." But for another eighty years after Miss Martineau was in America, peddlers in carts were still spreading not only goods but gossip; they not only brought knives and ribbons and calicoes, but were windows upon the world beyond the farm.

The peddlers' means of transportation changed from horseback and wagon to automobile. Even after the First World War the butcher's wagon (now a Model-T Ford), its driver in a straw boater and apron, stopped at every door at least once a week not only on back country roads but in villages and suburbs and on the rims of cities. The vegetable truck, with its wooden crates of fruits and vegetables and staples ranged along its sides, protected from the sun with an awning, the fishmonger's white wagon emblazoned with portraits of its contents, and the baker's truck were as taken for granted as the ice wagon until thirty years ago. Women shopping at the bottoms of their front lawns, surrounded often by children pleading for apples or cookies, had a pleasant and sensible air.

The store that comes to the housewife is by no means entirely a thing of the past. It has become big business. One corporation, the Jewel Tea Company, that operates supermarkets, for example, also operates what it calls Home Service Routes in thirty-eight states and the District of Columbia. "Merchandise offered on our 1,881 routes," says its annual report for 1961, "now includes 263 staple grocery, cosmetic and household items, and almost 3,000 general merchandise items, sold with the help of modern catalogues, sales cards and point-of-purchase basket displays." Miss Martineau would have been surprised, but it is unlikely that she would have found the process picturesque.

The most humane contribution that the nineteenth century made to the kitchen, and the most unsung, was window screening. Compared with its contribution to comfort, to sanitation, to the preservation of sanity and good temper, the gas range, the electric range, the refrigerator, and the freezer pale into nothing. Flies were a far worse trial to the housewife of the last century than the pump in the kitchen sink or the scuttle that needed filling with coal. The literature of the nineteenth-century household is filled with them.

They were primarily a summer problem, of course, a problem of "the dog days." It was then that "your kitchen ceiling looked like huckleberries and milk." It was then that children weren't allowed to bring apples into the house because they attracted flies, when the housewife made a member of the family stand by the dining-room table waving a peach-tree branch back and forth so that the other members of the family could eat in relative peace. There were various contraptions and dozens of recipes for dealing with flies. Some households had devices that hung from the ceiling, gadgets from which long strips of paper descended and which could be operated by a foot treadle that made them swing back and forth over the table. There were cone-shaped traps baited with sweetened water and syrup. There were others, something like circus slapsticks, on which the housewife smeared molasses and when flies collected on them the boards were clapped together. Each household manual had its own formula. Miss Leslie suggested: "Flies may be destroyed by the following preparation: dissolve four drachms of extract of quassia (to be procured at the druggist's) in a pint of boiling water and then mix in a little brown sugar or molasses. Set it about in old saucers." In *The House Servant's Directory* of 1828 its author recommended: "To remove flies from rooms: Take a half a teaspoon of black pepper, in powder, one teaspoon of brown sugar, and one tablespoon of cream; mix them all together, and place them in the room on a plate, where the flies are troublesome, and they will soon disappear." This same formula was still being recommended fifty years later; it also appeared in Todd S. Goodholme's *Domestic Cyclopedia of Practical Information* in 1877. He also suggested a formula of leeks soaked in soft water for twenty-four hours; this solution was applied to furniture and pictures as a way to keep them from being fly-spotted. Miss Martineau thought the most ludicrous scene she had ever witnessed was a hostess waving a "great bunch of peacock's feathers" to keep flies off the breakfast table.

The history of wire window screens is murky, to say the least, and the annals of those manufacturers who have an interest in their past are full of contradictions and the not-very-accurate reminiscences of men who were in on the beginnings of the screen business. But the story seems to go something like this:

Several historians seem to agree that the first wire netting for windows appeared in Nuremberg, Germany, in the 1660's. But it was difficult to make by hand, slow and costly, and as a consequence was a curiosity rather than a commodity. The first uses of wire mesh in this country were for cellar windows (to keep out rats) and for the protection of food against flies. In an 1818 almanac published in Baltimore by Shaeffer and Maund, Hugh Balderston advertised that he made all sorts of wire-work receptacles for the protection of food, but there was no hint of (or probably dream of) making a house flyproof. Like so many products that have been helpful to the household, the commercially successful window screen seems to have been a by-product of war production. During the Civil War a manufacturer of wire mesh for sieves found to his dismay that he had greatly overproduced, and in order to get rid of his surplus he gave the screening a coat of protective paint and put it on the market for covering windows. The product (produced by Bennett Company) was known as "wire cloth," and it is mentioned in *Knight's Mechanical Dictionary* in 1872 as useful for window screens, meat-safes, and dish covers. If Bennett was the first successful marketer of wire screening for windows, he does not seem to have been the first to manufacture it, and the argument of priority in the industry remains, for our purposes, unresolved. By the 1870's steel was being used for the screening instead of iron and by 1885 galvanized wire cloth was on the market.

So far as the householder was concerned, however, window screens were still a novelty in the 1880's, and most houses were as flyblown as ever. Mosquito netting, a sort of gross cheesecloth, was tacked to doors and windows and thrown over baby carriages. Mark Twain wrote to Willard M. White of Collinsville, Connecticut, who patented a "Portable Folding Fly and Musketo [sic] Net Frame" in 1872 (prices $1.75 to $3):

Mr. White,—Dear Sir:

There is nothing that a just and right feeling man rejoices in more than to see a mosquito imposed on and put down, and browbeaten and aggravated,—and, this ingenious contrivance will do it. It is a rare thing to worry a fly with too. A fly will stand off and curse this invention till language utterly fails him. I have seen them do it hundreds of times. I like to dine in the air on the back porch in summer, and so would not be without your portable net for anything; when you have got it hoisted, the flies have to wait for the second table. We shall see the summer day come when we shall all sit together under our nets in church and slumber peacefuly while the discomforted flies club together and take it out on the minister. There are heaps of ways of getting priceless enjoyment out of these charming things if I had time to point them out and dilate on them a little.

Flypapers were also in general use in the 1870's, but they were looked on with suspicion. "It is claimed for all of them that they are harmless to human life," said Goodholme's *Domestic Cyclopedia* in 1877; "chemical analysis, however, has shown that most of them contain ingredients which render their use far from safe, except with many precautions. It may be doubted whether any mixture or paper kills more flies than it attracts into the house; and the only way to be really rid of the nuisance is to fit frameworks covered with netting to the doors and windows."

In 1902 the DeWitt Wire Cloth Company advertised "Fine Screens for Fine Houses, Made to Order . . . ," and in their catalogue they said:

> You can keep your house free from *Fly Specks*, and can light your rooms at night without admitting a host of insects.

> Probably No Money Expended upon the fixtures of a house will make so large a return in saving repairs and in comfort, as that paid for wire screens.

> They save more than their cost in a Single Year, by keeping flies from disfiguring the interior of a house, its decorations, fixtures, etc.

During the nineteenth century and in the first decade of the twentieth, screens were "12 mesh" (that is, twelve wires to the inch) and this was fine enough to keep out houseflies. But when the number of horses began to diminish and the automobile became common, flies became fewer, and the populace became more aware of mosquitoes and other insects that could make their ways through coarse screens. The mesh was made finer; full screens, rather than those that fitted into the bottom half of the window, became more or less standard, and after the First World War the metal frame began to replace the wooden frame. Today, of course, aluminum frames are common and the screens, many of them, are made of plastic mesh rather than of galvanized iron or the more expensive copper. If air-conditioning were to become universal, which is improbable, screens would disappear.

In December 1930 the *Journal of Home Economics* published a survey made by sociologists at the Connecticut Agricultural College who were intent on discovering what household appliances were considered the most important by country families, and which they would least like to do without. Window screens ranked third (after running water and sewage disposal) and ahead of electric lighting, central heating, refrigeration, and even "sufficient house room." It was the kitchen that was the primary invitation to flies, and the kitchen that has benefited most spectacularly from their exclusion.

The nineteenth-century kitchen bore little resemblance to the enameled and shiny-surfaced laboratory of modern suburbia. It frequently had a high wainscoting of unpainted but stained boards above which its plaster walls were sometimes whitewashed and sometimes painted and crowned with a wallpaper border of cabbage roses. In prosperous houses kitchen walls were often covered to the ceiling with white tiles. Its table, where the servants ate (if the family did not), was covered with a checked tablecloth, and thoughtful housekeepers provided a bit of carpet, a bookcase with a few magazines and books in it, and a good light hung from the ceiling for the cook, whose sitting room as well as place of work it was.

In Miss Beecher's day (and in farm kitchens well into this century) the kitchen sink ideally had two pumps, one for well water "with a forcing power to throw water into the reservoir in the garret" (for baths and water closets) and the other for rain water, which was collected in a "rain barrel" from the eaves of the house because of its softness. The sink was made of wood and had a grooved wooden drainboard. By the 1870's painted iron sinks were considered the most practical; tin-lined copper sinks were often installed in the houses of the rich, and it was not until the end of the century that the enameled or porcelain sink came into general use. Even in 1904 the soapstone sink was recommended by architects as the most efficient for the heavy work of the kitchen.

Keeping the kitchen clean was (and in spite of detergents still is) a heavy chore. In the last century soap for heavy cleaning was made on the kitchen stove, but many farm wives preferred to scrub their floors with wood ashes because the lime in them whitened the boards more efficiently than soap. "Won't somebody please invent something for kitchen floors that can be easily washed, that will not hold dust, and that will be warm?" pleaded an anonymous writer in *Scribner's* in 1875. Oilcloth had been invented by then, but it was considered costly at $2 a square yard for the best quality, and only good quality was worth having. Most kitchen floors in well-built houses were made of hardwood, oiled and stained. In the 1890's such floors were recommended as being preferable to linoleum, a patented material invented in England in 1860 and made of solidified linseed oil, cork or wood dust, and pigments on a backing of burlap or canvas.

As the tyranny of the kitchen yielded little by little to more efficient equipment, it also yielded its size. Very gradually in the last eighty years the kitchen has grown smaller, more compact, and more efficient. The spacious kitchen of the nineteenth-century farm, in which not only the family but the hired hands ate their meals around a center table lighted by a kerosene lamp, gradually lost its social purpose. Even in large houses where the kitchen provided meals for a dozen servants and dinners for thirty or forty guests, the kitchen began to take on more and more of the aspects of a factory—some of its time-saving principles, some of its mechanization, and some of its orderly arrangement of functions. The cookstove, as we have seen, solved many cumbersome and infuriating problems and saved many steps; the refrigerator solved other problems, not the least of them the trips down and up the cellar stairs to fetch provender. Gadgets such as the apple peeler and meat grinder contributed to the efficiency of the kitchen; the galvanized-iron boiler attached to the stove, if it did not beautify the kitchen, gave the cook a copious supply of water for washing pots and pans and for scrubbing her floor.

None of these devices escaped the attention of Catharine Beecher, of course, but she added her own special kind of intelligence to the solution of the problems of the kitchen. She had a time-and-motion-study kind of mind, and her plans for the kitchen in *The American Woman's Home* in 1869 arranged sinks and cupboards and storage bins and stove with an eye to convenient work-surfaces and the fewest possible waste motions. Her arrangement would have done credit to the engineers now employed by General Electric and Westinghouse to plan "model kitchens"; indeed, household engineers owe more to Miss Beecher and her central utilities unit than they wot.

"Keep the kitchen as small as your fittings will allow without cramping," an architect wrote in 1906. "If the cook should be able to stand in the centre of the room and by revolving on her heels perform her duties, both time, space, and the cook may be saved. The principal trouble with the average kitchen lies in the fact that there is an unlimited amount of travel involved."

Mechanization had something to do with shrinking the kitchen; so, obviously, did the acuteness of the problems of finding and keeping servants. But it was not until about 1910 that the domestic scientists launched an offensive for the "efficient kitchen" that captured the public imagination. On the outskirts of Darien, Connecticut, a Mr. Charles Barnard conducted "a housekeeping experiment station"; he was concerned not only about the arrangement of equipment (he advocated alcohol stoves, fireless cookers, and "a white enamel icebox, round in shape" with revolving shelves), but with the "direction food should take on its journey from the hands of the delivery clerk at the back door to its ultimate appearance on the dining room table." In 1912 Christine Frederick, the author of a book called *Household Engineering,* argued that the primary need of the kitchen was for equipment that was not designed individually and hit or miss, but was, like that made for large hotel kitchens, "standardized and related by a definite system of work." She was against buying a table here and a cupboard there and a stove somewhere else when each of these pieces needed to be fitted with the other to make for efficiency.

According to Sigfried Giedion, the first industrial step toward standardizing kitchen equipment was made in 1922 when a furniture manufacturer put on the market a line of kitchen cabinets that could be fitted into a variety of combinations. In the 1930's manufacturers turned their attention to "the work-process" and the sink became an integral part of the complex of cupboards. It was not until the 1940's that the stove was integrated into the total scheme and the streamlined kitchen was suddenly a gleam in almost every housewife's eye.

What happened to the kitchen physically was certainly no more important than what happened to it socially. It is popular to assume that modern changes in social behavior have been the creatures of technology, but it is also true, of course, that the demands of manners have acted as a spur to technology. If the development of industry changed the nature of the servant supply by wooing domestic workers from their brooms and ovens to manipulate wrenches and lathes, the shortage of help demanded of technologists that they get busy and find solutions to domestic problems. The need of the family to maintain life without constant drudgery provoked invention just as it ultimately provoked changes in the basic plan of the house itself. Nowhere has this been more evident than in the kitchen.

Since the end of the Second World War, the kitchen has assumed a social acceptability that it had never had before in the well-to-do classes in America. In 1958 the head of the Market Research Corporation of Chicago reported to the American Meat Institute that "70 per cent of home meals were served in the kitchen" and that "the figure rises to 71 per cent in the summer." Two years later Poppy Cannon, a food expert, commented at a meeting of the National Homes Fashions League that, "The cook is in the parlor, and so are the cooking utensils." Mr. O. S. Fowler's observation of 1854 with which this chapter began ("The sight of a tidy kitchen is not so very disgusting, even to men of refined tastes") has been entirely justified.

The kitchens that were designed in the 1940's after the war were not only streamlined, they were also planned for the pleasure of the housewife. It was there that she spent a good part of her day, not only feeding her children, but telephoning her friends, often having coffee with her neighbors, and doing her laundry. Colors in the kitchen veered away from clinical white to pastel shades and window curtains became cheerful (and cute) and women demanded that there be a mirror somewhere handy and a picture window above the sink. (In the last century the authors of household manuals frequently warned against mirrors in the kitchen; they were a temptation to the cook to comb her hair with heaven-knows-what parlous results to the soup!) But even the kitchen that was one-third dining room and one-third office and living room still segregated the housewife from her family and her guests when she was preparing meals, unless she was to have them underfoot.

The logical answer to this was to incorporate the kitchen into the living room. The open plan by the 1940's had been fairly widely accepted as the means of achieving the illusion of space in the small house. Instead of being chopped into small self-contained segments, cut off by doors, the living room flowed into the dining "area," often an "L" of the living room. It was a brief step to open the dining area into the kitchen so that, in effect, they became one, divided only by a counter, below which were cupboards. The factory of the house and the parlor had finally become one. Guests were not only present at the final stages of the manufacture of what they would consume, but they were also on hand to help clean up after themselves. When the hostess is also the cook, class distinctions vanish; the servant and the served are one. The process of democratizing the household is complete.

We have ignored in this cursory examination of the kitchen the history and development of the cookbook, about which much has been written. But I would like to quote the titles of three cookbooks which, it seems to me, put brackets around the development of the kitchen from the First Age of the Common Man to ours, the second. The first cookbook written by an American for Americans and including for the first time recipes for American dishes such as johnnycake, Indian slapjack, and pumpkin pie was published in Hartford, Connecticut, in 1796. It was called: *American Cookery; or the Art of Dressing Viands, Fish, Poultry, and Vegetables; and the best modes of making Puff-Pastes, Pies, Tarts, Puddings, Custards, and Preserves, and all kinds of Cakes, from the Imperial Plum to Plain Cake, Adapted to this Country and All Grades of Life.* It was by Amelia Simmons. In the fall of 1960 Poppy Cannon, who is quoted above, produced *The Electric Epicure's Cookbook,* and in 1962 there appeared with every chance of almost universal appeal a housewife's culinary bible called *The I Hate to Cook Book.*

CHAPTER VIII

The Parlor

The parlor is usually the most Philistine of
all Philistine American institutions.
George Fletcher Babb in
A Domestic Cyclopedia, 1877

N o room in the American home has been more tenderly cared
for, more fussed over, more jealousy protected or, on the other
hand, more abused than the parlor. In has been the highly polished
apple of the housewife's eye, the butt of rude jokes, the pride of the
family, and the target of the architect and the reformer. It has been
the upholsterer's and decorator's gold mine, and, by the same token,
the bottomless pit of the family budget. It has set husband against
wife, daughter against father, and swain against maiden. It has been
a chamber of horrors for restless children, a rack of boredom for tired
men, and a family chapel for the sanctification of the household lares
and penates. We are likely to think of it now as an outdated nineteenth-century symbol of stuffiness, gentility, and decorum, though
it is merely the progenitor of the drawing room of the turn of the
century and the living room. Manners have changed and so have our
ways of entertaining ourselves and our friends, but the living room
is still the front parlor or, as it was often called, "the best room"; it is
still our domestic best-foot-forward, and in many households exists
more for impressing the neighbors than for comforting the family.

But it would be unwise and unperceptive to underestimate the
parlor as a reflection of America's determination to achieve "the good
life." In some respects it represented the very antithesis of "all work
and no play"; it was a determined grab for the symbols of civilized
living, and it is not surprising that in a society that was restless, ambi-

tious, and materialistic, the parlor, which represented quiet, calm, continuity, and culture, should have been set aside, its double doors firmly shut and its blinds drawn against the invasion not only of the sun but of the hurly-burly of daily life. To all intents and purposes the parlor was not a room in the house, but a room in a world apart, a sort of island filled with treasure to which one could on very special occasions retreat for refreshment among family memories, delights brought back from travels, precious objects preserved by forebears, presents from lost friends, mementos of anniversaries, the record of the dead in the family Bible, and all looked down upon by ancestors staring out of the black backgrounds and gilt frames of family portraits.

The parlor, a room in which to have conversation, not only derived etymologically from the French verb *parler*, but took its airs and graces from what was called in the early part of the last century "the French taste." In polite urban circles anything French was considered more fashionable than anything English, and it was not until late in the century when the word *parlor* had become an object of ridicule and rich Americans were buying titled Englishmen as husbands for their daughters that the British expression "drawing room" came into polite usage in America. In general the parlor meant a room set apart for formal occasions, for entertaining acquaintances, rather than intimate friends, and clergymen on their rounds of parish calls. The word, however, was ubiquitous, and even in log houses that consisted of two square cabins joined by a breezeway the room in which the family entertained guests, as opposed to the "family room" where the family cooked and ate and some of it slept, was called the parlor.

The parlor had many guises but only one meaning. In a Kansas log house in the 1850's it might be ornamented with a strip of Brussels carpet in front of the fireplace which "constrasted strangely with the coarse green and yellow stripes" of a homemade rug that covered the rest of the floor. Its wooden-seated chairs might be "scanty in number and dilapidated in condition" but it might harbor a "rosewood piano of elaborate workmanship" and an old-fashioned sideboard on which "there was quite a display of silver plate" and a pine table on which stood a "canister of shot and a few wax flowers in a glass case," but it was nonetheless a parlor, a space which for all practical purposes was largely wasted out of deference to convention and the need for maintaining in decency such household gods as there were. It was a need, reasonable or not, that demanded sacrifices, and in the particular log house that sported the rosewood piano and the wax flowers under glass, the "family room . . . was low and dark, scantily and even meanly furnished, the walls without paint or plaster, but hung with hanks of yarn, red peppers, articles of clothing and strings of dried apples," with a bed in the corner and a long table that left "scarcely any room to move about." Only in rich households was the parlor not maintained at some cost of inconvenience and some sacrifice of family comfort.

From the columned and gently tinted simplicity and restrained elegance of the Greek Revival parlor and the formality of the Gothic furnishings so warmly recommended by Mr. Downing, the parlor erupted in plush and velvet. It became a bower of fringe and needle-point, cabbage roses and lambrequins, ottomans and little spindle chairs on which a lady might perch in her crinoline and beribboned satins, but on which a man scarcely dared to risk his bulk. Even late in the century when the "artistic craze" was foisted on Americans by an Englishman, Charles Eastlake, and furniture became solid, doweled, and "sincere," the spirit of the parlor changed scarcely at all. It remained an island of formality in a turbulent sea of family comings and goings—set apart from baking and cooking and laundering and sweeping, from homework, muddy boots, and slop jars, sewing and mending, preserving, cleaning grates, and trimming lamps.

The trouble with the parlor—and a great many serious-minded people who took the cares of every American household as their very own thought it was a grave trouble—was that the island all too often occupied far too large a part of the family sea and, even more deplorable, far too large a part of the budget. One might expect this of the social butterflies and fops who lived in cities and to whom the niceties of fashion and etiquette were all-important. *Harper's Bazar* in the 1860's might fly into a rage of indignation because all too many families in New York spent a third of their incomes renting houses at fashionable addresses and had only enough money left to make a splurge in the parlor and dining room and leave the rest of the house in a state approaching squalor. But it seemed downright immoral of the farm family, not only the bulk but the backbone of the nation, to indulge in silly notions of the same sort. And yet such was too often the case.

Attempts to reform the parlor, if not quite out of existence at least into some sort of reasonable sense of proportion, nagged at nineteenth-century women decade after decade. It is a tribute to the guile of upholsterers and the "gentility" of the American housewife that so few women gave in. "Multitudes of persons," wrote Miss Beecher in 1841, "will cramp their bedrooms, kitchens and closets to secure a large parlor . . . to be shut up most of the time." She was only one of those who raised her voice and went unheeded. Thirty-five years later, Sereno E. Todd, that widely read advocate of the virtues of rural living, was still trying. "So far as *space* is concerned," he wrote in *Country Homes and How to Save Money*, "most people in the country should reverse the order of their parlors and kitchens. . . . Most farmers erect a nice and expensive house, with a costly parlor or two, and furnished with beautiful carpets, window shades and other adjuncts of a parlor, and go look into the—almost sacred—apartment about once a week. . . . What is the use of having a house without making fair and respectable use of it?"

Very few women bothered to answer, much less consider, his question. A parlor was a parlor, and that was that. What matter that its shades were usually drawn or its shutters closed for fear that the sun might fade the roses in the carpet and the velvet on the chairs? Who cared that what might have been the sunniest room in the house was off limits to children, so long as the bell glass that covered the twig of stuffed birds never felt the smudgy finger tips of little hands? What did it matter that the room smelled damp and the air was chill because the windows were kept tight shut against dust and flies for weeks on end? What matter that "for concentrated stiffness, weakness and the most glaring lack of welcome," as an architect late in the century wrote, "these rooms are famous and unequalled"? What difference did it make that there was a coldness about such rooms that "froze the enthusiasm of friendship," or that the studied display of ornaments and "gift books" stayed the visitor's hand lest he should upset the composition of the room? It was a parlor, the housekeeper's pride, and her means of telling the world that she knew how to be "refined" and understood the nicer things of life.

The limits to which women went to protect the sanctity of their parlors will always seem odd to a man and today seems odd to all but a few of the fussiest housekeepers if, indeed, any of the breed still exists. Some women, according to Miss Leslie, "were always uneasy when their visitors sat down on a sofa or an ottoman, and could not forbear inviting them to change their seats and take chairs." They were evidently afraid that "the more the damask-covered seats were used, the sooner they would wear out." But the care of the parlor went a good deal further than that.

In her delightful book *House and Home Papers*, Harriet Beecher Stowe ("Christopher Crowfield") wrote from a man's point of view of how the purchase of a new piece of Brussels carpet very nearly brought about the downfall of a family. The carpet made the furniture of the living room look shabby and this prompted the lady of the house and her daughters to reupholster every piece in the room. The husband was no longer permitted to smoke his pipe or read there in the evening lest he mess up the room with his newspaper, so he retired to his study, and soon the family followed him. "In fact," he said, "nobody wanted to stay in our parlor now. It was a cold, correct, accomplished fact . . . an undeniable best parlor, shut up and darkened, with all proper carpets, curtains, lounges, and marble-topped tables, too good for human nature's daily food." He was appalled at the lengths to which women went to put their parlors away for the summer: "Sophia . . . was warned of cockroaches, warned of flies, warned of dust; all the articles had their covers, made of Holland linen, in which they looked like bodies laid out,—even the curtain tassels had each its little shroud."

The cost of furnishing a parlor properly by nineteenth-century standards was nearly three times that of any other room in the house, and, of course, it was often a great deal more. In Goodholme's *Domestic Cyclopedia*, a fat tome of "practical information" published in New York in 1877, George Fletcher Babb, who wrote the article about house furnishings, and who said that "the parlor is usually the most Philistine of all Philistine American institutions," gave itemized lists of what should be in each room in the house with the cost of each item. Prices, he said, had fallen about 20 percent as a result of the depression of 1875, but to furnish a parlor in a house that cost four to five thousand dollars should cost about $600. The principal cost was Brussels carpet at $2 a yard. A divan sofa cast $75, small cushioned chairs $22 apiece, an overstuffed chair $30, and a "Centre table, covered with billiard cloth—a unique piece bought at second-hand" $75. There was also an "Oriental folding chair" at $11, a rocker at $35, two dwarf bookcases at $37.50 each, a $10 rug, and a gas chandelier with six globes at $54. (I suggest that you do not attempt to add up these figures; some of the carpet cost was spread into other rooms.) A master bedroom in this same house he estimated could be furnished for $254 including the bedding and linen, while in his estimate for the parlor he includes none of those ornamental plates, *bibelots,* brass pots, and peacock feathers or draperies which were considered essential in the "artistic" period of which he writes.

Mr. Babb's parlor was not meant for a rich household or for a poor one; it was thoroughly middle-class. With some ingenuity and a proper amount of do-it-yourself, such as making rustic picture frames and plant-stands of boughs decorated with clusters of acorns, it was possible to contrive a parlor for a comparative pittance. In the school textbook edition of their *Principles of Domestic Science* the Beecher sisters gave this budget for "anyone with 'a heart that is humble'":

Wallpaper and border	$ 5.50
Thirty yards matting	15.00
Centre-table and cloth	15.00
Muslin for three windows	6.75
Thirty yards green English chintz, at 25¢	7.50
Six chairs, at $2 each	12.00
	$61.75

Most female hearts, however, were at their least humble when it came to the parlor. "Was there ever an American woman who, furnishing a house, did not first lay aside the money for the parlor?" asked Mr. and Mrs. Stockton, who wrote about the home in the 1870's. "A parlor must be, even if after it there comes the deluge."

But if the financial cost of the parlor was nearly always enough to take a husband's breath away, the spiritual cost of it was downright inflationary. The demands of the nineteenth-century parlor were exacting and filled with pitfalls for the ill-bred or unwary. It was *sanctum sanctorum* or sit-down-and-mind-your-manners. It professed to provide a sweet-smelling (pomanders and rose-petal potpourri), calm, dignified, and cultured escape from the hurly-burly of the market place and counting room for men and from the endless details of children, servants, and housekeeping for women.

The parlor was the showcase of gentility and its code of manners was elaborate and exacting. There the most formal moments of family life were endured—the formal call (called a "morning" call if it took place any time between eleven in the morning and three in the afternoon), the tea party, the evening reception, the dreadful ten minutes while guests gathered before the dinner party, the hushed and lugubrious conversation when a member of the family had died, the proposal of marriage. The writers of books of etiquette had advice to offer on every aspect of behavior in the parlor, every situation, every innuendo. They anticipated every social *gaffe* and adumbrated every possible *faux pas,* some with an air of indignation, others with humor, and still others with the quiet indulgent tones of an older and wiser friend. There were a great many American families who looked upon their parlors as the indispensable anchor which held their households in the social stream, but who were unsure just how one should behave in them. It was at them that the behavior books were aimed, and there were rules, rules, rules. How could anyone learn them all?

There was nothing more difficult about the parlor than the problem of how to get in it gracefully and get out of it without fumbling. Emily Post in her first etiquette book in 1922 said, "Perhaps the best instruction would be like that in learning to swim. 'Take plenty of time, don't struggle, and don't splash about!' " Nearly a century earlier Mrs. Farrar in *The Young Lady's Friend* felt constrained to note that on entering the parlor, "Some girls have a trick of *jiggling* their bodies, (I am obliged to coin a word in order to describe it); they shake all over, as if they were hung on spiral wires, like the geese in a Dutch toy. . . . It robs a lady of all dignity, and makes her appear trifling and insignificant. . . . It must have originated in embarrassment, and a desire to do something, without knowing exactly what; and being adopted by some belle, it became, at one time, a fashion in New York, and spread thence to other cities."

The problem was by no means merely a feminine one. The author of *The Ladies' Indispensable Assistant,* which also included instructions for gentlemen, took a less humorous view than either Mrs. Post or Mrs. Farrar of this critical social moment: "You leave your overcoat, cane, umbrella, &c., and if the call is of any length, your hat in the entry. A graceful bow, a pleasant smile, an easy way of paying compliments, and suiting them to each person, no lesson can teach." The anonymous author, who was presumably a woman, was more concerned about how to get out of the parlor than into it. "It is well to know how to enter a room," she wrote, "but it is much better to know when and how to leave it. Don't stand hammering and fumbling, and saying 'Well, I guess I must be going.' When you are ready, go

at once. It is very easy to say, 'Miss Susan, your company is so agreeable, that I am staying longer than I intended, but I hope to have
the pleasure of seeing you again soon; I wish you good morning,' and
bowing, smiling, shaking hands, if the hand be proffered, you leave
the room, if possible without turning your back; you bow again at the
front door, and if any eyes are following you, you still turn and raise
your hat in the street."

Hundreds of thousands of words were devoted to what to talk about
in the parlor and, more emphatically, what not to talk about. Conversations for brief fifteen-minute calls, which consisted merely of
exchanging compliments, were outlined, and suitable topics for longer
interchanges were listed, along with topics that were considered
socially taboo.* To engage in an argument was, of course, the very
nadir of bad taste and ill-breeding, though the argument might be
about the name of a rose or the quality of a piece of ribbon or lace.
Gentlemen were cautioned not to talk politics in the presence of ladies
(though they often did) because ladies were expected to be both
uninterested in them and ill-informed. Religion and moral questions
were to be avoided as well, for they led, according to *The Illustrated
Manners Book*, "to angry, endless, and useless contests." Miss Leslie
advised women not to attempt to engage gentlemen in discussions of
finance or politics, because: "All the information that a woman can
possibly acquire or remember on these subjects is so small, in comparison with the knowledge of men, that the discussion will not elevate
them in the opinion of masculine minds." She most assuredly did not
share the views of her ardently feminist contemporaries like Margaret
Fuller. "Truth is," Miss Leslie wrote, "the female sex is really as
inferior to the male in vigour of mind as in strength of body; and all
arguments to the contrary are founded on a few anomalies, or based
on theories than can never be reduced to practice."

Ladies and gentlemen of the day were cautioned that the art of
conversation was not to be taken lightly or acquired easily. It required
"a cultivated mind, richly stored with a variety of useful information;
a good taste; a delicate sense of propriety; a good use of language;
and an easy and fluent expression." To achieve this artistic effect
Harvey Newcomb, the author of *How to Be a Lady*, published in
1863, provided eleven rules, among which were: avoid *affectation*

---

* A Baltimore friend of mine once overheard a maid in her house say after a
party, "When the quality meets, how the compliments fly!"

("it will expose you to ridicule"); avoid *low expressions* ("a dialect peculiar to low people"); avoid *provincialisms* ("For example, in New England, many people are in the habit of interlarding their conversation with the phrase, 'You see.' "); avoid *unmeaning exclamation* (such as "O my! O mercy! &c."), and so on. But the meat of the advice about conversational decency wherever it appears in manners manuals was to avoid talking too much about one's self and one's personal problems. Late in the century the forbidden topics of polite conversation were reduced to what one elderly lady of my acquaintance used to call "The five D's": they were Dress, Diseases, Domiciles, Descendants, and Domestics. It is a great deal more difficult to discover what the mentors of manners thought were suitable subjects for conversation than what were not. The weather, of course, was safe, so was the opera. It was polite to inquire about a visitor's children, though even this had to be undertaken with discretion, as Miss Leslie cautioned:

> As mothers are always on the *qui vive,* (and very naturally,) be careful what you say of their children. Unless he is a decidedly handsome man, you may give offense by remarking, "The boy is the very image of his father." If the mother is a vain woman, she would much rather hear that all the children are the very image of herself. Refrain from praising too much the children of another family, particularly if the two sets of children are cousins. It is often dangerous to tell a mother that "little Willy is growing quite handsome." She will probably answer, "I had hoped my child was handsome always!"

It was considered dangerous in the highly mobile society of America to ask questions that might remind a woman that she came from "humble" origins. It was a cliché at the turn of the century that one should not ask a prosperous San Franciscan who his grandmother was; it was quite possible that she had been a madam. But in the middle of the last century it was considered treading on thin ice to discuss household affairs with newly rich women because "Women who have begun the world in humble life, and have been necessitated to give most of their attention to household affairs, are generally very shy in talking of housewifery, after their husbands have become rich, and are living in style, as it is called. Therefore, do not annoy them by questions on domestic economy. But converse as if they had been ladies always." There were also taboos against gossip, of course, but few women, either ill- or well-bred paid much attention to them. "It is one of the greatest miseries of our life," wrote "Daisy Eyebright," the author of *A Manual of Etiquette*, "that scandal is the standing dish in society, and calumny stalks abroad with perfect boldness and impunity."

The occasions for conversation in the parlor were primarily those already mentioned, the "morning" call, the tea party, and the evening party, which was quite distinct from the dinner party, which started promptly upon the arrival of the guests and broke up, perhaps three hours later, almost at once when dinner was finished. The ritual of the call was an absolutely essential part of nineteenth-century manners, its propriety taken for granted, its uses very nearly universal. Even in the back country in the 1830's making calls was an essential part of a woman's day, and Captain Marryat when he was in Detroit in 1837, when there was not "a paved street in it or even a footpath for a pedestrian," found that "the muddy and impassable state of the streets has given rise to a very curious custom of making morning and evening calls." Detroit was then a town of many log cabins, but it was not without its proprieties. "A one-horse cart," Marryat recorded, "is backed against the door of a house; the ladies dressed get into it, and seat themselves upon a buffalo-skin at the bottom of it; they are carried to the residence of the party upon whom they wish to call; the cart is backed in again, and they are landed dry and clean."

Books of etiquette disagree on many details of making calls, but they were as one that they should be made. The morning call was generally a visit of about fifteen minutes; less than that was rude, more was inconsiderate of the person being called upon. "First calls" were paid on new arrivals after a "suitable" interval had been allowed them to settle their new homes. "When should a lady call first upon a new and desirable acquaintance?" asked Mrs. M. E. W. Sherwood in *Manners and Social Usages*. "Not hastily. She should have met the new and desirable acquaintance, should have been properly introduced, should feel sure that her acquaintance is desired. . . . Too much haste in making new acquaintances, however—'pushing,' as it is called— cannot be too much deprecated." It was, of course, the prerogative of the lady being called upon to decide whether she was "at home" or not. In the country where callers might well have come some distance by carriage, it was considered rude not to be "at home" and, worse than that, unfriendly. But in the city it was a lady's privilege to receive callers or not, so long as she exerted discretion, and was "at home" more often than not. In no city was calling more elaborate or more of a social burden than in Washington. "The American woman is making an heroic effort, here as elsewhere, to do what is expected of her," wrote the author of *Social Usages in Washington* in Teddy Roosevelt's administration. "A lady in official life sometimes devotes four afternoons in the week to the business of paying calls, making as many as thirty or even fifty in a single day." This kind of calling was merely "dropping cards" on people, an onerous task that had nothing to do with friendship or hospitality, and was merely a kind of tribute that women were expected to pay to the demons of etiquette.

The uses of the calling card grew to ridiculous proportions during the nineteenth century, and the rules for using them became so elaborate that scarcely anyone could master all of their nuances and idiosyncrasies. "However laughable it may appear to some persons, to see bits of pasteboard with names on them, left at the doors of houses," wrote Mrs. John Farrar, early in the century, "it is a most convenient custom, and the only way of being sure that your call will be known to your friend." Mrs. Farrar would have been astonished at what came eventually to be the tyranny of the card. Forty years later the anonymous author of *Social Etiquette in New York* devoted two chapters to the use of cards, one for gentlemen and one for ladies, and it was a solemn matter indeed. The discourse began: "To the unrefined or underbred person, the visiting-card is but a trifling and insignificant bit of paper; but to the cultured disciple of social law, it conveys a subtle and unmistakable intelligence. Its texture, style of engraving, and even the hour of leaving it, combine to place the stranger whose name it bears in a pleasant or disagreeable attitude, even before his manners, conversation, and face have been able to explain his social position. The higher the civilization of a community, the more careful it is to preserve the elegance of its social forms."

Mark Twain was certainly one of "the unrefined or the underbred" whom this author had in mind. Five years earlier in *The Gilded Age*, Twain, who took special delight in needling the socially pretentious, had written of the use of cards in Washington. "For instance," he wrote—

> Mrs. A. pays her annual visit, sits in her carriage and sends in her card with the lower right-hand corner turned down, which signifies that she has "called in person"; Mrs. B. sends down word that she is "engaged" or "wishes to be excused"—or if she is a parvenu and low-bred, she perhaps sends word that she is "not at home." Very good; Mrs. A.

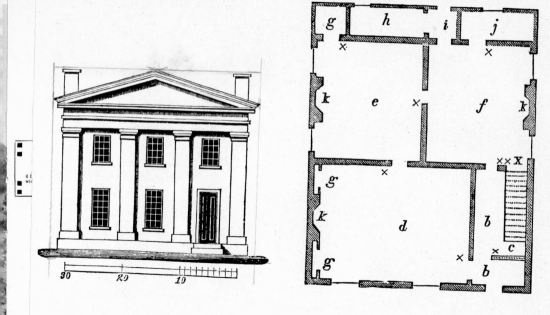

Our Templed Hills

No fad in domestic architecture has ever been so universally appealing to Americans as was the Greek Revival. The modest house above was considered suitable for a farmer in 1842. The splendid "temple" below is Andalusia, built by the banker Nicholas Biddle near Philadelphia in 1833.

Multiple Dwellings

Two-family houses, cheek by jowl, housed millions of families at the turn of the century and still do. The ones in Bethlehem, Pa., were photographed by Walker Evans in 1936. In big cities row houses began to give way to tall apartments in the 1860's. The famous Dakota, below right, was built in New York in 1881 and is still fashionable. The American predilection for circles and octagons, balconies and bays has never been given greater play than in Marina City in Chicago, completed in 1963.

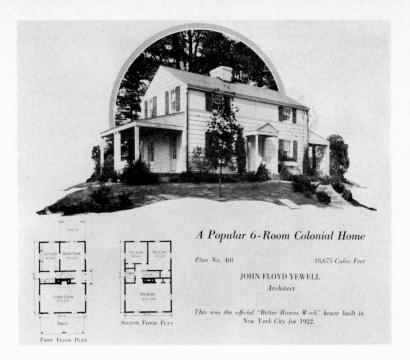

A Popular 6-Room Colonial Home

Plan No. 401   18,675 Cubic Feet

JOHN FLOYD YEWELL
Architect

This was the official "Better Homes Week" house built in New York City for 1922.

FIRST FLOOR PLAN   SECOND FLOOR PLAN

Yesterday's Up-to-date House

Not many colonists ever lived in anything that resembled the 1920's Colonial Home, but it was the ranch house of its day and the apple of millions of eyes. Surprisingly it still is, though in the 1930's Bauhaus Modern (also called the International Style) began to show up in scattered places. The house below, designed by William Lescaze, was considered wildly unconventional in 1936.

Today's House and Yesterday's Modern

Today's domestic architects have added almost no new concepts or ideas to those that Frank Lloyd Wright built into the famous house Falling Water in the mid-1930's. They have changed roof lines and experimented with materials and arrangements. But most Americans are content with something like the house below—a split-level ranch built in 1960 in Pontiac, Michigan. It could be anywhere.

drives on happy and content. If Mrs. A.'s daughter marries, or a child is born to the family, Mrs. B. calls, sends in the card with the upper left-hand corner turned down, and then goes along about her affairs,—for that inverted corner means "Congratulations." If Mrs. B.'s husband falls downstairs and breaks his neck, Mrs. A. calls, leaves her card with the upper right-hand corner turned down and then takes her departure; this corner means "Condolence." It is very necessary to get the corners right, else one may unintentionally condole with a friend on a wedding or congratulate her upon a funeral. If either lady is about to leave the city, she goes to the other's house and leaves her card with "P.P.C." engraved under the name—which signifies, "Pay Parting Call."

One can almost hear the author of *Social Etiquette in New York* sneering and saying "Tsk! Tsk! Doesn't he know that P.P.C. stands for *pour prendre congé?*" The language of etiquette, like the decoration of the parlor, was French. In fashionable circles the "party call," which one omitted to pay on a hostess within a week of a party at the cost of social ostracism, was called a *"visite de digestion."*

It was on the manners of the parlor that writers about etiquette concentrated their principal fire, though the manners of the dining room and of the street came in for their fair share of comment. The parlor was, after all, the principal private room in which public manners were most on display, and it was the place where guidance in proper behavior was presumed to be most needed. It is impossible to say whether the stuffiness of the room dictated the increasing stiffness of manners or if the determination to behave genteelly made the room more uncomfortable, more formal, and more forbidding. Visitors to America in the early days of President Jackson's administration were struck by the snobbishness of the self-appointed aristocracy of Eastern cities (especially in New York and Washington) and their incivility to anyone they considered their social inferiors. In the new cities of the West they were dismayed by how unentertaining the "entertainments" which took place in the parlor could be. In any case, the dictates of gentility coupled with a kind of sentimental piety tended to make the parlor and its amusements more and more restrained and constraining.

When Mrs. Trollope first arrived in Cincinnati in the late 1820's she noted that, "Whatever may be the talents of the persons who meet together in society, the very shape, form and arrangement of the meeting is sufficient to paralyze conversation." The trouble was that the men herded together in one part of the room and the women in another (a trouble that is still a common practice in many American households) and nothing seemed able to break the barrier between the sexes. Later Mrs. Trollope was surprised to discover that this practice of segregation was equally prevalent in cities east of the Alleghenies. "The gentlemen spit, talk of elections and the price of produce, and spit again," she wrote. "The ladies look at each other's dresses till they know every pin by heart; talk of Parson Somebody's last sermon on the day of judgment, on Dr. T'otherbody's new pills for dyspepsia, till the 'tea' is announced, when they all console themselves together for whatever they may have suffered in keeping awake, by taking more tea, coffee, hot cake and custard, hoe cake, johnny cake, waffle cake, and dodger cake, pickled peaches, and preserved cucumbers, ham, turkey, hung beef, applesauce, and pickled oysters than were ever prepared in any other country in the known world. After this massive meal is over, they return to the drawing room, and it always appeared to me that they remained together as long as they could bear it, and then they rise *en masse,* cloak, bonnet, shawl, and exit."

In New York, where dancing was often indulged in at evening parties, James Silk Buckingham found in the 1840's that, "The dancing was monotonous and indifferent; partly from languor, and partly, it is believed, from affectation of indifference, which is considered to be more genteel than vulgar vivacity." It was gentility that was taking the fun out of life, and it was gentility that continued until the end of the century to make the parlor and its amusements the kind of tribulation that leisure enforces on those who believe, as Americans did, that only work was a virtuous occupation. The functions of the parlor were social "duties" rather than friendly pleasures, and the more onerous, the more complicated by elaborate rules of etiquette, the more niceties and nuances there were to be observed, and the more silver there was to be polished, the easier it was for the American woman to justify the use of her leisure. Only among the very rich was the observance of social amenities a full-time occupation which demanded not merely extensive knowledge of the rules but the self-assurance to flout them and make new ones and the generalship to plan and execute the elaborate strategy of social campaigns.

For most men the parlor was one of the tribulations of life that one was expected to make the best of, keep a stiff upper lip about, and try not to make a fool of one's self in. It was part of the sacrifices that he grudgingly took for granted were due his wife. To children it was a place where they were to be seen and not heard, except when their mothers asked them to perform a newly learned piece on the piano for the benefit of a lady who sat stiffly with her gloved hands folded in her lap, or to show off a few French phrases they had just learned at school. They might "speak when spoken to," but if they ventured to speak on their own, they were hustled from the room. Even the parlor games which children had enjoyed in the early part of the century were obsolete or, as Miss Leslie said in a book about children's games, "only to be found in circles which are yet untouched with the folly and affectation of what is called fashion."

The downfall of a room which placed such a burden on so many members of the family was bound to come sooner or later, in form if not entirely in substance. Many of its values were false ones and its discomforts far outweighed its pleasures or even its returns in social prestige. Further than that, its proprieties were blown up into what seemed to most people a symbol that played hob with the best qualities of frank and casual republican manners and hospitality. As the century progressed and America grew in power and importance and became less self-concious about its cultural shortcomings, it felt less and less need to look over its shoulder to Europe for its standards of polite behavior.

There were practical considerations that militated against the parlor as well as cultural ones. For one thing, more and more people were living in cities and a smaller and smaller percentage of city families were living in houses. For the Eastern cities the value of land had made the cost of building a city house by the 1870's prohibitive except for the rich, and as a result the apartment house began to appear in earnest. Only in expensive apartments was there a room that could be shut off for only formal use, and the parlor became the sitting room used by all of the family every day. Its furniture became more comfortable, its atmosphere more relaxed, and the children were allowed to do their homework at its center table under a gas fixture which shed its blue-white light from a ceiling chandelier. Even in large houses and expensive apartments the word *parlor,* identified with parvenu wealth of the earlier part of the century, lost caste and, now decorated with "antiques" imported from England and France and Italy rather than American-made furniture, it became the "drawing room."

But the parlor did not die quietly all at once and without a prolonged whimper. It had to be beaten to death with words, some of
them indignant and some humorous. The attacks on the extravagance
of the parlor, its size as compared with other rooms in the house, and
its being preserved as a sort of family museum only for special use
started early in the century. By the 1870's the Victorian parlor began to
give way to the "artistic" parlor which gloried in the "quaint" and the
exotic. Cozy-corners and Turkish nooks, piled with cushions and decorated with cattails and peacock feathers, with brass pots and taborets
inlaid with mother-of-pearl, drove out formality and ushered in
romantic notions. One writer on the home called it "Yankee rococo,"
but whatever it was it combined clutter with comfort and substituted
polite sensuousness for the straight-spined piety of a few decades before. People looked back with few regrets to the time when the parlor
was a "temple of form and fidgetiness," when "the children were
watched with lynx eyes lest they should displace or soil something,"
and when "the entertainment of friends" was a "social discipline."
Even the manners books became more relaxed in their attitudes, and
though they continued to give advice on every conceivable aspect of
social deportment, they no longer thought it essential for a young man
when he got married to get rid of all of his bachelor acquaintances lest
his bride find them unsuitable to invite into her parlor.

Forbidding as the parlor was, it was an oasis, but more important it
was a gesture of civilization in a nation that was still more than half
wilderness—a counterpart of the British colonial's dinner jacket in the
jungle, a hedge against falling into habits of slovenliness. Such habits
of mind as the parlor represented are not easily shaken, nor are objects
once thought beautiful or special or associated with times of happiness
or tragedy quickly cast aside for the new and fashionable. One does
not have to look far in nearly any part of the country for a parlor in
which at least the echoes of a century ago are still alive. There are,
after all, still a great many men and women whose childhood was lived
in the late Victorian era and in whose houses the television set now
sits next to a whatnot and whose radio is planted on a rosewood table
with carved and twisted legs. Their forebears still watch them from
gilt frames and they still cherish their green-shaded student lamps,
long since wired for electricity. Fashions in decorating are continually
nudging each other out of the way, but manners have a way of

persisting, and those whose manners were tempered in the fire of the parlor are as dignified as they ever were.

"We are fast becoming a parlorless nation," wrote Lillian Hart Tryon fifty years ago. "The accidental limitations of space and of service in modern life, and the increased expenses of buildings as well as the noble intention of simplifying the house, have contributed to the result. . . . The parlor now is relegated to the cold and viewless side [of the house], or is crowded into a corner of the hall, with two chairs and a palm. We could not get our parlors back if we tried, because we ourselves have changed. . . . Life is too full to have patience with formalities. The cry of the time is for few friends and good ones." But even more important than the shrinking house, its mechanization, and the shortage of service was the change that had gradually come over women, how they viewed the world around them with a new interest, and strode through it with a quickened pace. "In this age of the feminist," Mrs. Tryon continued, "man has come into his own at home."

The parlor had been not only the forum over which the woman presided but almost the only arena in which she faced the world outside her home. When Harriet Martineau visited America in the 1830's, she had found only seven kinds of employment that were open to women—teaching, needlework, keeping boarders, work in cotton mills, typesetting, bookbinding, and domestic service. Of these only teaching and, possibly, keeping boarders were considered respectable occupations for ladies. Toward the end of the century came a shift of heart and of opportunity. The professions of law, medicine, and architecture grudgingly opened their doors, if only a crack, to women; offices wooed them to run the newfangled typewriter; the reputation of Florence Nightingale had made nursing honorable, and even being an actress was not considered as entirely disreputable as it had been only a few years before. Colleges like Vassar, Holyoke, Smith, and Bryn Mawr, which were determined to give women an education not only equivalent to that given to men but of precisely the same sort, had begun to make women impatient with the drudgery of housekeeping and the finicky world of the parlor. ("Only our failures marry," said the militantly intellectual M. Carey Thomas, first woman president of Bryn Mawr.)

The American woman was moving again, not to the forest and the prairie this time, but into a world as filled with adventure and with as many unfamiliar kinds of weariness, drudgery, and boredom as the wilderness had imposed on her mother a generation before. But this time her dream house was not built around a parlor—elegant, formal, sweet-smelling, and immaculate. The dream became not of a place to sit with your ankles neatly together, but a place to put your feet up. It took a feminist revolution to make women see that there was some sense in men's attitude to the parlor after all.

CHAPTER IX

Below Stairs

"Why did you leave your last place?" I en-
quired of an applicant.
"The lady says I was sassy to her, ma'am."
"Were you?"
"Yes, ma'am; but she was sassy to me first."
Mrs. Shillaber's Cook-Book, 1887

I

The men who founded our Republic conscientiously saw to it that the United States would always have a "servant problem." In insisting on equal rights for all men, they wrote the servant problem into the Declaration of Independence and they confirmed it in the Constitution.

Obviously we would much rather have a servant problem than a servant class. We wish the problem would go away, but we cannot abide its alternative, and so, rather than solve it by means that seem to us unhumanitarian and undemocratic, we have managed during the last century and a half to change the ground rules in a characteristically American way. We have treated the servant problem as though it were a mechanical one, which to a very considerable extent it is, and by and large have done quite well with it on that basis.

The story of our intentionally insoluble servant problem has agonized its way through three chapters in the last century and a half, and in some respects we are right back where we started. Our present domestic arrangements are not unlike those of the frontier house, and we get along by organizing the family to do the domestic chores and by getting in occasional "help." We have moved a long way mechanically; we are almost where we started humanly.

155

The first chapter of the saga of the servant problem starts more or less with the outburst of the republican spirit in the 1820's, when no one would admit to being anyone else's creature and when, as Mrs. Trollope said, it was "more than petty treason" to call anyone a "servant." A dearth of willing domestics coincided with the upsurge in the spirit of "gentility," with the result that there was a sharp conflict between the "help" on one side and those who were determined to be politely useless on the other. The quarrel, essentially, was between those who had not the slightest intention of forfeiting their dignity to fostering anyone else's pretensions and those who, though they often paid hearty lip service to the great American experiment in equality, bent every effort to be as doggedly upper class as their incomes would permit. This first chapter takes us roughly from the inauguration of Andrew Jackson in 1828 to the Civil War, though it would be a mistake to attempt to put hard and fast time brackets around it.

The second chapter, as is commonly true of social history, was begun before the first chapter was finished. It coincides with the era of massive immigration from Europe to the East Coast of America and from China to the West Coast that poured hundreds of thousands of domestics into the country. This is a story of ignorance and inefficiency (on the part of both help and helped) in conflict with increasing domestic sophistication, mechanization of the household, the cult of "refinement," and the determination of the newly arrived to "arrive."

It was the First World War that ushered in the third (and almost surely not the final) chapter, which might be called the Age of Creeping Informality. It was not democratic pressures or immigration that this time changed the complexion of the servant problem; it was the mass emigration of women from the washtub to the lathe, from the parlor and kitchen to the assembly line. Industry, which was making more money and more goods for more people, was also seeing to it that the servant class was all but done away with.

II

The American house in the first chapter of our saga was a constantly demanding structure with very few alleviating graces. The only way to keep a house was the hard way, and the only way to keep up with its demands was to carry on an unremitting war with its refusal to stay clean, orderly, warm, ventilated, nourishing, and pleasant. The main power was woman power, and one woman was not enough to tame the house, much less make it the "genteel" surroundings in which most women wished to disport themselves. It was taken for granted that almost every family, including the families of farmers and mechanics, had some kind of domestic help. What we now call "middle-income families" had two "in help" at least (a cook and a maid) and the rich from five to a dozen or more.

The Greek Revival and Gothic houses and the Tuscan villas, for all their high-ceilinged elegance, their leisurely air, and sense of well-being, were the antithesis of efficiency. They almost seem by our standards to have been designed with the intent to aggravate the servant problem. In city houses servants' quarters more often than not were dark, low-ceilinged rooms in the basement near the kitchen, with high, small windows that looked out on the hoofs of horses passing in the street, and opened to the clatter of clicking heels and the rumble of wheels on cobblestones. If servants' rooms were not in the basement, then they were under the tin roof, three or four flights from the casual caller at the front door and a long way up to haul a pitcher of water and a slop jar. The country servant was little better off. Her room was likely to be in the attic, or she might live in a cubby on the back of the house reached by its own flight of stairs, making it necessary for her to go down and up again by the front stairs to reach the other bedrooms. If the admonitions to housewives are accurate, all too often the servant's room was hot and airless, rugless, uncurtained, and unadorned, with a straw-ticked bed and leftover and broken furniture.

Some houses, especially those in which the kitchen was below the dining room, had dumbwaiters from kitchen to pantry; some had dumbwaiters that went to the bedroom floors as well, which eased the burden of lugging baskets of clean linen up steep, narrow flights. Some houses had speaking tubes in which the mistress of the house first blew to make them whistle, and then, having summoned the maid, gave her orders. All houses had grates to be cleaned and fires to be lighted the first thing in the morning. Hot water from the boiler attached to the kitchen stove had to be carried in pitchers to the master's bedroom. Slop jars and commodes had to be emptied. There were no buttons to push to make light, no switches to flick to make heat, no faucets to turn to bring water. There were lamps to clean and wicks to trim; there was wood or coal to haul; there was water to carry. And except in a few rich houses which boasted housemen, it was the sinews and muscles of housewives and hired girls that supplied all the power there was.

The house servant's day started an hour before the rest of the family got up and it was not finished until after the last member of the household had gone to bed. The day began with the fires, of course— not just the kitchen fire, which had been banked for the night and which the ministrations of a good cook could bring to life in a minute by adjusting the dampers and throwing on some wood or coal, but the parlor and dining-room fires as well. Wood fires presented few problems, but coal fires were seemingly cursed with a temperament that demanded cajolery, flattery, artfulness, patience, and humor to make them respond. Furthermore, the grates had to be cleaned, and brasses of the andirons (or firedogs) polished before the appearance of the family. The boots and shoes had to be shined, the table set, and the master's coat brushed and ready for him when he left the house after breakfast. Once breakfast was over and the ladies of the family retired to their chambers to dress, there were silver and plate to polish, *bibelots* to dust with feather dusters, tables to be rubbed with oil, and a hundred other chores. The day ended as it began, with the fires. After the family had gone to bed, it was the function of the house servant to turn down the lamps (not blow them out), push down their keys so that the oil in them would not overflow, and then see that the fireguards were secure in front of the fires.

But the design of the house, its seeming disregard of the convenience of those who had to make it behave, was not at the root of the servant problem; neither was the length of the day. No self-respecting American wanted to be anyone else's creature, and there seemed to be no getting around the idea that unlike any other kind of service or labor one might perform for another man or woman, domestic service was somehow demeaning. Part of this attitude can unquestionably be traced to the plight of the indentured servants of colonial days. They were often riffraff shipped out of England as good riddance, and they were little better off (and sometimes a good deal worse) than slaves. The status of servants changed with the Revolution; indeed, the word *servant* all but disappeared. Those who were caught up in the new republican spirit had their work done by "helps" or by "domestics" and not by servants. But a mere change in name far from solved the problem of how to find men and women who were proud of being free citizens and who were at the same time willing to live and work in other people's houses.

The word *help* persists in our common parlance, whereas *domestics*, now rarely used, has a pretentious sound to it and overtones of self-conscious "gracious living." *Help* and its plural, *helps,* had an honorable history. It is of New England origin and it was used everywhere in the First Age of the Common Man, except in the South, where the word *servant* was always used of Negroes, slave or free, who worked in the house. *Help* implied the very opposite of the master-servant relationship; help and helped were on the same social footing. Help worked for an employer, not a master, and, except in the fancier households, worked side by side with the mistress of the house, who did her fair share of the physical chores. In some cases, especially in the country, housewives took into their households young girls, often about eleven years old, who were "bound" to them like apprentices until they were eighteen. In exchange for this they were clothed, taken to Sunday School, given "a certain amount" of ordinary schooling, and trained. If they behaved themselves, they were presented with a cow, or fifty dollars, or the equivalent, when their term of service was done. But more often the girl who came into the farm family as help was not bound. She was frequently the daughter of a neighbor. She worked hard and she became, to all intents and purposes, a member of the family, ate with them, went to church with them, shared their pleasures, was often married from their houses, and might even be buried in the family plot. James Russell Lowell in a letter to a friend said that he loved "our Yankee word" help, "teaching, as it does, the true relation, and its being equally binding on master and servant."

Mrs. Trollope, the indefatigable ambassador of middle-class English morality and manners, ran head on into the American concept of "help" as soon as she arrived in Cincinnati in 1828. "The whole class of young women," she wrote with characteristic exaggeration, "whose bread depends upon their labour, are taught to believe that the most abject poverty is preferable to domestic service." Indignant at the difficulty of finding help and appalled at the outrage to her gentility, she added: "Hundreds of half-naked girls work in the paper mills, or in any other manufactury, for less than half the wages they would receive in service; but they think their equality is compromised by the latter." The young girl she hired, and who arrived with a single dress that

Mrs. Trollope thought entirely unsuitable to a servant, was upset because she was not allowed to dine with the family. "I guess," the girl said, "that's 'cause you don't think I'm good enough to eat with you. You'll find that won't do here." Mrs. Trollope paid her the standard wage of a dollar and a half a week. "I found afterwards," she said with surprise, "that she rarely ate any dinner at all, and generally passed the time in tears." Obviously, Mrs. Trollope thought that the distinction between "help" and "servant" was republican tommyrot.*

Men, as well as women, worked as domestic help, and like the women they had no intention of letting this fact in any way change their social status or limit their activities on their time off. Some rich families tried to get their male help to wear the traditional servant's costumes but, as Francis Grund said, few Americans "would submit to the degradation of wearing a livery, or any other badge of servitude. This they would call becoming a man's man." Harriet Martineau was surprised and pleased to discover, for example, that the man who waited on her when she spent an evening at the house of the president of Harvard was also Major of the Horse in the local militia. "On cavalry days," she reported, "when guests are invited to dine with the regiment, the major, in his regimentals, takes the head of the table, and has the president on his right hand . . . ," after which "he goes home, doffs his regimentals, and waits on the president's guests at tea."

This sort of relationship between what Europeans would have considered "master and servant" existed nowhere else in the civilized world, and to the forward-looking it seemed to offer great promise—greater promise, indeed, than time proved was justified. "The condition of domestic service," de Tocqueville wrote in *Democracy in America*, "does not degrade the character of those who enter upon it, because it is freely chosen, and adopted for a time only; because it is not stigmatized by public opinion and creates no permanent inequality between the servant and the master." But most Americans could not abide even an impermanent inequality, and they never considered domestic service as anything more than a stepping stone to something, if not better paying, at least more independent. The result was that, unlike his European counterpart, the American servant had "his mind

---

* Francis Grund, another foreign visitor, on reading Mrs. Trollope's account of this incident, wrote that the young lady exhibited "a nobility of sentiment, of which certainly not a trace is to be found in her lady's writings."

constantly engaged in making plans for the future" and as soon as he had collected a few dollars set out on his own.

The outcome of this attitude was salutary for the country but hard on the housewife with her multiplicity of domestic problems and her ambitions to lead a pious, albeit genteel, life. To the housewife the nub of the matter was not economics but the shortage of servants. It was considered the prerogative of ladies to be waited on hand and foot; it was the dream of every mechanic's wife to raise her daughters to a life of suitable indolence, the mark of social achievement and the condition of gentility. The more airs and graces the ladies attempted to put on, the more stringent became the servant problem. The daughters of farm families, who early in the century had been the best kind of help that a family could find, took to the factories and the needle trades, so that wages in those jobs were depressed by too many available hands, and wages for "help" went up. "They did it," Catharine Beecher said, "mainly because they would not take positions in families as an inferior laboring-class by the side of others of their own age who assumed as their prerogative to live without labor." She gave as an example this exchange between two proud women:

> "I can't let you have one of my daughters," said an energetic matron to her neighbor from the city, who was seeking for a servant in her summer vacation; "if you hadn't daughters of your own, maybe I would; but my girls are not going to work so that your girls can live in idleness."

> It was vain to offer money. "We don't need your money, ma'am; we can support ourselves in other ways; my girls can braid straw, and bind shoes, but they are not going to be slaves to anybody."

To the helped, the "help" were inefficient, imperious, rude, independent, and insolent. To those, like Catharine Beecher and Miss Leslie, who were trying to knock some sense into the heads of American women, the fault was that of the housewives and not of their employees. How could you expect servants to be respectful and efficient if you hadn't the vaguest idea how to explain their jobs to them; if, when the bread was sour, you hadn't the slightest notion what made it so, or, if the carpets were dusty, you couldn't even explain how a broom should be used? The servant problem belonged squarely on the shoulders of the housewife and not on the independence of the American laborer, male or female.

III

Such was the state of service in the household at mid-century. One might have thought that the importation of a ready-made servant class from Europe, which began to arrive then, would have solved the American servant problem. It didn't of course, but it gave it an entirely different complexion. It took some of the solemnity out of the battle between householder and domestic, if none of the fury, and made it one of the wryest jokes of the last century. Crusaders for improving the lot of servants developed a whole new set of theories in keeping with the changing attitude toward the rights of labor. Lip service to the republican ideals that had made Americans drop the word *servant* was forgotten, and people began to talk quite frankly about servants again and were not embarrassed to do so; on the contrary, as America became more generally class-conscious after the Civil War, as the gap between the rich and the poor widened alarmingly, and Society began to solidify its position, the "badges of servitude," so distasteful a generation before, blossomed out as elaborate liveries for coachmen and footmen, butlers and waiters, and as uniforms for parlormaids. The servant problem, both literally and figuratively, took on a quite different look.

It was famine and political unrest in Europe in one direction, and treaty negotiations between the United States and the Chinese, in the other, that ushered in the second chapter of the story of America's servant problem. What had been a trickle of immigrants from Europe became suddenly, in the late 1840's, a harassed but hopeful wave of hungry, penniless Irish and Germans pouring into our northeastern ports in the steerage of ships. During the first year of the potato famine in Ireland (it struck in 1846) fifty thousand Irish gathered together a few clothes and a few trinkets and made their way across the Atlantic. During the next year, a worse one in Ireland, more than double that number came, and by 1851 they were arriving at the rate of more than 220,000 a year. The Revolution of 1848 had a similar effect on Germans, and soon they were arriving in very nearly the same massive numbers as the Irish. In the year of unrest before the Revolution about seventy-five thousand Germans came to America; six years later they were being joined by their compatriots at the rate of 215,000 a year.

The Irish stayed for the most part in the already crowded cities of the East, though some went into the hinterland to help build canals and turnpikes. Most Germans, on the other hand, headed for Wisconsin and Ohio and Illinois, where the majority (but by no means all) became farmers. At the other side of the continent the treaty with the Chinese in 1844 opened the doors of the West to the Orient. The Gold Rush a few years later acted as such attractive bait that by 1870 there were fifty-six thousand Chinese in America (and there were also the beginnings of an ugly race problem). These were merely the first great waves of immigration. By 1880 America had a foreign-born population of nearly seven million, of which about two million were Germans and another two million were Irish, and half a million were Scandinavian. If all had become servants, as a certain class of Americans thought they should have, it is still unlikely that there would have been more of them than the households of America could absorb.

Prosperity which puts many families in a position to afford service in their houses also puts those who might be servants in a position to do jobs more to their liking. A great many of the Irish and Germans who started life in America as domestics quickly caught the spirit that made native-born Americans revolt against servitude. They took to mills and factories and shops to earn their livings. But even in 1890 when almost 60 percent of all white women of foreign birth in America who had jobs were engaged in domestic service, there was still a scramble for cooks and maids. Cooks were getting $3.80 a week and "second girls" $3.04 plus their lodging and board, which families figured at twice the cost of their servants' wages. Employers, wrote Lucy Salmon in 1897, "expected perfection at twelve dollars a month and positive genius at thirteen." A houseman made eighty-seven cents a day plus his keep.

Yet housewives thought that they were being outrageously persecuted by servants. Bridget or Biddy was generally accused of "surly independence amounting in many cases to aggressiveness." She willfully broke the ivory handles off the family's best knives; she washed the silver in greasy soapsuds; she chipped the fragile china that was the family's pride; she shook out "showers of ashes from the grate, forgetting to cover the damask lounges" in the parlor. She wasted soap and food and fuel. There was no household sin too heinous for her to commit.

It was still true, as it had been in the 1830's, that there were a great many women who had not the slightest idea of how a servant should be trained. So they complained and they competed with one another for the services of the servants who claimed to have any proficiency. They took servants into their households without ever inquiring into their references, and they would give servants who had made their lives miserable glowing "characters," as they were called, in order to get rid of them. They demanded long hours of work, expected Bridget to put up with a tiny bedroom and no place to sit but the kitchen, and objected to her having friends, and especially men, come to visit her. Indeed, if the housewife did not think it was part of her duty to look out for the comfort and pleasure of her servants, she most certainly did think that she should supervise their morals.

The influx of a great many untrained young women, and some not so young, and the importation of a relatively few professional servants from Europe helped to overthrow entirely the old ideal of "help" and all that it implied. America had acquired a "servant class," and class snobbery, which had been kept reasonably well under wraps in the era of republicanism, became more or less taken for granted. It had been there all along, of course, because snobbery is as characteristic of class-less societies as those with rigidly and traditionally defined social levels; indeed, it is sometimes more so. Snobbery is not, as many people think, just a matter of looking down one's nose at other less well-placed people; it implies social climbing as well, and the more mobile a society is, the more social climbers there are in it.

New fortunes were being made with astonishing alacrity after the Civil War, some of them vast, and it became chic for Americans to imitate the manners and mannerisms of Europeans, and especially of the English. Families who had always done their own chores found themselves in a position to hire servants. They treated them with the loftiness and imperiousness which, they guessed, was typical of English gentlemen and ladies, and demanded servility in return. The very rich insisted on hiring servants who had been trained abroad, and they paid dearly for it, not in exorbitant wages only, but in the sufferance of impudence as well. In their elaborate palaces of granite and marble, the châteaux of Fifth Avenue and Newport, and the crenelated conceits of Chicago and St. Louis, they were waited upon and sneered at by servants whose techniques of insolence had been aged in long tradition. "Yellow-plush" was Thackeray's name for the British flunky, and the editors of *Harper's Bazar* insisted that if "he is bad enough in Europe, he is a hundred times worse here." There were some restraints of class on him there, they observed, but "in this country he is free to exercise all the viciousness and vent the insolence with which he has been thoroughly saturated." German and French servants were often offensive, they noted, but they were no match for the English.

But it was not only the rich who took the servant class for granted; so, indeed, did nearly everyone who could afford to own a house, live in a boarding house, or, at the end of the century, in an apartment or an apartment hotel. The common attitude became a proprietary one, even though the difficulties of acquiring servants often made women in pursuit of them lose their dignity. Servants in the North had once more become creatures, as the Negroes in the slave states had always been and continued to be.

Books of etiquette are given to exaggeration, to be sure, but as they are meant to instruct the unsophisticated, they do reflect in some degree sophisticated attitudes. The anonymous author of *The Complete Bachelor*, for example, was in no doubt in the 1890's what one's stance in relation to servants should be. "In the treatment of servants," he wrote, "a man must exercise an iron will." And he continued:

> He can be kind and considerate, but he must never descend to dispute with one, and certainly not swear at him. To be on familiar terms with one's servants shows the cloven foot of vulgarity. . . . Encourage your servants now and then by a kind word, and see that they have good and wholesome food, clean and comfortable quarters. Once in a while give them a holiday, or an evening off, a cash remembrance at Christmas, and from time to time some part of your wardrobe or cast-off clothing. They are just like children, and must be treated with the rigor and mild discipline which a school-master uses toward his pupils. In all their movements they should be noiseless and as automatic as possible in their actions.

Treat them like children, indeed! No wonder there was a scarcity of servants.

Mrs. M. E. W. Sherwood's attitude was somewhat different, but it was scarcely what we now think of as democratic. "We cannot expect perfection in our domestic service," she wrote in the 1887 edition of *Manners and Social Usages*, "but it is possible, by painstaking and patient teaching, to create a respectable and helpful servant class." Even a serving man's person was not his own. "Those who are particular in such matters," said Mrs. Sherwood, "do not allow a waiter or a footman to wear a moustache, and require all men-servants to be clean shaven, except the coachman, who is permitted to wear whiskers. Each must have his hair cut short, and the waiter must wear white gloves while waiting at table or when handling refreshments; even a glass of water on a silver salver must be brought with a gloved hand." To the bride she gave the following advice:

> A young housekeeper beginning her life in a great city finds herself frequently confronted with the necessity of having four servants—a cook, a laundress, a waiter or parlor-maid (sometimes both), and a chamber-maid. None of these excellent auxiliaries is willing to do the other's work; they generally quarrel. So the first experience of housekeeping is not agreeable. But it is possible to find two servants who, properly trained, will do all the service of a small family, and do it well.

The process of finding those who would do it well, or would do it at all, well or ill, meant that housewives spent a good deal of time seated in straight-backed chairs interviewing servants in domestic-employment agencies where they often felt that it was not the prospective cook or parlormaid but they who were being interviewed. Bridget had her own snobbishness and her own quite definite ideas about the conditions under which she would work. Sometimes she insisted she would not accept a position in a household that did not employ a manservant; sometimes she insisted that the family have its own carriages and not depend on the livery stables. Occasionally servants advertised for work in the newspapers in such a manner as this:

> WANTED—SITUATIONS IN A PRIVATE
> FAMILY by two young ladies; one as
> cook, and the other as chambermaid.
> Inquire at, etc.

This kind of advertisement provoked an article in a New York newspaper about a housewife who applied to an agency in the following words:

> A WOMAN, living on Fifth Avenue,
> who can give good references from
> the last lady who worked for her,
> wishes a situation as mistress over two
> young ladies. . . .

It was a running fight between the servers and the served. "American women are now divided into two classes," wrote Elizabeth Jordan in *Harper's Weekly* in 1908. "Those who have servants and those who are trying to find them. You'll know the first by their apprehension, and the second by their agony." But there was a greater depth of despair. "You don't know yet what it is to have one of them come, stay three months, win your affections, make herself absolutely indispensable, and then leave because she has suddenly decided to 'specialize' and work exclusively for 'de four hundert.' When that has happened you will have touched the bottom of the deepest abyss known to the American homemaker."

The jokes about servants and their employers cut both ways. On the one hand:

Knicker: What's the matter?
Bocker: The cook has divorced us and wants alimony.

and

Mistress: Bridget, do you spoil *every* piece of meat you cook?
Maid: Oh, no, mum. Sometimes it comes bad from the butcher.

On the other hand:

Maid: Please, mum, may I go out for an hour or two?
Mistress: No, you must stay in, but you may wash all the windows.

and

Maid: Please, mum, could I have one o' yer red geraniums to kape in me bedroom?
Mistress: Oh, no, Bridget, your room is too dark. It would die. Plants must have sunlight and fresh air.

These four bitter items of hilarity all come from *Harper's Bazar* in 1912. There is one other that is worth quoting because of one of the main accusations leveled at servants by housekeepers. It is this:

Green: Misery loves company.
White: But the cook won't allow us to have any.

Since they could not entertain in a manner that they thought becoming, a great many families did not entertain at all. One of the byproducts of the perpetual servant shortage was a decline in American hospitality. "We are afraid or ashamed to conform honestly and hardily to a state of things purely American," Harriet Beecher Stowe observed. Hospitality, she said, was "much neglected." Nearly fifty years later, in 1910, an Englishwoman visiting in America still found this to be true. "Weekend stays," she wrote, "are exclusively the indulgence of the rich in America. There is one thing that militates mightily against private hospitality in the United States." It was the gradual disappearance of the servant. "The trouble with the servant-girl in America," she said, "is that she wants an easy job terminating in an easy husband."

All sorts of devices and schemes and admonitions were used in the attempt to keep the servant class from disappearing altogether. The promoters of efficient housekeeping lectured the housewife roundly on her responsibilities to the help who worked for her. She was told to plan her servant's day so that the poor girl would know what was expected of her and when. Architects lectured her on the subject of attractive and healthful servants' rooms and sunny kitchens. The clergy encouraged her to see that her servants had a decent amount of time off, uplifting books to read, and a place and time to entertain their friends. The Emily Posts of the day told her to mind her manners when dealing with servants. If the servant problem grew worse, it was surely not because there was any shortage of advice. But since none of the advice seemed to have any effect, drastic schemes were proposed.

One desperate band of housekeepers seriously suggested that public schools be abolished after the primary grades. Too many girls, they believed, were educated "beyond their station," and they refused to hire anyone in their homes "who had been beyond the third reader and the multiplication table."

Another group advocated the introduction of courses in housework into all public schools, so that there would be a continual supply of properly trained housemaids and cooks.

Mary Rankin Cranston recommended in 1906 in *Craftsman* magazine that we should establish here a counterpart to an experiment that was being carried on in London under the name of Guild of Dames of the Household. It was a school that trained carefully selected young women to be house servants, provided them with a uniform and a badge, and insisted that they work in houses where there were no ordinary servants. So far as I have been able to discover, the notion of Dames of the Household never caught on in America, though a number of schools for domestic service were tried. "The training school for servants," wrote Lucy Salmon, a professor at Vassar at the turn of the century, and the principal historian of the servant problem in America, "means the introduction of a caste system utterly at variance with democratic ideas."

Democratic means were tried, though, in a variety of ways. In the 1860's Melusina Fay Pierce attempted to organize "Co-operative House-keeping," a scheme for a dozen or more families to get together, open a grocery store, a bakery, a laundry, and a kitchen, and pool all of their energies and housewifely talents so that the chores of cooking, sewing, and laundry could be carried on at some central point, thereby eliminating the necessity of servants. But not everyone wanted to patronize the cooperative store, or have their meals at the same time, or work as hard as their neighbors, and such schemes came to nothing. The problems they created were more aggravating than the servant problem which they sought to solve.

Some families decided that the only answer was to have their servants sit at the table with them, as servants had done in the days of "helps." But the climate was quite different in the 1890's from that in the 1830's. No longer was there any trace of the apprentice system which had made this kind of relationship a usual one. The factory had not only changed the means of production and consumption; it had changed the nature of the class structure as well.

In the seventies a few people were beginning to talk about the "living-out" servant as the democratic answer to the problem. "Servants would be relieved from that constant interference with their independence . . . that insufferable consciousness that they are never . . . in free possession of themselves," said the authors of the *Bazar Book of the Household* with uncommon good sense and prophetic insight. There was also talk of a servants' union, which housewives found alarming, and satirists found funny.

But the real and lasting reform in the household came from a quite different source. Since it seemed impossible to reform either the house-keeper or the servant, it was the house and its equipment that gradually and tacitly adapted itself to the change, among other things, in the nature of service. Gradually the basement kitchen disappeared, or, where it was considered an economic necessity, as in some city houses, dumbwaiters were greatly improved. Furnaces took the place of open fires. Water, which at first was piped just into the kitchen and pantry, was made to run to the upper floors; long before the end of the century the bathroom (usually just one) was standard equipment in a great many houses. The washstand with its basin and pitcher had disappeared in such houses (except for emergency use and often in servants' rooms) and so had the commode. The Argand kerosene lamp had replaced the oil lamp and the candle, and was in turn replaced in cities by gas and not much later by electricity. The icebox replaced the cold-cupboard. The washing machine, though hand-operated, changed the character of Monday. The carpet sweeper took over many of the duties of the broom. The telephone reduced the number of errands to be run. The gas range supplanted the wood or coal stove. Each of these innovations took over part of the work that had been done by servants. The house was rapidly becoming mechanized, though its design continued, basically, to be that of a house which belonged to the era when servants were more plentiful than they had become by the end of the century. The house that had once needed five servants now ran pleasantly enough with two, and the one that had needed three made do with one.

IV

If the servant problem had been serious in America for a century, the First World War made it seem to housewives all but hopeless. War factories were magnets that drew women out of kitchens and parlors like so many steel filings. The pay was good, and though the hours were long (sixty hours was standard), they were not as long as the servant's day that started at seven in the morning, or earlier, and usually lasted until eight or nine in the evening, with Sunday afternoons off and "maid's night out" on Thursdays. The exodus from the household did not stop with the Armistice in 1918. Too many women had had a taste of a more independent kind of life; their men had good jobs, and the crest of what turned out to be a false prosperity was rapidly rising. In 1922 the *Literary Digest* announced "The Passing of the Household Servant," and based its pronouncement on the findings of Paul W. Brown's book *America at Work*. "If the present tendency keeps up," Mr. Brown said, "there will be literally nobody there but the family." The census of 1920 showed that the number of cooks had dropped by 21.5 percent, chambermaids by 26 percent, maids-of-all-work by 20.5 percent, and laundresses by 25.7 percent. Mr. Brown viewed this as a triumph for democracy. "An age is dead: an age is born," he said. "The shadow moves on the dial. Of all the new things given to the world by the United States, the well-to-do servantless house holds perhaps the biggest significance."

A good many families that had always taken for granted that servants were essential to their happiness and respectability began to discover that there were some delights in the privacy of the servantless house. They also found that with the new gadgets to do so much of what had once been heavy work, it was more pleasant to spend their money on travel and gramophones and occasional dinners in restaurants than on maids and cooks. They found that they could do quite well with "a woman to come in and do the heavy cleaning," and occasionally hiring a maid or "a man in a white coat" when they gave a party. The tea party with its lace doilies and paper-thin sandwiches and highly polished silver pots and jugs and sugar tongs gave way to the cocktail party, and any husband could learn to shake up a white lady or an orange blossom or a sidecar, or any other of those sweet and frothy drinks so popular in the flat-chested and bell-bottomed gaiety of the twenties.

The crash of 1929 spoiled the fun but it did not reverse the seemingly inexorable decline of the domestic supply. There were, of course, a great many desperate people who would take any sort of job they could get, and some ugly employment practices developed. But there were also fewer people who could afford servants, and young couples starting out on their married lives took it for granted that there were much more important and interesting things on which to spend what little extra money they might have than service. Even the prosperous young, who were getting handouts from their parents, got along happily with an occasional "cleaning woman." They would have been embarrassed to have made any more of a display of prosperity than that.

That is not to say that all households were servantless. At the time of the Lindbergh kidnapping in 1932 Mrs. Lindbergh's parents, the Dwight Morrows, who lived in Englewood, New Jersey, had twenty-nine in help, and, compared with the Whitneys and Astors and Hearsts and other spectacularly rich families of the day, they did not live ostentatiously. Instead of the $12 a month that the average parlormaid was earning in 1890, the maid of the twenties was earning $70 to $80 a month; and instead of $15, a cook was getting $75 or, if she lived in a house of the Morrows' sort, she might well be getting $150. It was a simple matter of supply, demand, traditions of social acceptability, and the state of the stock market. Forty years before, half of the women in America who had jobs were working in other people's kitchens and parlors and bedrooms; by the twenties, of the almost nine million women who had jobs only about one-ninth, or a million, were cooking, cleaning, and answering doorbells. The Irish were still the most plentiful, and presumably the most content to stay in service, but it was generally conceded that the best cooks and chambermaids came from Finland and Sweden, and especially those who had been trained in the Swedish schools of domestic science.

Just before the Second World War there was a spate of attempts to get the servant problem to make sense. On November 29, 1939, the *New York Times* reported under the headline "How to Get a Maid Debated by Women": "Five hundred women eager for a solution of the problem of a shortage of household help despite the extent of unemployment crowded the conference rooms of the Hotel Roosevelt yesterday for a symposium in which delegates from twenty-four organizations participated. An all-day discussion failed to offer any panaceas. . . ." The best they seemed to be able to do was to advise the delegates, many of whom came from women's clubs, to go home and tell their friends what the nineteenth-century reformers had been saying all along—both housewives and servants needed to be educated "on the factors involved." Attempts were made by the Woman's Trade Union to get laws passed that would regulate the number of hours a week that domestic servants could work "because many women persist in being unfair to their household help. . . ." The good women of New Jersey organized a Household Employment Standards League in hopes of establishing "standards" of hours, duties, and facilities. This was by no means greeted with enthusiasm by all housekeepers.

The Second World War certainly did not help to solve the old problem, but it changed it. If the First World War had reduced the supply of servants and pushed up the wages of those who were willing to work in other people's houses, the Second World War altered the nature of service itself. It introduced a new kind of domestic helper (indeed, several new kinds); it made a reality of at least one of the nineteenth-century suggestions for revising the patterns of service, and it sent some people back to living as their grandparents and great-grandparents had.

The new kinds of domestic helpers were teenagers and married men. The "baby sitter" on whose head has been poured all of the old vituperation that used to be the lot of Bridget (slovenly, greedy, insolent, and so on and so on) came to save the family from the bondage of small children. And husbands, who a generation earlier had never been expected to raise a finger to a domestic chore, found themselves in aprons washing dishes, down on their knees waxing floors, and in chef's caps presiding over back-yard barbecues. I have told the story in some detail of how this came about in another book,* but it is worth noting here that the change in the domestic stance of the husband was largely based on what happened to the young men who came back from the army to their young brides. In a great many cases they went back to school on the G. I. Bill and their young wives took jobs to help them pay their college bills and to support the family. While mother was at work, father was at home studying, taking care of the baby, and doing the dishes. He became, in other words, a part-time wife and part-time Bridget. Having once established himself as domestically competent and useful, there was little chance that he would ever again be able to avoid sharing at least some of the responsibilities of the house servant.

But both the sitter, usually the daughter of a neighbor, and the husband-maid had a status that was quite unknown in the old servant classes or, at least, unknown since the days of "helps." They were both socially the equals of the women for whom they worked, a very important factor in changing the nature of service today. Though it is now half a generation from the time when the young men first took advantage of the G.I. Bill, the pattern has become firmly established. As young couples are marrying earlier than they did a generation or two ago and many of them are continuing their education in graduate schools (sometimes both husband and wife), the domestic responsibilities continue to be divided on the postwar basis. Almost the only "living-in" servants today are husbands.†

The suggestion that was bandied about in the 1870's, but not taken very seriously, that the way to solve the servant problem was to have maids and cooks that lived at home and came to work by the day, has to a very considerable extent been the solution to today's servant situation. From the point of view of the domestic worker the ideal family is one in which both husband and wife have jobs and are out of the house all day and thus are not in a

---

* *A Surfeit of Honey,* 1957.
† One definition of the suburban husband is "a groundsman with sex privileges."

position to meddle in the affairs of the household. The servant in such households is no longer called cook or maid or general house-worker; she is a housekeeper. If you will look at the "Help Wanted" columns in a newspaper today, you will find advertisements for "housekeepers"; you will find very few for cooks and maids. You will also find some kinds of listings that would have been impossible a couple of decades ago. Employers advertise that they not only supply "own room" but also "own bath, TV, and air-conditioning." They advertise the fact that they are "working parents" and have a "happy comfortable home." It is not uncommon to find a request for a couple (a "housekeeper-cook" and a "handyman-gardener") at $500 a month, or, in this day of pensions and pre-occupation with tenure, to find ads including the words "secure future." There is still a trickle of foreign-born and trained professional servants that can be hired at tidy wages through agencies. In general, it is considered not proper today to make the distinction between white and Negro servants, and some agencies get around this by saying that they have on their lists both "local" and "Southern" maids. Those who advertise for work in the "Positions Wanted; Domestic" want, for the most part, a five-day week (Monday through Friday) and to "live out." Some want nine-to-five jobs.

Those who have reverted to the mode of life of their grandparents have set up a manner of housekeeping in apartment hotels in which meals and maid service are supplied by the management. The old-fashioned boarding house, as I have said, has all but disappeared; the apartment hotel in this era of prosperity is thriving, though its tenants are in the top 10 percent of the nation's wealth. There is also a reversion to nineteenth-century customs at a quite different financial level: the kitchen has again come into its own as a center of family life, so that those who have to do the household chores are not isolated from the rest of the family. No one would design a house that built the cook into the living room unless the cook was also the mistress of the house and the wife of the homeowner.

But we have gone a step further than that. We have taken over many of the ideas of the cooperative housekeeping movement of the 1870's, without its aggravations. A great deal of our food is cooked in central kitchens, packaged, canned, or frozen, and made available to us with almost no effort at any moment we want it.

The laundress has disappeared in favor of the commercial laundry (a suggestion made by Catharine Beecher and her sister in 1869 in *The American Woman's Home*), the "laundromat," or the home automatic washer and drier. Our rugs and clothes are cleaned, our windows washed, and our household pests exterminated by companies that do nothing else. All of these were servants' jobs.

The mechanization of the house and the organization of all sorts of services to supply the home and to reduce the amount of physical labor that it demands has in some ways forced, and in other ways compensated for, the vanishing of the servant class. But in a great many respects (social not physical ones) we are right back where we started, and better off because of it. With the exception of a very slim slice of people at the very top of the financial pyramid, we are again relying on "help" whom we treat with the respect that is due them. The domestic worker today is an "employee" not a servant, and certainly not a creature.

CHAPTER X

The Dining Room

Whether a meal is humdrum or festive, can-
dle-lit or sunlit, every family feels that their
way of doing it has unique and individual
importance.
Robert Woods Kennedy, *The House*, 1953

"I remember hearing it told of a very accomplished gentleman," Mrs. Farrar wrote in *The Young Lady's Friend* in 1838,
"that when carving a tough goose, he had the misfortune to send
it entirely out of the dish, and into the lap of the lady next to him;
on which he very coolly looked her full in the face, and with admirable gravity and calmness said, 'Ma'am, I will thank you for
that goose.'"

The dining room, even more than the parlor, has been the prov-
ing ground of poise. Emily Post is said to have told a woman whom
she had been coaching in manners in order that she might take
her place in Boston society (which seems unlikely on the face of
it) that above all things she must remember not to put her elbows
on the table at dinner parties or luncheons. When the woman came
back from her first such social occasion and said with alarm that
the other ladies had put their elbows on the table, Mrs. Post is said
to have remarked, "Ah, my dear, but they know enough not to."

Of all the rooms in the house, the dining room is the most ritu-
alistic. Like the altar of a church, the table is set according to rather
rigidly accepted patterns; on special occasions it is lighted with
candles; the manner in which those who serve it is scarcely less
formalized by custom than the routine prescribed for acolytes. The
rules of behavior for those who partake of the meal are intricate,

elaborate, and must be so thoroughly learned that it is obvious that those who break or at least bend them "know enough not to." It is not surprising that books on manners and the "compendiums of forms" (like Hill's *Manual* and Gaskell's encyclopedic guide) should devote extensive chapters to the arrangement of the table, the placement of forks, knives, spoons, glasses, casters, and to the various acceptable methods of serving meat and vegetables, bread, wine, soups, and desserts. But if the advice on the arrangement of the table is elaborate, so is it on such matters as who sits where at the table, whether the hostess should be the first or the last to enter the dining room, whether it is better to serve the meal *à la Russe* or in the English manner, whether when there are two kinds of soup there should also be two kinds of fish, and, of course, how a fork should be held, a finger bowl used, and a conversation conducted. Don't talk with your mouth full. Don't reach across your neighbor for the bread. Don't cool your coffee by pouring it in the saucer. Don't blow your nose at the table. Don't slump in your chair. Don't eat with your knife . . . or in Mrs. Farrar's day: "If you wish to imitate the French or English, you will put every mouthful into your mouth with your fork; but if you think, as I do, that Americans have as good a right to their own fashions as the inhabitants of any other country, you may choose the convenience of feeding yourself with your right hand, armed with a steel blade; and provided you do it neatly, and do not put in large mouthfuls, or close your lips tight over the blade, you ought not to be considered as eating ungenteelly."

The dining room was a relatively new "essential" of the household in Mrs. Farrar's day. It was not until it established itself as a *sine qua non* of genteel living that it began to develop intricate rituals and codes of service and behavior which it behooved everyone with any pretensions of "getting ahead in the world" to understand and observe. The nineteenth century did not invent the dining room, to be sure, but it made it almost universal. In the simple colonial house the family ate in the kitchen, as it continued to in the farmhouse, except on special festive occasions in larger houses. Even in somewhat elaborate houses before 1800, the eating room, as it was called, also served as a sitting room. In the grand houses of prosperous merchants in the North and in the plantation houses of the South where slaves were plentiful, a dining room big enough to seat at least twenty was an appurtenance of gentlemanly domesticity that was taken for granted. By the middle of the nineteenth century the dining room appears in the plan books as a normal part of all but the simplest farm cottages. Its size was usually about the same as the parlor. Even as late as 1906 Charles Edward Hooper in *The Country House* observed that "the exclusive dining room is a comparatively new thing. The demand for a separate room is due to different conditions and of social intercourse." Hooper's grandfather, who was born in 1800 in Maine, was one of those, he remembered, who resented the newfangled notion that there should be a room separate from the kitchen for eating. "He tolerated the dining room from necessity only," Hooper said, "and when dragged from his chosen retreat, the kitchen . . . evinced stormy symptoms of restlessness."

Once the existence of the dining room was taken for granted, its placement in the plan of the house and its decoration occupied the prayerful attention not only of the architects of grand houses but the designers of small ones. In the city house, as we have already noted, it was sometimes above the kitchen on the back of the house and not infrequently was a projection into the back yard with no other rooms above it. Sometimes it was in the basement on the front with high windows that looked out on the street. (As the city dining room rarely commanded a view worth looking at, it was not uncommon toward the end of the nineteenth century to provide it with a large stained-glass "picture window" which let in jewel-like splotches of color and provided the diners with a vision of fruits and autumn leaves, or the features of a pre-Raphaelite damsel.) It was far easier for the designer of a country house to put the dining room in a pleasant place, as he was not confined by the rigidity of a city lot, and his first concern was to locate it so that the morning sun flooded through the windows and made the glass and silver on the table and sideboard sparkle. Ideally, it faced the east so that, as Oliver Coleman said in *Successful Houses* (1899), "the dreariest of the meals, a breakfast, should have the fullest benefit of all the morning sun. In the winter this is good, of course, while in the summer the early morning is often the only time of day worth living. . . ." If possible, it should also let out upon a garden, not only because it is pleasant to look upon but "pleasant to smell the fragrance of the honeysuckle and the lilac bush."

The relationship of the dining room to the kitchen was, of course, of paramount importance for purely logistic reasons. It was not, however, considered proper or practical for the kitchen to open directly into the dining room, and so the "butler's pantry" was common even in many houses that never saw a butler. It was in this passageway of a room between the kitchen and the dining room that the dishes were washed, the cruets filled with oil and vinegar and placed in casters, along with catsup, soy, black pepper, cayenne, and other sauces for meats or vegetables. There the butter balls were made with wooden paddles chilled in ice water (this was maid's work not cook's), trays were set up, wine was decanted (or "decantered," as the process was sometimes called a century ago), and china and glass were stored in cupboards. The butler's pantry was a workroom, quite different from the kitchen pantry, which was for storage of preserves and dry foods and staples, or from the "buttery," where cheese, butter, milk and cream were kept cool and fresh. It was essential in those houses where meals were brought from the downstairs kitchen by dumbwaiter or stairs. It was considered desirable in any sort of house as a buffer between the formality of the dining room and the mechanical operations (and smells) of the kitchen. It divided the functions of service from those of preparing the food.

No room in the house has been more subject to fads in decoration than the dining room. It was not open to the same pressures of nostalgia that kept the parlor stuffy; it was a museum only in a secondary sense—only for the purpose of displaying the family's best china and crystal and silver. Consequently, it was quick to follow the whims of fashion. It skipped blithely from the machine-made furbelows and fripperies of the "French style" of the 1850's to the ponderous, puritanical Elizabethan oak made popular by the Centennial Exposition. It boasted imitation stamped Spanish-leather walls which it deserted for gold and red paper, and around 1900 for green grass cloth (which has recently been revived). The "plate rail" which ringed the room two-thirds of the way up the wall or higher with rows of platters, plates, steins, pitchers, and bric-a-brac became a standard cliché around the turn of the century. It was contemporary with the leaded glass lamp shade that hung from a heavy chain over the center of the table and spread its colors, sometimes as subtle as Louis Tiffany could make them, and sometimes as gaudy as the plumage of parrots. "That room," said *Harper's Bazar* of the dining room in 1912, "more than any other tends toward the deadly conventional type." It was, after all, the room in which conventions were most closely observed.

The conventions of the dining room are not wholly accounted for by the expression "table manners," but it encompasses most of them. From the moment one enters the dining room to one's ultimate escape from the table, etiquette dictates in some respect every move one makes; it defines the manner in which one walks into the room, pulls a chair from the table (or stands still while someone else does it for one), sits down, uses the implements and napery conventionally placed at one's disposal, speaks to one's fellow feeders, rises, and departs. Etiquette sets limits to the appetite, ordains the speed of consumption, and dictates the nature and volume of conversation and sometimes even its content. Table manners are essentially a set of conventions devised to make the fulfillment of a basic biologic need something which people can bear to perform in public. Bared teeth and grinding jaws are not a pleasure to watch, and table manners are intended to distract attention from them by ritual means.

Nineteenth-century books of etiquette, while they were inclined to devote a good deal of attention to the more finicky details of table manners, started, for the most part, from the assumption that their readers had everything to learn. They went to the very root of the matter, as had George Washington when as a boy of fifteen he wrote out a list of rules of behavior that he copied from a French manners book. He had said, among other things,: "Put not another bite into your mouth 'til the former be swallowed," and "Cleanse not your teeth with the Table Cloth, Napkin, Fork or Knife." Well over a century later a manual by "A Gentleman" entitled *The Laws of Etiquette; or, Short Rules and Reflections for Conduct in Society* cautioned that ladies "may wipe their lips on the table cloth, but not blow their noses with it," and on the subject of implements said, "The ordinary custom among well-bred persons is as follows: soup is taken with a spoon. Some foolish fashionables employ a fork! They might as well use a broomstick."

Soup and implements seem to have been a continuing problem. In 1881 Gaskell's *Compendium of Forms* advised: "Eat soup with your spoon, holding a piece of bread in your left hand; cut your food with your knife but use your fork to convey it to your mouth. Break your bread, do not bite it. Drink from your cup, not from the saucer. . . . When you send your plate away from the table remove your knife and fork and allow them to rest upon a piece of bread." *How to Behave and How to Amuse* published by the *Christian Herald* in 1895 under "Notes for Diners" gives these hints:

Never gesticulate with your knife or fork in your hand, nor hold them pointing upward, keep them down on your plate.

Never load up your fork with food until you are ready to convey it to your mouth.

Tea, coffee, chocolate, etc., are drunk from the cup and never from the saucer. Never blow your tea or coffee; wait till it cools.

The question of what to do if you broke or upset something at the table preoccupied the writers of manuals of etiquette. Mrs. Farrar suggested: "If you break anything belonging to the person you visit, you should express regret, and blame your own awkwardness; but even then, take care not to say too much about it." The *Christian Herald* goes further: ". . . should you unfortunately overturn or break anything, make no apology, but let your regret appear in your face." In any event, the point was to preserve your composure, for only by doing so could you avoid seeming uncouth, naïve, or vulgar.

Of these three social sins the last, vulgarity, was the one to be avoided at all cost, and a great many pages of books of etiquette have been devoted quite openly to pointing out to the reader which of his bad habits were the most obviously vulgar ones. The fact seems to have been that nowhere more than at the dining-room table did one's vulgar origins show (the vulgarities of the well-born and well-bred were of no concern to writers of books of etiquette for the most part). The *Golden Manual*, published in 1891, summed up this attitude:

Persons new to society may master its simpler forms—such as dropping cards, paying visits, mixing in evening parties, and so on, but dining is the great trial. The rules to be observed at table are so numerous and so minute in respect to detail, that they require the most careful study; and the worst of it is that none of them can be violated without exposing the offender to instant detection, and for this reason, that those accus-

tomed to good society cannot err in particulars in which others are pretty
certain to commit themselves.

Just what "particulars" Mr. Northrup, the author of the manual,
had in mind he does not say. The anonymous author of *The American Chesterfield*, however, has no reticence about calling a spade
a spade:

> Eating quick or very slow, at meals, is characteristic of the vulgar; the
> first infers poverty, that you have not had a good meal for some time;
> the last, if abroad, that you dislike your entertainment; if at home, that
> you are rude enough to set before your friends what you cannot eat your-
> self. So again, eating your soup with your nose in your plate is vulgar.
> . . . If it be necessary then to avoid this, it is much more so that of smell-
> ing of the meat whilst on your fork, before you put it in your mouth
> [to see if it is spoiled]. I have seen an ill-bred fellow do this, and have
> been so angry, that I could have kicked him from the table. . . .

On the other hand, excessive "gentility," which was as much
a sign of vulgarity and social insecurity as smacking one's lips, came
in for its own criticism. In *The Young Lady's Friend* Mrs. Farrar,
whose touch is always gentle and amused, and never sarcastic,
mentions a young lady of her acquaintance who thought that chewing was rather vulgar and spoke "with great disgust of some of
her acquaintances for chewing their food so much." She found it
not "very refined and pretty."

Table manners changed rapidly in the nineteenth century (as
they have changed rapidly in the last twenty-five years in directions of informality). In 1874 *Scribner's Magazine* found that "some
things that were in vogue a generation or two ago, are no longer
deemed polite." And the explanation it gave was that the mechanics
of eating had improved. "Twenty or thirty years since," the article
said, "everybody was accustomed to use the knife to carry food
to the mouth, because the fork of the day was not adapted to that
purpose. Since the introduction of the 4-tined silver fork, it has
so entirely supplanted the knife that the usage of the latter in
that way . . . is regarded as a vulgarism." (There were the die-hards
who thought the fork an affectation and who in the 1860's still insisted that eating peas with a fork was like "eating soup with a
knitting needle" or "sipping tea with a hair-pin.") Also the butter
knife had been invented, which meant that it became obsolete to

use one's own knife to cut butter from the butter dish. And from being a quite ordinary and commonly accepted custom, "turning tea and coffee from the cup into the saucer" to cool it became, like eating with a knife, a vulgarism. I have not been able to discover at precisely what point it became considered genteel to shift one's fork from one's left hand to one's right before using it to convey food to one's mouth, but it is a nineteenth-century genteelism that is purely American and that has persisted.*

The formal dinner party, of course, presented a great many details of etiquette that were absent from the ordinary family meal. The manuals of manners are by no means always in agreement on what is correct, which must have left the insecure hostess in a jelly of uncertainty. Should the hostess, escorted by the guest of honor, be the first to enter the dining room? Or should the host, accompanied by the oldest lady, the lady from farthest away, or the wife of the guest of honor, enter ahead of the others? Books of etiquette were of diametrically opposite opinions on this matter a century ago. (We seem to have solved that problem by avoiding it, except for state dinners, and the problems of protocol are no business of ours here.) Or what about the delicate matter of a lady's and a gentleman's gloves? One had to be up-to-date. In the 1820's both men and women wore gloves into the dining room, and it was not uncommon for ladies to eat with their gloves on. (Miss Leslie in her *Behavior Book* was delighted to see the passing of this nonsensical, as she believed it to be, affectation.) In the 1830's a lady wore her gloves into the dining room and did not remove them until she was seated at the table. Mrs. Farrar warned her, however: "Be sure to get through with your dessert and have your gloves on, all ready to move, by the time the lady of the house gives the signal [for the ladies to leave the dining room]." Sixty years later the custom had changed only in one respect. "Gloves are removed by both ladies and gentlemen," according to *How to Behave and How to Amuse*, "after being seated at the table, and they need not be replaced during the evening." In 1921 Emily Post was still advising ladies to remove their gloves after they got to the table and to place them and their fans on their laps and cover them with their napkins. She warned that unless

---

* Walter Hoving in *Tiffany's Table Manners for Teen-Agers* (1961) says: "Don't keep shifting the fork from the left to the right hand. This is clumsy and awkward."

ladies tucked their napkins around themselves like carriage blankets, gloves and fan were bound to slip off their satin knees to the floor. "This ought not to be put in a book of etiquette," she wrote, ". . . but it is either do that or have the gentleman next you groping under the table at the end of the meal." (Miss Leslie in her *Behavior Book* in 1853 had another answer to the napkin problem, at least at lunch. She advised a lady to pin her napkin to her belt to prevent its slipping to the floor. "Bring with you a spare pin or two . . . ," she advised, "or keep a pincushion in your pocket.")

Dyspepsia is a word that has more or less disappeared from the American vocabulary in favor of such pill-makers' preferences as "acid indigestion" and "nervous stomach," but it was a national complaint a century ago. The Americans invented the "quick lunch" partly because they were in a hurry to get on to the next thing but partly because the American tradition of eating was, quite simply, a bore. The Puritan tradition which saw to it that all sensual pleasures were sinful made family meals more or less silent affairs where children were seen but not heard, and conversation of any levity whatsoever was frowned upon as unsuitable. Because this was so, Americans learned to dive into their food silently, and even when the board groaned with delicacies, it was likely to be swept clean in a hushed twinkling of an eye.

When Count Carlo Vidua reported on his visit to America (he was here in the 1820's), he took a typical American meal as an indication that "paternal and filial affection is not lively" among Americans. "In a large family," he reported, "the sons gather together at meal time, each coming from his business; each enters the room, says not a word to father or brother; opens not his mouth, in fact, except to put something therein; devours in a few instants the few ill-cooked dishes, and whosoever is first satisfied, without waiting till the others have finished, rises, takes his hat and is off." Lack of filial affection seems less likely to have caused this eat-and-run attitude than what prompted Sir Charles Lyell to suggest that our national motto should be "All Work and No Play." Meals were merely an essential stoking process—a peremptory grace, a gulp, and a belch. Breakfast was taken on the run, lunch was snatched (though it was often a stout meal) as often as not standing up, and dinner (or supper) was put away in a state of exhaustion. "What time, I would ask you," wrote Francis Grund in the 1830's, "has one of our young men to be unhappy?—when in the morning he rises, to read the papers; then takes his breakfast, at which his fair partner presents him with her own white hands two cups of hyson or pekoe, with the trifling addition of a steak or chop; then goes to his counting-room where he remains until one; then passes the hour from one till two on the 'change'; then returns home to eat his beef and pudding, which he accomplishes in about ten minutes; then returns once more to his counting-room where he remains till sunset; then comes home to swallow his two or three cups of tea; after which . . . , he is heartily glad to go to rest. . . ."

Such a schedule may have been good for the gross national product, but it was certainly not good for the digestion, and no amount of advice in household books, health books, books of manners, or magazine articles against bolting one's food seemed to stay the American in the swift completion of whatever was set before him. No one expected to accomplish the miracle of reform merely by saying "Slow down." The answer seemed to be in making meals pleasant occasions at which people actually conversed with one another and laughed and enjoyed themselves. "It is not at all an extravagant belief," wrote C. E. Sargent in a book called *Our Home* in 1884, "that much of the dyspepsia of today had its remote origin among the Puritans in their cruel suppression of mirth at the family board. . . . Our meals should be scenes of uninterrupted merriment. It is a fact universally acknowledged that the American people eat too rapidly for the good of their health. . . . One of the evils of Puritanism, which we have not yet outgrown, was the idea that cheerful conversation is unbecoming at meals. The children were taught to eat in silence at the second table, under the awful superintendence of their parents, who had eaten up all the good things." About twenty years later Maria Parloa, the *Ladies' Home Journal's* high priestess of the household, said: "The worry, haste, lack of conversation, and often the ill temper shown at table have much to do with the national disease known as dyspepsia." Obviously, the situation had not improved greatly. Obviously, from the number of television commercials devoted to dyspepsia today, it still has not much improved, though no one would contend that it is because children are repressed.

Haste alone, of course, could not account for the national inclination to heartburn; it was not merely a matter of how fast but of how much and of what quality. American produce was plentiful and of excellent quality, but we were inclined to fry it until it was stiff and dressed in a kind of union suit of flour and grease. We invented monstrosities like the "chicken-fried steak," an indelicacy that is popular today in the Southwest, and especially in Texas. We threw away our beef bones without getting the good out of them for soup; we threw them indeed to the dogs. (A writer in the *Atlantic Monthly* in 1879 who advocated that the wives of factory workers should be instructed "in economical methods of preparing wholesome and appetizing food," observed that "They throw out to their dogs what would give them the basis for a valuable and delicious soup. The operatives keep a great many dogs, as is the custom among poor people generally, in this country." Today it is not the dogs who get the bones but the "mechanical pig" in the kitchen sink.) But if dyspepsia was a by-product of overfrying, it may also have been the result of magnificently inspired gluttony, for there were delicious dishes in which the American household used to excel. Mrs. Trollope in a shocked tone of voice had this to say of the American diet in the 1830's:

The ordinary mode of living is abundant but not delicate. They consume an extraordinary quantity of bacon. Ham and beef-steaks appear morning, noon, and night. In eating they mix things together with the strangest incongruity imaginable. I have seen eggs and oysters eaten together; ham with apple sauce; beef-steak with stewed peaches; and salt fish with onions. The bread is everywhere excellent [Miss Beecher most assuredly did not agree with this!], but they rarely enjoy it themselves, as they insist upon eating horrible half-baked hot rolls both morning and evening. The butter is tolerable; but they seldom have such cream as every little dairy produces in England; in fact the cows are very roughly kept, compared with ours. Common vegetables are abundant and very fine. . . . They eat the Indian corn in a great variety of forms [all of which she detested]. . . .

There is a great want of skill in the composition of sauces; not only with fish, but with everything. They use very few made dishes, and I never saw any that could be approved by our servants. They have an excellent wild duck called the Canvas Back. . . .

They seldom indulge in second courses . . . , but almost every table has its dessert (invariably pronounced desart) which is placed on the table before the cloth is removed, and consists of pastry, preserved fruits and creams. They are "extravagantly fond," to use their own phrase, of puddings, pies, and all kinds of sweets, particularly the ladies; but they are by no means such connoisseurs of soups and ragouts as the gastronomes of Europe.

When Mrs. Trollope was in America and for about sixty years after that, breakfast was a very heavy meal even for those people who were known as "the fashionables." Since then the American breakfast has been dwindling, and though in diners, especially in the West, fried eggs and bacon are served in a nest of fried potatoes, breakfast is not the universal feast it once was. On the farm, where breakfast was eaten in the kitchen and not in the dining room, of course, it followed an hour or more of heavy chores (and still does) and was a meal suited to the appetites of men who worked with their backs and hands, but even in the more genteel atmosphere of houses, such as that of Andrew Jackson Downing, breakfast was a hearty meal. "The breakfasts here, in the country, are much more substantial than with us in Sweden," wrote Fredrika Bremer, who was visiting the Downings in Newburgh in the 1840's. "Besides coffee and tea, the table is supplied with fish, fresh meat, buckwheat cakes, omelets, and so on. Besides which here is bread of Indian corn, and a kind of sweet potato. . . . It is commonly brought to table unpeeled, and is eaten with butter."

Breakfast was a far more leisurely repast in the country, and particularly in the South, than it was in the Northern cities and in the bustling new towns of the West. ("The South is less governed by commerce," declared Gaskell in his *Compendium*, "and does not save five minutes from the breakfast-room, at the cost of a life-long dyspepsia.") Breakfast was, as a writer in *Scribner's Magazine* noted impatiently in 1874, "a hurried half-way place of entertainment between bed and business: a mere halt for supplies before taking the road; a glimpse at the new day through the medium of a frumpish dressing-gown, buckwheat cakes, and a damp newspaper—a whispered colloquy with the cook going on at one end of the table, and the children scuffling off to school from the other." It would be far better, he thought, if breakfast could be a leisurely occasion to which one invited one's close friends. ". . . at break-fast we stand at ease in mind and body," he said, and how much better to talk with one's friends then than at the end of the day when one was carrying "all the burden of anxiety rolled up since morning."

By the last decade of the century breakfast was becoming far less of a feast and far more like the Continental breakfast of Eu-rope than it had been. It was sparser and more chic and less likely to include a steak than cooked cereal, or a slice of apple pie than a three-minute egg. (Dry cereals—shredded wheat, wheat flakes, corn flakes and the like—first appeared on the market in the 1890's.) Breakfast started with fruit, fresh if in season but otherwise stewed. Orange juice was a seasonal luxury, and juices were not widely used until frozen concentrated juices hit the market after World War II.

Breakfast is the most stereotyped of all meals in the sense that many persons are quite content to eat an identical breakfast day in and day out who wouldn't think of eating the same thing for lunch every day. In that respect, breakfast, which is the least formal of meals, is the most conventional.

In the part of the country from which I come (western Massa-chusetts) the midday meal was dinner, the evening meal was sup-per. Lunch was a word that was rarely used at all, except that the boys might take a "lunch" with them when they went fishing. The workman did not carry a lunch box; he carried a dinner pail. Sum-mer people ate lunch in the middle of the day and had dinner at night, and they not infrequently entertained at "luncheons" in their houses or at the country club. This use of the words and times of eating a heavy meal as opposed to a light one was not (and in-deed still is not) restricted to my part of the country. It is, how-ever, a ruralism, and applies largely to those places where the men of the family come home for the midday meal. This has not, how-ever, always been so in America. The nineteenth-century city fam-ily ate, as we have seen, a heavy breakfast which was meant to hold them until a substantial lunch at about two o'clock. This lunch was, to all intents and purposes, "dinner." The evening meal was a light supper, often not much more than what we would con-sider a "hearty tea." In a book called *Breakfast, Luncheon and Tea*, published in 1875, the author describes "a real old-fashioned New

England tea table." "During one delicious vacation I learned, and reveled in knowing," she said, "what this meant. Black tea with cream . . . rounds of brown bread, light, sweet and fresh; hot short-cake in piles . . . ; a big glass bowl of raspberries and currants that were growing in the garden under the back window an hour before; a basket of frosted cake; a plate of pink ham, balanced by one of shaved, *not* chipped, beef—and sage cheese!"

Lunch in the latter part of the last century was frequently a formal occasion for entertaining friends (both men and women), though not as formal or as formidable, as we shall see, as the dinner party. The *Ladies' Home Journal* in its February 1892 number gave this "simple" menu "that can easily be served."

LUNCHEON
CONSOMMÉ IN CUPS—BREAD

OYSTERS AU GRATIN—BREAD

BROILED CHICKEN
FRENCH PEAS   POTATO BALLS

SALAD
OLIVES   CHEESE
CRACKERS

PRESERVES, CAKE AND TEA OR CHOCOLATE

Compared with lunches earlier in the century it was, indeed, "simple," but by the nineties, which we are likely to think of as somewhat stuffier and more steeped in gravy than they were, the author of a discourse on the dining room in *The Woman's Book* (1894) was able to say, "We take our food now more sparingly and with greater gayety." The dining room, which she called "the temple of the family," was becoming a far more cheerful place. Even dinner parties were less ominous than they had been, though the dinner party was the most formal thing, short of a funeral or wedding, that ever happened in the American household.

The formal dinner party (which takes place today only in a dwindling number of American homes) was a nineteenth-century means of casting off a Puritan tradition which ruled that men and women should mingle socially as little as possible. Mrs. Trollope observed in 1828 that: "Mixed dinner parties of ladies and gentlemen are very rare." She thought it contributed little to the festiveness of the occasion when it did happen "to set the gentlemen at one end [of the table], and the ladies at the other; but," she added, "it is very rarely that you find it otherwise." This provincialism (for that is what Mrs. Trollope considered it to be) did not persist long in an America that was hell-bent on becoming genteel, and in which gentility was interpreted as the adoption (or often adaptation) of many European customs.

When the Americans decided that the dinner party was a *sine qua non* of domesticated, not to say sophisticated, living, they went at it with a vengeance that was more wholehearted than sensible. They managed to make the dinner party into one of the most boring social traps—endless and unendurable—ever devised by a presumably civilized people. "Is there in this world," wrote Fredrika Bremer, Downing's Swedish friend, who was lavished with hospitality wherever she went on her American travels, "anything more wearisome, more dismal, more intolerable, more indigestible, more stupifying, more unbearable, anything more calculated to kill both soul and body, than a great dinner in New York?" It seems unlikely from her description that there was. "People sit down to table at half-past five or six o'clock; they are still sitting at table at nine o'clock, sitting and being served with one course after another, with one indigestible dish after another, eating and being silent. I have never heard such a silence as at these great dinners."

There was, obviously, a happy (or at least endurable) medium between the sexually segregated parties of Mrs. Trollope's day and those Miss Bremer encountered about twenty-five years later in the 1850's. It is not surprising that the dinner party became not only a subject for endless discussion by writers on manners, but a heady preoccupation of hostesses, chefs, satirists, gourmets, and novelists. It became a matter for serious consideration (sometimes with the tongue slightly in the cheek) in magazines like *Harper's* and *Scribner's* and the *Century*, which were family magazines and not above instructing the naïve in the ways of sophisticated society. Gradually, the formal dinner was brought within reasonable bounds—less lengthy, smaller, less silent (that is, more conversational) and, above all, less of a burden on the digestive system.

Refinement of details became a substitute for grandioseness of conception. The transition was a gradual one. Methods of setting the table and serving the food changed, as did the hours at which dinner was served, the number of courses, kinds of wines, and suitable clothes. It is not possible to strike an average of the nineteenth-century dinner party and say "this is the way it was"; one cannot equate the vast dinners given by Mrs. Astor at 350 Fifth Avenue in the 1870's or those given by Mrs. Vanderbilt at The Breakers in Newport in the 1880's with dinners in the household of a reasonably prosperous middle-class family, but they had some things in common, and it is these that I would like to invite you to consider.

If you were to have walked into a dining room in the 1840's, the table would have looked very different to you from the one you would have seen fifteen or twenty years later. The table was set for service in the traditional English style. The anonymous author of *The American Chesterfield* in the 1848 edition of his book gave these instructions for setting a dinner table:

> Every person at table should be provided with knife and fork, plate, bread &c; and before every meat dish, a carving knife, fork, and spoon; and a spoon for every dish of vegetables. At the corners of the table, spoons, a salt-cellar, and small spoon for salt; and if pickles are there placed, a small knife and fork. If the table is large, the furniture of the corners should be likewise placed at short and convenient intervals. It has lately become common, in our Atlantic towns, and particularly where light wines are used with water, as a *long drink*, to place at convenient distances around the table, bottles of Sauterne, claret, or other light wine, (the corks previously drawn, and inserted lightly in the bottle,) and goblets of water. This is found, by experience, to be an admirable arrangement for convenience, and gives the waiters more time to attend, among other duties, to the frequent changes of plates, which modern refinement has introduced.

The introduction of what was called "service *à la Russe*" changed not only the appearance of the table with its platter of meat ready for carving and vegetable dishes, but the method by which the meal was served. It took the vegetable dishes off the table and sometimes put the process of carving into the pantry. By the old system (sometimes referred to as English and sometimes as French) the roast was put on the table and was carved there by the man of the family; plates were passed to him for servings of meat, and then the vegetable dishes were passed from hand to hand by those who were dining. (The person who sat in the center of the side of the table, which was called the "ferry" seat, often spent most of his time passing and had little for eating.) The Russian system provided that "meats &c., are not handed around until they have been carved, then the servants pass them to the left of each person. Vegetables [were] served in a similar manner, and then the various sauces and pickles follow[ed]." According to "Daisy Eyebright," whose *Manual of Etiquette* was published in 1868, ". . . serving a dinner in the Russian style" was "quite *à la mode* in the United States" then. The method is now, of course, so taken for granted that its Russian origin has long since been forgotten, though it was still being referred to as "Russian service" by Emily Post in 1932.

The change from the English to the Russian style introduced to the formal dinner the custom of putting a menu at each place, "so that the guest may see what will be handed around, and may be prepared to select, or wait for whatever dishes he may prefer." ("Bills of fare in English are better than those written in French for this side of the Atlantic," said the author of *Sensible Etiquette* in 1878.) Service *à la Russe* was not necessarily an all-or-nothing method. "The combination of the French and Russian mode of serving dinners is to be preferred," Gaskell said, "if the dinner party is small." In that case: "Soup is put opposite to the lady of the house; if there are two soups a tureen will be at each end and be succeeded by two kinds of fish. It may be that the soup is before the lady and the fish at the same time placed before the gentleman. . . ." The Russian of it was that the servant held the soup plate to the tureen and it was filled by the lady—or sometimes by the gentleman at her right, who took this arduous job off her hands. Gaskell explained further: "The soup and fish are succeeded by the meat and chicken, or turkey. The mutton or lamb is put before the gentleman; the chicken or turkey before the lady, who is assisted in carving by the gentleman beside her, but before either of the dishes are [sic] uncovered the servants hand the *side dishes* which are *not* now put on the table." But whether the method used was all *à la Russe* or a mixture of Russian and French (or English), it presupposes a waiter for each four guests, and the waiters, unlike the guests, did not, of course, remove their white gloves. An ungloved waiter was unthinkable.*

The hours of arrival for dinner, the length of the repast, and the departure of the guests were matters that received a great deal of attention from manuals of behavior and from magazine writers. In 1858 a writer in *Harper's* set the proper hour for dinner as seven-thirty, which assured the diners of "enjoying as long as possible the pleasures of anticipation." (Seven-thirty was considered very late then, but formal dinners frequently started far later than that in the nineties and in the early years of this century. "Dinner at eight" was common; later than that was rather grand.) "Punctuality, however," the *Harper's* writer said, "whatever the hour, is indispensable." It was customary to allow ten or fifteen minutes between the arrival of guests and the announcement of dinner. ("This interval will give time for introductions and greetings, and for the assignment of escorts to the table"). To be late was considered an "unpardonable rudeness"; to be early was to run the risk of finding your hostess "not yet ready to receive." If your carriage or hansom cab arrived at your hostess's door five minutes before the hour for which you were invited, you somehow killed the time. The "dreadful ten minutes," as it was often called, between arriving and going in to dinner was eased by no sherry or cocktail. *Century Magazine* in the 1870's reported on a new and "pretty custom" which had recently been introduced to cheer up the interval: ". . . each gentleman [is presented] in the dressing room a button-hole bouquet tied with a ribbon, the color of which he finds, on reaching the drawing room, corresponds with that on the bouquet of the lady he is expected to attend to the dining-room."

The length of the dinner hour varied according to the pretensions of the host and hostess, the number of guests, and the decade. In the 1870's a rule of thumb was: "Limit the time occupied in serving dinner to the two hours which form prescribes. For small dinners one hour, or at most one hour and a half, is the allotted time." It was still not unusual, however, to hear people (not sophisticated people, to be sure) "speaking of the number of hours [sometimes four or five], as the gauge of a successful dinner." It was,

---

* A vestigial remnant of this custom can be seen in some restaurants today where the bus boys, not the waiters, still wear white cotton gloves.

furthermore, considered a sign of either ignorance or arrogance to serve more than ten courses at a formal dinner.

Samuel Eliot Morison in *One Boy's Boston* gives the menu of a proper Boston dinner party held on October 20, 1888, and recorded in his grandmother's notebook. It was a dinner for ten and consisted of

OYSTERS
BROWN SOUP
SMELTS, SAUCE TARTARE
SWEETBREADS IN CUPS
CHOPS BROILED, MACÉDOINE
CHICKEN ZEPHYRE WITH PEAS
DUCKS, CELERY AND LETTUCE
WATER ICE
SAUTERNE, SHERRY, CHAMPAGNE, BURGUNDY

Twenty-two years later in 1910 an American woman, Katherine G. Busbey, writing on *Home Life in America* for a British audience, said: . . . the simplest dinner deemed 'proper' by the American hostess in Washington is along the following lines:

GRAPEFRUIT OR HORS D'OEUVRES
RAW OYSTERS
SOUP
FISH
ENTRÉE
ROAST
BIRDS
SALAD
FROZEN PUDDING, CAKES, BON-BONS, ETC."

To this must have also been added coffee, and probably cheese. The meal was accompanied by only four wines, far fewer than would have been considered suitable a few decades earlier. It was preceded by cocktails and followed by liqueurs.

The optimum size of a dinner party undoubtedly received so much attention from writers on manners because ambitious hostesses had a way of letting the number of guests run away with them under the impression that the larger the party the more elegant it must be and the more it must contribute to their social standing. Miss Busbey, with justification, shook her head. "In America," she said, "the scale of entertainment is the rating of the socially elect. The elaborate menu, the rare musical talent for after-dinner recital, spectacular decorations—these are the lances with which the newcomer must enter the society jousting that is ever in session in America. . . . The constant effort to make our entertaining represent not ourselves or our income, but the income of the class above us in earthly possessions, honey-combs our hospitality." It was also death on conversation; too many people at dinner made good talk impossible. M. Anthelme Brillat-Savarin, the author of *The Physiology of Taste* and one of the most quoted gourmets of the last century, declared that the number of guests at dinner should not exceed twelve; if a dinner were larger than that, he contended, general conversation was impossible. "Bright conversation," wrote one of his American contemporaries, "is the best of all sauces, and a good supply of that is worth a hundred delicacies."

The sauce was rare. The American man of the nineteenth century was notorious for his inability to make conversation. He could pontificate; he could hold forth on business and politics, but conversation was, he believed, something fit only for "lightweights" and "lady-killers." Henry Adams in his *Education* said quite forthrightly that "the American woman of the nineteenth century was much better company than the American man." It was more or less taken for granted that the busy, energetic, single-minded American man found social life not only a bore but a situation in which he felt uncomfortable and gauche. "He has no small talk for his dinner partners," Miss Busbey wrote. "He is almost always absorbed in some scheme to make more money, and naturally is in no mood to make it a topic of conversation . . . and then he is, as a rule, too exhausted to look upon any effort of entertainment to which he must contribute as anything but torture." (*The Woman's Book* took a more optimistic view in 1894: "The old man is dead whom his neighbor tried to engage in conversation over his soup. At last he spoke: 'That there piece of green has gone down without my knowing it,' and spoke no more.") The male attitude toward dinner conversation was part and parcel of the notion that anything that smacked of culture—of the arts in any form—was women's business, and unfit for manly attention. As a result, even fifty years ago the social lions in America were said to be "a few men doing light literature, the foreign diplomats accredited to America and

. . . the actor of scholarly success." (This was a step forward; in the 1850's no self-respecting "lady" would have dreamed of inviting an actor to sit at her table, no matter how "scholarly." Editors and authors were also looked upon by careful hostesses with an uneasiness amounting to embarrassment and consequent avoidance.)

If most dinners were dull and conventional, at least when they were over they were over. It was customary for the hostess to rise as a signal that the ladies would leave the dining room for the parlor (or withdraw to the "withdrawing room") so the gentlemen might drink their wine. The author of *The American Chesterfield* explains the custom thus:

> Habit having made a pint of wine after dinner almost a necessity to a man who eats freely, which is not the case with women; and as their sitting and drinking with the men would be unseemly, it is customary, after the cloth and dessert are removed, and two or three glasses have gone around, for the ladies to retire, and leave the men to themselves. . . .

The Illustrated Manners Book of 1855 noted a change in the custom which it regarded with approbation. Anything, its author believed, was better than the old custom of dividing the ladies and the gentlemen. "Formerly," he said, "when ladies were supposed to be deficient in intellect, and gentlemen were truly deficient in decency, as soon as the dinner was over, and the gentlemen were ready for drinking, talking, smoking, and vile stories, and viler songs, the lady of the house gave the signal, the ladies rose, the gentlemen also, someone opened the door, and the ladies retired to the drawing room while the gentlemen enjoyed their own peculiar pleasures." Times and manners, he noted, had changed, and he added: "But now that ladies can talk quite as well on most subjects as their lords, and that gentlemen think it as well to be decent in their own society, ladies remain at the dinner table, take champagne very prudently, if at all; coffee is served last and at the dinner table; and all retire together to the music, conversation, or the flirtations of the drawing room."

Mrs. Farrar regarded the division of the sexes after dinner from a different perspective. "A dinner, well-performed by all the actors in it," she said, "is very fatiguing, and, as it generally occupies three hours or more, most persons are glad to go away when it is fairly done." The arrival of the gentlemen in the parlor, "the young ones first and the politicians last," was the signal for departure. "The sooner you depart after taking coffee," she said, "the better."

This custom of the men remaining in the dining room for their coffee and cigars and brandy is still observed in some households at formal dinners, but it is increasingly rare. It presupposes adequate service. However, it is not in the least uncommon to find the men and the women gathered immediately after dinner in opposite corners of the living room, as though some rigid social convention held over from Mrs. Trollope's day prescribed it. There is usually "man's talk" going on in one corner and "woman's talk" in the other, and conversation in neither.

The etiquette of wine received a great deal of attention in America a century ago (as it is beginning to again), and it was a topic of conversation upon which it was considered essential for a gentleman to be able to express himself knowledgeably. Though the names of many of the great wines that were bandied about then are the same ones that connoisseurs regard with favor today, many of the customs of serving and drinking wine have changed.

In the 1860's it was customary at dinner parties to put the wines on the table, and each gentleman served the lady next to him. Under no circumstances must a man or a woman to whom wine was offered refuse it. If they did not wish to drink it, they must at least touch their lips to it. It was customary "on raising the first glass of wine to his lips . . . for a gentleman to bow to the lady of the house." He must be sure, however, not to "offer to help a lady to wine" until he had seen that she had finished her soup or fish. At large dinners, especially those served in the Russian manner, wine was passed by the waiters, and it was considered something less than hospitable to place fewer than four wineglasses at each person's place. ("It is a great breach of etiquette, as well as a sign of vulgarity, to drink more than one kind of wine out of a glass.") In the 1870's and 1880's the "authority" whom Gaskell falls back on to discuss this delicate subject, said: "The taste for light wines which is now prevalent makes a great variety indispensable." He prescribed sauterne and sherry for the fish and soup, and "with the joints the choice of hock, chablis, and one or two kinds of claret; with game, burgundy . . . and there should be port on the table for those few who choose to take it at this time. Then the 'ladies' wines,' as they are sometimes called, still or sparkling champagne and moselle. For dessert provide port, sherry, madeira, and claret. Port accompanies cheese."

In the middle part of the last century burgundy, according to the anonymous author of *The Perfect Gentleman* (he wrote about wines with eloquence, delight, and obvious relish and understanding), was usually unfit to drink in America. "When it arrives in this country," he said, "it is generally brandied, which is most injurious to its flavor and smell. Pure Burgundy is a very delicate wine, that is not very common in the United States." Clarets, on the other hand, were excellent and "a great favorite in this country, in hot weather especially . . . light, agreeable, gently exhilarating, and an excellent quencher of thirst." The matter of *chambré*-ing a wine was somewhat different when room temperature was colder than it became with the introduction of central heating or even with iron stoves. It was customary to put a claret "near the fire before uncorking, as without a moderate degree of warmth it lacks the soft and delicious flavor which makes the chief merit of this wine." Wines that had to be cooled, on the other hand, offered no problem in winter. For summer, Roberts' *House Servant's Directory* recommended: ". . . dip a cloth in cold water, and wrap it round the bottle two or three times; then place it in the sun; renew the process once or twice." The wine cooler, a mahogany icebox suitable for the dining room, was already being recommended in the 1840's by Miss Leslie, as we have seen.

Not only was the order in which wines were served different a century ago from the order today (in 1860 red wines preceded white ones and champagne was commonly drunk with the meats), but the manner of serving them was also different. "Hock, champagne, moselle and chablis," said Gaskell's "authority," "and some few other wines are brought to the table in bottles [as today], the choice varieties of claret in the baskets in which they are imported; port, sherry and madeira are decanted; ordinary clarets and burgundy wines are handed around in claret jugs, either of glass or silver." There are very few people today who go to the trouble of decanting port or sherry and even fewer who serve Madeira at all. The wine basket in which a bottle is placed (not in which the bottle was imported) is chic in Upper Bohemian circles and in some posh restaurants. The custom of wrapping chilled white wines in a napkin before serving them goes well back into the last century. Some wine fanciers insist that it is proper to use a napkin only when the wine is champagne, some others say it is never proper. But in any case, it is extremely rare today to be served more than two wines at any meal, however formal.

The decline in wine-drinking in America seems to have started in the 1880's under the pressures of the temperance movement, which was largely a female crusade against the "demon rum." (Actually, most Americans drank whisky, not rum, as there was plenty of grain to make it from and as it was so extremely cheap.) Less than twenty years after the author of *The Perfect Gentleman* had said that it was a heinous breach of manners to refuse an offer of wine whether you drank it or not, another book of etiquette says: "One of the greatest privileges of the present age is liberty of opinion, and if you are disinclined to drink wine you can avail yourself of it . . . you accept it or decline it at your pleasure. If you do not drink it, quietly cover the top of your glass with your fingers, and say, 'Please, excuse me.'" In the early 1890's the *Ladies' Home Journal* ran an article on the decline of wine-drinking, and the manners manual published by the *Christian Herald* in 1895, which was obviously on the side of the temperance movement, had the following to say on "The Wine Question":

> The wine question is one that disturbs many a dinner-giving family. Shall wine be served or not is a growing problem. Society has at last reached the point where it is not considered a breach of good form to serve a dinner without wine. Such a course is sanctioned by the example of many high social leaders; and when it is the result of a temperance principle it has the respect of every diner-out. . . . Apollinaris can be made to take the place of stronger waters, and no embarrassment follows. The hostess who simply does not offer wine to any guest under any circumstances, is using her influence effectively and courageously in the cause of temperance in support of Christian principles.

In 1906 in a manual called *The Up-to-date Waitress* the author remarks on the passing of the profusion of wines that were customary on the Victorian table merely by remarking: "Formerly at dinner a different variety of wine was poured for each distinct course. At the present time this is rarely seen. In many houses, where means are unlimited, but one wine—claret—is served throughout the meal. When guests are bidden, often champagne takes the place of the claret."

Dyspepsia unquestionably contributed to the decline of wine-drinking. So, obviously, did the introduction of the predinner cocktail in the first decade of this century. Prohibition in 1918 did it in completely except in a very few households of families rich enough to put away cellars filled with delectable bottles, and a few families who made their own dreadful brews. Since the Second World War there has been a considerable revival of interest in wines, both domestic and imported, but it saddens the hearts of today's domesticators that the greatest sales of wine in America should be cheap fortified wines and the sweet table wines that taste like slightly spiked and highly sugared grape juice.

Since the turn of the century the dining room has waxed and waned and now shows signs of waxing again. In the Edwardian era, during which meals were still ponderous, the dining room in rich households was richly ornamented with marble mantels and imported paneling, chandeliered, carpeted with Persian rugs, and presided over by butlers in tail coats, footmen in striped waistcoats, and maids in black or lavender dresses frothed with white aprons. But in many houses that were less than palaces and mansions the dining room began to lose its importance and in some cases even its identity. It vanished completely in a great many summer cottages (now called "second homes," like second cars), where the family ate on the screened porch or, when the weather was inclement, in the corner of the living room nearest the kitchen. This was true not only in the simple cabin whose front porch was lapped by a lake, but in the very substantial summer home in an expensive (if not the most expensive) resort. No one called it the "dining area," as it has recently come to be called, but as summer living was a mild sort of "roughing it," it is not surprising that the accommodations for eating should revert to a polite version of frontier living. It seems likely, according to Edgar Kaufmann, Jr., that it was from the summer house that Frank Lloyd Wright got the idea of making the dining room merely a part of the living room. In any event, Wright did not invent it, or even revive it, and he did not use it in the houses that he built before 1910, though it became a standard practice with him in his later domestic building.

Indeed, in 1910 all but the very least expensive houses that were built in towns and villages had dining rooms, though in the bungalow, which was so ubiquitous then, the dining room and living room very frequently opened into one another through a wide entrance with only a screen or a curtain to close one off from the other. The "dining area," a logical next step to the dining room that was scarcely separated from the living room, came into its own with the introduction of the "open plan" in the 1930's.

This extension of the living room to include a place for the family to eat (it was often a sort of "L" in the living room) was, obviously, partly a matter of economy, partly an attempt to make the living room look larger than it actually was, and partly a matter of exploiting a fashionable belief in the validity of flowing spaces. The open plan, which seemed so important to the advanced architects of the period following the First World War and continues to be important to many of them today, was only grudgingly accepted by a vast majority of home builders and purchasers. They considered it a blow against privacy. How, they wanted to know, can you close a door on the children and get some peace? Housewives worried about the mess in the "dining area" after their guests moved to another part of the living room; there ought to be some way to close a door on it—especially in the servantless household, which, of course, was by the 1940's very nearly all households. After the Second World War the family room began to become increasingly popular; it made it possible to keep the living room all fixed up so that it was, in effect, the old-fashioned parlor. It was also a place where the family could eat if it didn't eat in the kitchen. It was, indeed, very like the "eating room" which doubled as a sitting room when the table was cleared. In apartment houses, where the cost per room went up and up after the war, the dining room vanished from all but the most luxurious apartments and, indeed, from many of them as well.

But the sentiment for the dining room did not disappear, and it did not disappear from the plans of development houses, whatever may have happened in the plans of houses built by architects for specific families. In 1956 Albert M. Cole, who was then the chief of housing for the federal government, invited a large number of housewives to say what they thought of the current state of house-planning. Some of the reactions he received had to do with the dining room, and here are a few of them:

"I want a dining room, not just a dining area in the living room or kitchen," a Kentucky housewife wrote. "I just can't understand why many medium-priced [$11,000 to $15,000 at that time] homes in this country are arranged to 'sleep' so many people when you couldn't possibly feed everyone at the same time."

Then there was the matter of manners; a Washington, D.C., woman wrote: "My preference is a separate dining room, as we feel children should not be brought up eating a life-time of meals in the kitchen, no matter what size."

There was also the matter of festivals. "As far as I am concerned," said a Pennsylvania housewife, "a family seated around a dining table on such occasions as Thanksgiving, Christmas, etc., is still an integral part of the American way of life and omitting this room is as serious an offense as forgetting to put in the bathroom."

In the annual collections of house plans and photographs that are published by architectural magazines to demonstrate what they believe is the very best in domestic architecture each year, you are not likely to find houses with dining rooms or, in any case, dining rooms that can be closed off from "living areas." If, however, you will look at the houses that are reproduced each week in the real-estate sections of many newspapers, you will find dining rooms in ranch houses, split-levels, raised ranches, in "colonials," and in something called the "splanch" (which is a split-level ranch, of course). In other words, the developers who, whatever their architectural standards may be, have an eye for building "dream houses," seem to believe that most families want to have a dining room. You will also find in the slick magazines for the carriage (or three-car) trade, that a good deal of attention is given to the decoration of the dining room, and to discussion of its "revival," as though it had been somewhere and had just found its way home. You will find it spoken of as a "status symbol," along with everything else these days.

But if the dining room has not ever quite been away, many of the objects that we associate with it, if we are of middle age, have gone for good, or if not gone entirely are increasingly rare. In closing this chapter I think a few of these are worth mentioning, not merely for the sake of nostalgia, but because they say a good deal about the changing pace and style of American life, in how brief a time it has changed, and how little we regret what has disappeared. How rarely if you look around a dining-room table today do you see:

Napkin rings
Butter balls
Butter chips (except paper ones in inexpensive restaurants)
Cruets and casters
A bell on the table or a buzzer under it

A soup tureen
A cut-glass or silver rest for a carving knife
Finger bowls, to say nothing of the doilies under them
Horn spoons in the open salt cellars
Table crumber
Candy dishes
Epergnes of fruit

When I was a child there was a silver gadget that looked like a sort of coarse spider web on the breakfast table. If you pushed it down over an apple it took out the core and cut it into six or seven equal segments. The list I have given above could be expanded by anyone who remembers white tablecloths and linen dinner napkins, or even the recent days when orange juice came out of oranges, not cans, and hot baking-powder biscuits were a miracle of personal artistry and not of corporate ingenuity.

CHAPTER XI

The Bedroom and the Bath

> The odor of cone-bearing trees has a well-
> known influence upon the fruitfulness of wed-
> lock. Those who live in pine forests have
> ordinarily large families of children.
> George N. Napheys, M.D.
> *The Physical Life of Women*, 1869

Getting into the world and getting out of it not so long ago was a domestic affair that took place upstairs. Birth happened in a four-poster or a sleigh bed or a gleaming confection of brass and enamel curlicues, amid steaming basins of water and piles of clean linen. From the same room, often from the same bed, death seeped through the closed door into every corner of the house, hushing it and turning its smell sweet. Many a man died in the bed in which he was conceived and born, and where, when he had inherited it from his parents, he had in turn conceived his children. It is now considered safer for the mother and her child that birth should take place in a hospital; it is now considered more scientific and certainly more convenient, except perhaps for the one most concerned, to die in the hospital. As a result, some of the joy and some of the melancholy that have for ages attached themselves to the bedroom have gone.

But they are not all that has gone. Some more prosaic functions that used to belong to the bedroom have gone along with some of its minor pleasures. Its major pleasures have, perhaps, been enhanced.

The master's bedroom (which more accurately should be called the mistress's bedroom) of the middle-class household which had one or more servants was commonly the office from which the household was run. It was where the lady of the house had her desk; it was there that she decided what the family would eat and what she would serve to guests. It was there that the cook came for her instructions in the morning. It was there that the lady of the house wrote her notes, paid her bills, and starting about 1900 telephoned the markets to order the food. The room was a combination of boudoir, love nest, office, command post, dressing room, and retreat. (In some houses it was also the sewing room, though in the days when a seamstress used to come in once a week to many households, there was a separate sewing room where the sewing machine was kept along with dress forms and other such equipment as sewing baskets, strawberries for sharpening needles, and darning balls.) As it was the citadel of the lady of the house, the bedroom was decorated usually without regard to the taste of the gentleman of the house, on the theory, perhaps, that he enjoyed the role of intruder even in the most congenial of households and that he slept in his wife's bed not she in his. The decoration of the bedroom has changed greatly and frequently in the last century and a half, but I do not believe that it can ever have been said that its nature was masculine, unless that be the case today. There is, perhaps, something rather more masculine about the undecorated furniture of many modern bedrooms than about the ornate bedsteads, bureaus, wardrobes, and dressing tables of a few decades and more ago. (There is also something more masculine about the deportment of women, a point not worth exploring here.)

The only bedroom in the house which is intended just for sleep is the guest room. The small child's room is a playroom and storeroom with a bed in it. The infant's room adds to that some of the atmosphere and equipment of a hospital room as well; it is as much cage as room and is furnished more for protection than for comfort. The room of the school-age child is a study, a recreation room, a museum of precious trifles, a music room, and a library, characterized usually by a kind of clutter that is a direct reflection of the catholicity of children's taste. They love everything equally but nothing for very long. The room of the post-school child (by that age called the unmarried son or daughter of the family) continues to retain many of the attributes of the school child's room, but in somewhat restrained and domesticated terms. "A room of one's own" becomes more and more of a home within a house as its occupant grows older and his possessions and his privacy become more cherished. The guest room, however, by its very nature is almost invariably the most impersonal room in any house. Nobody lives in it; nobody is expected to live in it; and usually nobody would want to live in it. It has all of the attributes of a bedroom—a place to sleep, to store clothes, lights to read by, warmth, air, and, with luck, an adjoining bathroom—but it usually has about it none of the qualities that make a bedroom the room in the house that follows most closely the mood of its occupants. The bedroom is a chaos of mussed bedding, dropped clothes, discarded letters, newspapers, magazines, towels, hairbrushes, underwear, and keys one minute; and half an hour later is a placid, orderly, and sweet-smelling reflection of inner calm and emotion put in its place.

The bedroom has, of course, come in for somewhat more than its share of advice, counsel, and admonition from those who have tried to domesticate the American family. It is, such writers have pointed out again and again, the place where "one-third of life is passed in sleep." Sleep is a dangerous occupation; it is then that one is most vulnerable to attack (bedrooms should have stout locks); it is then that "we are much more susceptible to injurious influences . . . than when awake, and these accumulate with startling rapidity in an unventilated chamber" (don't sleep with the windows closed); it is in the bedroom that damp accumulates and therefore "no room should be slept in in winter that has not had a fire in it at least three times a week, [and] . . . the temperature of a bedroom should never be suffered to fall below 40°" (if it does, for heaven's sake, don't forget the bed-warmer or at least a brick wrapped in carpet that has been heated by the fire). Two people should not sleep in the same room (unless married, of course), because they should not be exposed to each other's "night exhalations." But even if they are married they should, perhaps, consider that there are circumstances under which husband and wife should not occupy the same bedroom. A marriage manual of 1890 advised:

A great deal has been written upon the effect on health and happiness of occupying separate apartments, separate beds in the same apartment, or the same bed. This vexed question it is impossible to settle by absolute rules, suitable to all cases. In general, it may be asserted that there are no valid physiological reasons for desiring to change the custom which now prevails in this and most other countries. When both parties are in good health, and of nearly the same age, one bed chamber if sufficiently roomy may be used without any disadvantage to either. Such an arrangement is also to be commended, because it assures closer companionship, and this develops and sustains mutual affection. [However] . . . very young and very old people should never occupy the same bed. When the married couple hold the relation to each other, in regard to age, of grandfather and granddaughter, separate apartments should be insisted on.

The bed itself, for obvious reasons (but not for sexual ones), was the primary focus of those who were concerned not only with the comfort and looks of the bedroom but with its contributions to health. In the Greek Revival house the bed in the master's bedroom was most commonly a tall four-poster, as it had been in colonial days, though the posts grew, as the historian Talbot Hamlin said, to "elephantine" proportions, and the rest of the room was furnished with "great dressers and wardrobes with huge cornices" and with chairs more or less in the Empire manner. But what its frame was like had little to do with whether or not a bed was comfortable, or, indeed, healthful, and it was upon these qualities that most advice was expended. In the days when Miss Beecher wrote her first book (that is, in the 1830's and '40's) there were, of course, no metal bedsprings. (The "springs in the form of woven-wire mattresses," Giedion says, "were invented around 1870.") But all the same there was a variety of kinds of mattresses that might be placed on the network of cords that stretched from one side of the frame to another, and not only did these mattresses vary in their contents, but also, it appears, in their social acceptability.

In the order of their warmth (and also of their cost) nineteenth-century mattress materials were rated by Goodholme's *Cyclopedia* in this way: "1st, down, 2nd, feathers, 3rd, wool, 4th, wool-flock, 5th, hair, 6th, cotton, 7th, excelsior, 8th, sea-moss, 9th, paper-shavings, and 10th, straw." Down and feathers were particularly recommended for the young and the old. Wool and hair were considered best for "healthy persons of middle age"; and for people "who perspire freely or for warm weather, the sea-moss and paper-shavings." It was hair, however, that was considered "the best of all materials for beds." It was "more healthy than feathers, more comfortable than any of the cheaper materials," and was "equally serviceable in summer and winter."

(The author of the marriage manual quoted at the head of this chapter was a physician and was concerned with problems of fertility, and in addition to the mattress materials listed in Goodholme he suggested the following: "A number of ancient writers have alleged —and it has been reasserted by modern authorities—that sleeping on sponge is of service to those who desire to increase their families. The mattresses of compressed sponge recently introduced, therefore, commend themselves to married people thus situated. Hemlock boughs make a bed which has a well-established reputation for similar virtues." This same physician warned against feather beds and against "beds long saturated with the night exhalations of their occupants.")

A very great many Americans slept on straw mattresses for a very long while. In the *American Frugal Housewife* (1838) Mrs. Child insisted in her parsimonious way that "Barley straw is the best [kind of straw] for beds; dry corn husks, slit into shreds, are far better than straw. . . . Straw beds are much better for being boxed at the sides; in the same manner upholsterers prepare ticks for feathers." In her day, and for many decades after, the "straw man," who peddled the material for making mattresses, was a common sight on village and city streets and his cry, "Straw! Straw!" was a familiar one. In a reminiscence of Grand Rapids, Michigan, of a century ago, Charles E. Belknap insisted that: "One way to tell the rich man or woman was by the feathers in whiskers or hair, while the others . . . reveled in wild oats. Wheat straw did not sprout so readily as oat and was cheaper."

Straw was a nuisance. It had to be changed once a month by the conscientious housekeeper, and it had to be carefully selected by the fastidious. ("Mother," says Mr. Belknap, "for her spare bedroom would use nothing but the best oat that had been threshed by flail.") It was the wide promotion of wire springs and the wool mattress in the 1870's that put an end to the general use of straw ticks.

An extraordinary amount of ingenuity was expended on the design and improvement of the bed in the nineteenth century, ingenuity that produced the most elaborate "convertibles" and the most luxurious systems of springs. This was no minor matter of converting, as we do today, from a love seat or a sofa into a bed. It went to such lengths as the "piano bed which looked like a spinet and not only opened to be a bed but contained," as Giedion says, "a bureau and two closets to hold bedclothes, a wash-basin, pitcher, towel, etcetera." The folding bed that during the day looked like a wardrobe against the wall was common as a means of converting the living room into a bedroom and was the precursor of the "roomette" bed on sleepers.

The mechanical bed, which seemed to have an independent life of its own and to harbor the threat of snapping shut against the wall like the jaws of a trap, was the source of elaborate spoofs and speculations on the extent to which the mechanization of sleeping equipment could (and would) be stretched. None of the jokes, so far as I have found, was more elaborate or more characteristic than one concocted by a wine merchant named Frederick S. Cozzens, who for the amusement of his customers wrote what he called *The Sparrowgrass Papers* in the 1850's. His concoction was the "Wake-up" bed. "It is a bedstead," Cozzens wrote, "with a clock scientifically inserted in the headboard. When you go to bed, you wind up the clock, and point the index-hand to that hour on the dial, at which you wish to rise in the morning. Then you place yourself in the hands of the invention and shut your eyes. You are now, as it were, under the guardianship of King Solomon and Doctor Benjamin Franklin." Its mechanism worked like this:

> The "wake-up" is a combination of hard wood, hinges, springs, and clock-work. . . . It is a bedstead, with all the beautiful vitality of a flower —it opens with the dawn. If, for instance, you set the hand against six o'clock, in the morning at six the clock at the bed's head solemnly strikes a demi-twelve on its sonorous bell. If you pay no attention to the monitor . . . the invention within the succeeding two minutes, drops its tail-board and lets down your feet upon the floor. While you are pleasantly defeating this attempt upon your privacy by drawing up your legs within the precincts of the blankets, the virtuous headboard, and the rest of the bed, suddenly rise up in protest; and the next moment, if you do not instantly abdicate, you are launched upon the floor by a blind elbow that connects with the crank of an eccentric, that is turned by a cord, that is wound around a drum, that is moved by an endless screw, that revolves within the body of the machinery. . . .

". . . this machine," he continued, "is one of the most remarkable evidences of progress, the ingenuity of man has yet developed. . . . I have no doubt, in a short time, we shall see the finest attributes of the human mind superseded by machinery."

This Rube Goldbergian concept of the overelaborated machine conceived for the sake of its own fanciness did not, of course, precisely evolve according to Mr. Cozzens' flight of fancy, though in July 1961 the *Wall Street Journal* reported: "Now comes a silent alarm clock which wakens sleepers by vibrating the bed." The elaborate headboard into which is plugged a jungle of reading lights and night lights, a percolator, a clock radio, and a telephone, and which stores books, pills, magazines, water carafe, eyeshades, earplugs, and other nocturnal equipment, is not far removed from what the designer of the convertible piano bed had in mind. The bed itself, however, has grown simpler in most respects than it used to be, and more comfortable. The looks have been a matter of taste; the comfort a matter of technology, most especially in the construction and control of the steel coil spring which was used a century ago in chairs. The bedstead, once a massive construction of mahogany or cherry or oak, has become a box-spring on inconspicuous legs, often with no footboard, and usually with a readily detachable headboard. Sometimes, as I have suggested above, the headboard is the bedroom equivalent of the dining-room sideboard (or buffet); often it is merely something against which to prop pillows rather than leaning them against the wall.

The characteristic master's bedroom suit (and it was called a *suit* and not a *suite*) of the late nineteenth century, consisted of a double bed, a washstand, and a chest of drawers or bureau with an attached mirror. John Wanamaker's in Philadelphia in its catalogue of 1887-88 offered twenty-four different bedroom sets ranging in price from $230 for a two-piece mahogany set (all the other sets had three pieces) to $32 for a three-piece "ash, finished antique oak, highly polished, wood tops." For $140 you could buy a suit that was "very heavy and richly carved walnut" with the tops of the bureau and washstand covered with Tennessee marble. Not infrequently the machine-made baroque headboards of the beds of such sets stood well over seven feet high. Double beds that folded up into gigantic boxes on the wall ranged in price from $175 for solid mahogany to $45 for ash treated to look like oak. A small single folding bed that looked for all the world like a mantelpiece when standing against the wall could be had for as little as $24.

In the late 1880's Wanamaker's, which was one of America's greatest suppliers to the individual householder, included in its furniture catalogue not a single item that could have been considered one of "twin" beds. It was taken for granted that husband and wife shared a bed or, possibly, slept in separate apartments. But by the end of the nineties, twin beds were considered suitable for the master's bedroom, and they very soon became not only the fashionable but also the hygienic thing for the modern family to insist upon.

The furnishings of the nineteenth-century bedroom make ours look spare indeed, but they changed greatly as the century progressed and they became simplified. There were no closets in the bedrooms of the first half of the century, except occasionally in very sophisticated dwellings, and the wardrobe, usually a bulky closed cavern of a piece with shelves above and drawers below (and sometimes called a "clothes press"), was the common substitute for a closet. Women, to be sure, kept many of their garments folded flat and put away with dried lavender in old-fashioned chests, and of course, in chests of drawers. Even after architects and development builders began to put closets in bedrooms, the wardrobe continued in general use throughout the century. Another essential of the bedroom was the washstand, on which stood a basin and pitcher, a china mug for teethcleaning, and a tumbler; and which secluded in its cupboard below a slop jar and foot-bath. Towels hung from rungs that projected up and out from either side. Next to the bed in properly appointed houses was the commode, in which was sequestered the chamber pot covered tidily with a linen towel. The bedroom, in other words, served not only as a place to sleep but as a sort of bathroom as well, and even after most households had running water upstairs and a real bathroom, it was not uncommon to have a marble-topped sink in the corner of every bedroom, with its towel rack next to it, and a shaving mirror above it, or sometimes a shaving stand beside it.

The concoctions which both men and women, especially citified and sophisticated ladies and gentlemen, saw fit to have on their dressing tables, in bottles fancily labeled with flowery decalcomanias, were of almost infinite variety. Meade Minnigerode in his extremely entertaining account of *The Fabulous Forties* wrote of a fashionable couple rising in the morning to make their toilets in New York:

> She probably soaked it [her hair] in Dr. Roley's Brazilian hair curling liquid, and washed it in Guerlain's lustral water, while her husband was treating himself with Rowland's essence of Tyre, or Jones's oil of coral circassia, and anointing his locks with bear's grease, bull's marrow, or macassar oil, balm of Columbia, bandoline, cream of lilies, or pomatum in brown, black and auburn sticks.

> And while he was shaving with Lubin's almond paste, or Ring's Verbena, or Henry's Chinese cream, she performed her ablutions with Brown's Windsor or Piver's soap, and improved her complexion with

esprit de cedrat, eau de Botot, or sirop de Boubie, with blanc de neige and citromane, or, if necessary, with Micheaux's freckle wash.

The list of cosmetics goes on and on ("bergamotte, frangipane, patchouly; caprice de la mode, bouquet de Victoria, Portugal water, or honey amber; . . .") but cosmetics were not just for those who lived in cities and were rich. In household manuals and cookbooks for the farm wife there were tucked in among the instructions for keeping apples for winter use, making rat poison, and preserving cheese from insects, recipes for cologne water ("Take two drachms of oil of rosemary, two of the oil of lemon, one of lavender, ten of cinnamon, one teaspoon of rose water. Pour on these one quart of alcohol; put all in a glass bottle, and shake it up well; to have it very clear, put some cotton in a funnel, and place a piece of clean tissue or printing paper over it, and strain the contents through.") There were other recipes for making cold cream and smelling salts, for removing freckles (". . . take one ounce of lemon juice, a quarter of a drachm of powdered borax, and half a drachm of sugar; mix, and then let stand a few days in a bottle, then rub it on the face and hands occasionally"), for making pomades, and for converting an orange into a pomander with cloves to scent a lady's underwear. In 1836 Mrs. Child offered this bit of practical advice:

> SHAMPOO: New England rum, constantly used to wash the hair, keeps it very clean, and free from disease, and promotes its growth a great deal better than macassar oil. Brandy is very strengthening to the roots of the hair; but it has a hot, drying tendency that New England rum has not.

There were in addition to the concoctions for enhancing the persons of those who occupied the bedrooms, those for keeping the bedroom itself livable. Mrs. Child's formula for bedbugs was "an ounce of quick-silver, beat up with the white of two eggs, and put on with a feather." This, she said, was the "cleanest and surest bedbug poison." Eliza Leslie in her *Behavior Book* (1853) approaches this problem as a social one, and in her advice to people who were visiting friends, she cautioned: "Above all things, avoid letting her [your hostess] know that you have found or felt insects in your bed; a circumstance that may chance sometimes to happen even in the best kept houses. In a warm climate, or in an old house, the utmost care and the most vigilant neatness cannot always prevent it. It may be caused by the

The Way to a Man's Heart

This kitchen with its great fireplace and cylindrical oven could have been modernized by 1847 when this picture was used as the frontispiece of a cookbook for economical New Englanders. The first cast-iron cookstove had been patented in America thirteen years before.

This stove that Catharine Beecher recommended in 1869 was a very sophisticated machine. It could "keep seventeen gallons of water hot at all hours, bake pies and puddings . . . heat flat irons . . . boil a tea kettle and one pot . . . bake bread in the oven, and cook a turkey in the roaster . . ." all at the same time.

This electric kitchen ("sketched from one in operation") was pictured in 1896 . . . but it was a rare sight indeed. The first such kitchen ever seen in America astonished visitors at the great Columbian Exposition of 1893 in Chicago.

Bathing in Luxury

Plumbers dream luxuriously. The bath at the top is a Greek Revival fantasy advertised by a plumber about 1845. Standard Plumbing offered the one below it (including stained-glass window, sitz bath, and ingenious shower) in 1907. At the bottom, water spews from gold dolphins in a bath designed by Sherle-Wagner for a Long Island home in 1957.

bringing of garbage from boats, or ships, or by servants neglecting their own beds; a too common practice with them. . . ." The spring mattress was considered a menace because "it almost inevitably becomes the harbor of bedbugs and other vermin which cannot be got at without destroying the mattress."

The literature of the bedroom in the nineteenth century was of two sorts; it was, on the one hand, practical advice on its arrangement, care, ventilation, and other such down-to-earth matters; on the other hand, it was a sort of misty, pious, romantical collection of sermons on the responsibilities of matrimony, the sacredness of love, piety, self-sacrifice, and endurance. The approaches might be called the muscular and the spiritual; sex seems to have fallen somewhere in between, but wherever it fell it was very little written about in any way that would have been a help to the uninstructed bride or her astonished groom. She could learn that there was no better exercise than to make her own bed (in England, she was told, it was recommended to young ladies of fashion by their physicians), and she would also learn that the bed should be stripped every morning, its sheets and blankets spread out over the furniture, the windows thrown open and freshness allowed to permeate everything. She most assuredly could not learn what might be expected of her when she got between those same sheets with her husband, except to put up with whatever she encountered (there were no hints what this might be) as well as possible under the circumstances, and to remember that marriage was ordained by God, and that on the whole there was nothing morally wrong with propagating the race if it was done in the right spirit of piety. Frank discussions of sex in the Van der Velde or how-to-do-it manner did not begin to appear until well into this century, though by 1890 Dr. Napheys in his two volumes (one intended for women and one for men), *The Physical Life of Woman: Advice to the Maiden, Wife and Mother* and *The Transmission of Life, Counsels on the Nature and Hygiene of the Masculine Function*, had been widely circulated. Indeed, a quarter of a million copies had been sold.

So far as I have been able to discover, no serious study has been published on marriage manuals of the last century, and reason for this may well be that they are for the most part such a wash of piety, sentiment, and circumlocutions that no scholar can bring himself to spend any considerable time with them. Dr. Napheys' volumes were bright beams of illumination in a murky sea of misinformation and no information. "The field," wrote a contemporary of Dr. Napheys, "had been left to quacks or worse, who, to serve their own base ends, scattered inflamatory and often indecent pamphlets over the land; or else, had one or more of the points been handled by reputable writers, it was in such a vague and imperfect manner that the reader gained little benefit from the perusal."

Dr. Napheys, who was trained at the Jefferson Medical College in Philadelphia, and fought as a captain in the Civil War, was only twenty-seven years old when he wrote *The Physical Life of Women* in 1869. It was heartily acclaimed by the Surgeon General of the United States Army, by Dr. Noah Porter, the president of Yale College, by Catharine Beecher's famous brother, the Reverend Henry Ward Beecher, and by a host of other physicians, health officers, divines, and educators of almost equal eminence. Not all of the reaction was favorable, of course. It was a time when most God-fearing people believed that "a sound treatise on these topics . . . could not be written in a proper style for the general public," and some journals assumed a position of shocked condemnation when the volume appeared. The book for men, *Transmission of Life,* appeared the following year with equally respectable support. Dr. Napheys' career, though he became quickly famous for his audacity, clarity, and scientific accuracy (by the standards of his day), was a short one. He died in 1878, at the age of thirty-six, "through some toxic agent, the nature of which was not ascertained."

One of the writers who preceded Dr. Napheys as an adviser on the problems of the marriage bed was the very same ubiquitous O. S. Fowler, phrenologist, who felt so passionately about the octagonal house as "a home for all." It is worth quoting a bit of Fowler's advice to women, not as an example of piety, but of nineteenth-century circumlocution. He wrote in a little volume called *Love and Parentage*:

> Reciprocity is a constituent ingredient in its very nature. Without it neither can ever be happy in either love or wedlock. Its absence is misery to the ardor of the one, and repugnance to the coldness of the other. [Here follow about five or six hundred words of expansion and elucidation which expand but do not elucidate.] . . . This being "the tie that binds" the absence of reciprocity here is, of course, *the* bone of contention. . . . Matrimonial felicity can no more be had without reciprocity and mutual pleasure here, than noonday without the sun, nor can discord

co-exist with reciprocity here any more than darkness and sunshine; because those who cannot make each other happy in this, the *ultimatum* of love and marriage, cannot in minor matters. [Skip another several hundred words.] Oh! If I could catch the matrimonial ear of the whole world, I would say, in the language of this *law of love*, to the blooming bride as she enters upon the nuptial relations: By all the happiness you are capable of conferring and receiving in married life, note every invitation to the banquet of love, and cordially respond. [And so on.]

This is a good deal more forthright in its intention than most nineteenth-century writing on sex, but it serves to show how conscientiously a writer had to (or, perhaps, chose to) beat about the bush to avoid using the language that is now characteristic of marriage manuals.

Advertisements having to do in one way or another with sex—either the promotion of fertility or the curtailment of it—seem to be out of character with the prudery of the nineteenth century, but they were, compared with modern advertising, downright flat-footed. The lady of the house could buy (and presumably conceal under her intimate garments in her bureau) Portuguese Female Pills, which were on sale in the 1840's, and which were advertised as "the wonder and admiration of the world" but "they must not be used during pregnancy as they are certain to produce miscarriage during that period." Madame Restell's Preventive Powders were more forthright both in name and in how they were presented. "These valuable powders," said Madame Restell's advertisement in the New York *Herald* (also in the 1840's), "have been universally adopted in Europe, but France in particular, for upwards of thirty years, as well as by thousands in this country as being the only mild, safe and efficacious remedy for ladies whose health forbids a too rapid increase of family. . . ." Or if the problem was not prevention of conception but fertility, there was Lucina Cordial for curing incipient consumption and barrenness, and later in the century there was a variety of medicines guaranteed to restore male potency. Harriet Martineau, in the 1840's, commented in shocked tones at how many abortions there were among those classes who could well afford to have large numbers of children, as we have noted earlier. Obviously, the bedroom of the nineteenth century witnessed some rather odd contradictions between the overt prudery and the normal sexuality of the men and women who slept in its mammoth beds.

Changes in sexual mores, and most especially those that have come about as the result of a very general use of effective (not Madame

Restell's) contraceptives since the beginning of the century, have had an enlivening effect on the way the house of today is thought about and most especially, of course, on the bedroom and its adjunct, the bath. In his book *The House and the Art of Its Design,* published in 1953, Robert Woods Kennedy is refreshingly more forthright about this than any other writer on architecture whom I have encountered. He quotes Lewis Mumford as saying that contraception "has vastly increased the erotic possibilities of marriage . . ." and so, "Every part of the dwelling must be arranged equally with an eye to sexual privacy and untrammeled courtship. Private bedrooms alone are not enough; sound-proof partitions are equally important. . . . Sexual intercourse must not be forever doomed, except for the luxurious rich, to take place only, like burglary, under cover of darkness, in that part of the day when the energies are fast ebbing away; but before it can occur at any other times many weaknesses in house design will have to be rectified."

The nineteenth century was not in the least shy about introducing the exotic and the erotic into the ornamentation of the bedroom, which not infrequently resembled, with its curtained bed, taborets inlaid with mother-of-pearl, heavy draperies, and elaborate gilt mirrors, something like a harem. It would never have occurred to them, however, to say that this was what was in their minds. Mr. Kennedy, however, says this:

> A bathroom . . . is an essential requirement for love making. It is needed not only as a concomitant to contraceptives. Urinating, and drinking are frequently performed as a by-product. To have to get dressed and leave the bedroom for any of these three functions adds nothing to what should be the pleasantest of occupations, and can be irritating or result in extreme embarrassment. It goes without saying that privacy from without and within, freedom from interruption, are also essential. The full enjoyment of nudity cannot be realized without some light. It is a visual as well as a tactile sensation. Making love, whether for its functional purpose of reproduction or not, is pure pleasure. . . . A part of its pleasure is seeing; the room should create a good background for the nude body. Its color and texture should be designed to compliment the body's modeling and softness. . . .

Actually, of course, the nineteenth-century house was in many respects a great deal more private than the house today, not only because of the stoutness of the partitions with which a good house was built, but because all rooms could be closed off from all other rooms (except the back parlor from the front parlor in some cases), and because there were nooks and crannies of concealment which have disappeared from the modern house. There is certainly no less private dwelling in the world that makes any pretensions of being architecture than the modern luxury apartment, through the walls of which travel the whispers of love along with the gushings of flushed toilets. But the nineteenth-century house was private for other than architectural reasons: its manners were more private. There is a certain privacy in the relationship between a woman and her husband when she always addresses him in the presence of others as Mister Smith; their intimacy is reserved for intimate occasions and is not broadcast. There is privacy in the segregation of children to their own parts of the house and for certain times of the day. There was privacy in the care with which nudity was never exposed, often not even by husband and wife to one another, and certainly never by a child much beyond the age of infancy. It would not have occurred to anyone to sleep without nightshirt or nightgown or pajamas or, until about 1870, without a nightcap. The distinction between the privacy of the nineteenth century and the kind that Mr. Kennedy speaks of in the paragraph I have quoted above is that the emphasis today is on privacy with intimacy; then it was privacy at the sacrifice of intimacy.

There is no question, however, that the double bed is more intimate than the single "twin bed," and as twin beds were not known in America until the end of the last century, it was not uncommon for husband and wife to occupy separate bedrooms. One of these bedrooms was very likely to be a dressing room that adjoined the master's bedroom, and was fitted up with the lady's dressing table and bureau, her washstand and comfortable chairs and sofa (if the room was large enough), so that it became a sitting room by day. In expensive households the man of the family also had his own dressing room, so that there was a three-room master's suite. The accouterments for a gentleman's dressing room were very like those of a lady's. (Neither, incidentally, had hangers for clothes. Dresses and suits hung on pegs, or were put away folded flat.) In general, a man's clothes took less room than a woman's, especially in the days of crinolines, but he had to have rather elaborate shaving equipment—"razors [preferably seven of them, one for each day of the week], shaving soap, shaving brush, and a small tin pot for hot water, also packages of paper on which to wipe razors." He also needed a razorstrop, a bootstand, boot-jack, buttonhook, and shoehorn. One manual says: "A couple of hair gloves, with a flesh brush, may be added."

THE BATH

Americans have long professed a strong belief in the efficacy of bathing as a cure of ills of all sorts and as essential to a good character. There is a traditional story that William Penn's butler was deaf and, moreover, "long vexed with wandering pains and anguish accessions." In his desperation, so the story says, "he leaped from his bed on a cold night, threw off his night shirt, jumped into cold water, ran naked round the garden, into the water again, twice more round the garden; then taking 'a good swig o' brandy,' back to bed." When he awoke in the morning not only had his wandering pains and anguish departed but so had his deafness.

Roughly two hundred years after this incident is supposed to have occurred, another American who revered the curative powers of nature, Thoreau, found that his compatriots did not take bathing nearly as seriously as they should. He noted on July 8, 1852:

> I am inclined to think bathing almost one of the necessaries of life, but it is surprising how indifferent some are to it. What a coarse, foul, busy life we lead. . . . Truant boys steal away to bathe, but the farmers, who most need it, rarely dip their bodies into streams or ponds. M——— was telling me last night that he had thought of bathing when he had done his hoeing,—of taking some soap and going down to Walden and giving himself a good scrubbing,—but something had occurred to prevent it, and now he will go unwashed to the harvesting, aye, even till the next hoeing is over.

There was some dispute in those days about whether a daily bath was, perhaps, not quite dangerous to the system, and though almost no one took a warm bath every day, general opinion seems to have been in favor of one warm bath a week and a thorough washing in cold water once a day. "Warm bathing," said Mrs. Farrar in *The Young Lady's Friend* (1838), "is highly useful to the health, and if properly indulged in has no debilitating effect. Dr. Combe says, 'When it is not too warm, and not prolonged beyond fifteen or twenty minutes, the tepid bath may be used daily, with perfect safety and advantage by persons in good health.'"

Warm bathing was a great nuisance. It presupposed heating a great deal of water on the kitchen stove (or in the open hearth in Mrs. Farrar's day) and then lugging it to wherever the tin or zinc tub should be placed on a piece of oilcloth to protect the floor from the splash of water. It meant toting heavy pitchers; it meant emptying the tub after the bath. Those who had servants to do this for them bathed in their bedrooms or dressing rooms or in special bathrooms on the bedroom floor of the house. Those who had no servants bathed in the kitchen on Saturday nights or, as Mrs. Farrar was sad to confess, did their only bathing "at the pump in the yard, or at the sink in the kitchen," a practice so likely to be done hastily that it was "not favorable to cleanliness or health." She feared, as a matter of fact, that a great many young women who should have known better, young ladies, indeed, who trod on Brussels carpeting and wiped their hands on damask towels, did "no more washing in her china wash-bowl than . . . the farmer's daughter at the sink."

Even in the 1870's there were a good many conservative people who looked suspiciously upon too frequent baths. "The virtue of frequent bathing, one might think, would be universally admitted," said a writer in the *Century Magazine* in 1874. "Nevertheless, there are ultra-conservatives who earnestly believe it detrimental. . . . It may be safely asserted that all persons of sound constitution and unimpaired health are greatly benefitted by daily baths." Ten years later C. E. Sargent in his book *Our Home* still was not convinced about the sense of daily bathing. "We would not advise one to adopt radical views on this subject," he said, "and take a daily bath through life, although we doubt if such a course would injure most people, yet it probably would be unnecessary, and would be a needless waste of time. A full bath once or twice a week is, perhaps, all that is necessary to escape the charge of being ungodly in consequence of filth."

There were a good many kinds of baths that preoccupied the bathers of the nineteenth century and each was believed to have its special therapeutic purpose. There were, for example, the cold foot bath, the sitz bath, the half bath, the douche bath, the cold, warm, and hot bath, the sponge bath, the shower bath, the drop bath, and the wet-sheet or pack bath. The shower bath, for example, was something of which to be careful, because if it was cold it resulted in a greater shock to the system than a plunge in cold water. Indeed, "its effects are more speedy, and extend more to the internal organs than those of the common bath.

. . . For delicate persons, the tepid shower bath is preferable; and salt added to the water is an improvement." Goodholme in his *Domestic Cyclopedia* goes into considerable detail about the values of each sort of bath. He says of the cold bath, for instance:

> The diseases for which cold baths are valuable as a remedy are morbid irritability and sensibility, accompanied by general debility; also for asthma, in the intervals between paroxysms, when the system is in other respects in a proper condition for it.

And he adds such cautions as this:

> It [a cold bath] is improper in the case of those who have a tendency to consumption, or who are constitutionally liable to bowel complaints, and it should never be ventured on by anyone suffering from chronic inflammation of the mucous membranes of the bronchia and intestinal canal, etc. etc.

In no case was bath water used lightly; it was hard to come by.

The story of the origin of the bathtub in America is responsible for one of the nicest of all American literary hoaxes and one that it seems almost impossible to root out of our history. During the First World War, H. L. Mencken was casting around for a subject for a piece for the New York *Evening Mail* and entirely for his own amusement he produced an elaborately (if imaginatively) documented account of the introduction of the first bathtub into America by a gentleman in Cincinnati, named Adam Thompson, who had acquired plans and specifications for its construction from an imaginary Englishman named Lord John Russell. Not only did Mencken describe the gadget (the water was heated by passing a pipe through a chimney), but he gave a full account of its debut to the astonished citizenry of Cincinnati, told of the prejudices against bathing in early nineteenth-century America, of legislation in Virginia putting a $30-a-year tax on bathtubs, of how President Fillmore had introduced the first tub into the White House, and so on and on. If you should have occasion to read histories of American domestic architecture you will find, as I have found, that Mencken's wholly trumped-up story has become accepted as gospel.

"The success of this little hoax," Mencken wrote when he reprinted the piece in *A Mencken Chrestomathy* in 1949, "vastly astonished me. It was taken gravely by a great many other newspapers, and presently made its way into medical literature and into standard reference books." Mencken tried repeatedly to set the record straight, but it persists as the most entertaining if the least accurate account of the origins of the modern bathroom in America.

Obviously, one of the reasons why historians have swallowed Mencken's story is that the origins of the first American bathtub are obscure and, furthermore, unimportant. In her *Domestic Economy* (which happened to be published in 1842, the very year that Mencken chose for the arrival of his mythical tub in Cincinnati) Catharine Beecher gave a diagram of a bathtub which in the way it was supplied

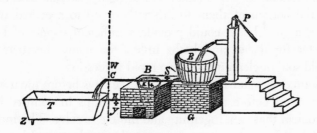

with hot water was astonishingly close to the one Mr. Thompson is supposed to have imported. Miss Beecher intended this contraption to be located in the basement of a house. The Reservoir (R) "may be a half-hogshead," she said, "or something larger, which may be filled once a day, from the pump, by a man, or boy."

To put a specific date on the arrival of the bathroom that had a tub supplied with hot and cold running water is difficult to do. According to Lawrence Wright, an English architect and student of plumbing, a hotel in Boston had bathrooms and water closets in 1827, but they were all in the basement. However, the Mount Vernon Hotel in Cape May, New Jersey, in 1853 boasted a bath with hot and cold running water for every bedroom. "This costly idea," Wright says, "was so slow to spread that not until 1906 did the Ritz in Paris follow suit, and in 1908 the Statler Hotel in Buffalo made a big stir when it advertised 'A Room With a Bath for a Dollar and a Half.'" In 1855 George Vanderbilt in his New York house had a bathroom with a tub, basin, and flush toilet, the three items set along a wall, but it was a rarity for an American to possess such a luxurious arrangement. Tubs with cold running water supplied from a cistern in the attic were not uncommon after the middle of the century, though the hot water had to be supplied to them by pitcher from the kitchen stove or hot-water jacket and many of them had no drains and so had to be bailed out. The hot-water boiler which stood in something like an openwork egg cup next to the kitchen stove (it was fed from the attic cistern, sometimes filled by rain and sometimes by forced pumping, which took a strong back, from the well under the house) became common in the 1870's. This kind of boiler, if it was not properly installed or not made of sufficiently strong materials, had an unpleasant way of exploding under pressure. (Boilers were bought by weight, which was meant to indicate the strength of the plate of which they were made, but there were unscrupulous manufacturers who made them of light materials and then put lead in the bottom of them to bring them up to specified weight.) However, a good boiler could provide a sufficient supply of hot running water for dishes and baths unless too many members of the household sought cleanliness in too rapid succession.

The source of water for the house in the days before town and city reservoirs (and before automatic electric pumps in country houses) was a problem that took ingenuity and muscle to solve. The individual well which served a house was customarily supplemented by a cistern for rain water, and the rain-water barrel which caught the run-off from roof gutters and spouts was at a corner (usually by the kitchen) of every village and country house. Calvert Vaux, the architect, observed in 1857 that "Rain water pipes, as generally planned, are most unsightly accessories to a country house. They need never be so. On the contrary they may often be made valuable helps in design. . . ." But the problem of design concerned far fewer people than the purity of the water. "Cistern water," said one manual, "may be purified by charcoal put in a bag and hung in the water." (It also cautioned: "Never use water which stood in a lead pipe over night. Not less than a wooden bucketful should be allowed to run," and "Never use water from a stone reservoir for cooking purposes.") In winter the pump at the well had a way of freezing. Catharine Beecher was adamant, you may remember, about the virtues of having the well below the house and the pump in the kitchen or in the basement, but this was not always practical and many families ignored its obvious advantages. Therefore, in Miss Leslie's *House Book* (1840) it is not surprising to find:

HYDRANTS AND PUMPS—To prevent a hydrant in the yard from freezing, cover it closely . . . with straw above and below, leaving nothing exposed but the handle and the spout, and lay over the top several folds of old carpet or coarse blanket . . . always turn the handle as far as it can possibly go.

If you have a pump, you may prevent its freezing, during the night by setting the handle as high as it will go. . . . [If that doesn't work] thaw it by pouring a kettle of boiling water around the handle and the spout.

With water such a problem, it is no wonder that the bath was customarily a once-a-week affair. Indeed, it sometimes seems a wonder that, when it was necessary to break the ice in the washstand pitcher on winter mornings, anyone washed at all.

Solving the problem of supplying running water to bathrooms was less difficult and far less worrisome than the problem of proper drainage from the fixtures in the bathroom to the sewer or the septic tank. "Deadly sewer gas" was a common and frightening expression in the American household as late as the first decade of this century, when householders were still being warned against the possible dangers of having a sink in the corner of the bedroom for fear of the noxious gasses that might come up through its drainpipe. Pictures warned of not permitting a baby to sleep in its crib in a room next to the bathroom, for fear of the seepage of deadly sewer gasses. "Though unquestionably a great convenience," said Goodholme in 1887, "water-closets, as now usually placed in houses, are an invention of which no one has any special reason to be proud. With a show of cleanliness they combine essential nastiness and a good deal of real danger. In cities, perhaps, their use cannot at present be dispensed with; in the country, with imperfect drainage and water-supply, they are simply a nuisance." But that was not the worst of it. "Fixed basins," he also said, "in bedrooms, however, kill ten to the water-closet's one. The water trap is a very indifferent barrier to sewer gas, and the overflow of the basin is a perfect gateway for contagion—especially in bedrooms having no fireplace and with closed windows."

In 1899 the architect Russell Sturgis in an article in *Harper's Magazine* observed: ". . . all architects know of good houses where the waste-pipe of the wash basin is simply a foot long, emptying into a common pail. When this is the case, the wash-basin must be in a closet or else the space below the slab must be enclosed. . . ." He then went on to say that "traps" were by then so well understood that there was no excuse not to have them. The fear, however, died slowly and many people were still frightened of them.

There was a time, starting in the 1860's and continuing for several decades, when the "earth closet," invented by an English clergyman, the Reverend Henry Moule of Dorsetshire, and highly recommended by Catharine Beecher, was considered far safer than the flush toilet in any community where "water cannot be obtained in sufficient quantities for cleaning the drain, or that it cannot be carried away with the deposit of the closet to a situation where it will not be injurious to health. The latter is especially the case in small towns and villages where there are not sufficient sewer arrangements." The earth closet which Miss Beecher described at length but which she summarized in a few words "consists, essentially, of a mechanical contrivance (attached to the ordinary seat) for measuring out and discharging into the vault or pan below a sufficient quantity of sifted dry earth to entirely cover the solid ordure and to absorb the urine." It was far preferable to the custom "prevalent in many places," as Mrs. Parloa put it nearly forty years after Miss Beecher's book, "of throwing all the slop water of the household upon the ground near the dwelling itself," which resulted in the poisoning of wells. It was better than the old-fashioned privy. "I suppose," Mrs. Parloa said in 1906, "it is no exaggeration to say that one half of the people living in country places suffer from impaired health on this account." She might also have added that there were no bathrooms at all in the tenements of New York at this same time.

When bathrooms began to appear in the nineteenth-century house equipped with everything we now think of as belonging in a bathroom, they almost immediately blossomed into extravagance where money permitted and into imitation fanciness where it did not. No sooner was there a workable toilet than it turned into a sculptured porcelain dolphin holding a conveniently shaped shell in its mouth. Washbasins and their surroundings were gilded with petals and painted with roses (as the old pitcher and basin so often had been), and bathtubs were housed in elegantly carved imitations of period furniture. In the seventies it was considered proper to conceal the pipes of the bathroom. Washbasins, sunk in their marble slabs, rested on constructions of mahogany that looked like bureaus with heavily-framed mirrors above them or like dressing tables; toilets were boxed in. In the nineties there was a reaction against this; housewives, architects, plumbing manufacturers, and building inspectors decided that concealed pipes were "lurking-places" for "dirt, germs, or vermin," with the result that the bathroom took on a much more airy, open, and sanitary look. Its pipes were now exposed; its floors and walls were often tiled; its tubs sat up on ball-and-claw feet, and in general it had a far less sensual and more clinical look in spite of the fact that by no means all of its fancy elements had disappeared. Stained-glass windows were considered appropriate for bathrooms at about the turn of the century; the shower bath (of the kind that comes at one from all directions at once) was popular, and the separate foot bath was a very nearly standard piece of equipment. It is perhaps a little surprising that a people that enjoyed washing itself a piece at a time never got up its nerve to adopt the French bidet.

The bathroom has undergone a great many changes since the beginning of this century, but none so important as the shrinkage of its size. When the demand for two or three baths on the bedroom floor replaced the old notion that one large bath was sufficient for a family, the compactness of its use of space became a primary concern to designers. The apron-front tub was introduced by the Standard Sanitary Company about 1910. It had the advantage of reducing the amount of floor space that had to be kept clean and also the amount of floor and wall space that had to be tiled. It worked admirably for a shower as well as a tub, and other units could be fitted in with it with a minimum of waste space. The bath, from being a family institution, began to become a personal adjunct to the bedroom. For a long time it maintained a clinical look—white tub, basin, and toilet, white tiled walls, white enameled medicine closet, and usually white towels and washcloths. "Decorator colors," as they are mysteriously called, began to creep into the bathroom in the 1920's, and now the bathroom has become, like the once clinically white kitchen, a bower of blossoms on wallpapers, bath mats, and shower curtains, and it is draped with towels of every conceivable color from chic to pretty. In expensive houses the bathroom has become a most extravagant display of conspicuous consumption—in very much the same spirit as the bathrooms of a century ago. The fixtures are the heads of gilded beasts spitting water; basins are ornamented with garlands; mirrors are baroque; tubs are again buried in carved and ornamented woodwork, or are sunken into the floor—circular pools with plexiglass domes above them, ringed with hanging baskets of ferns and tropical flowers.

The bathroom has not always been the pharmacy of the house any more than it has always been the beauty parlor. There was a time a century ago when remedies were kept in the kitchen and, indeed, were very often concocted there as well. In the 1830's, for example, if you pricked yourself with a sharp instrument it was believed that "a rind of pork bound upon a wound occasioned by a needle, pin, or nail prevents the lock-jaw." If you had a sudden attack of quinsy or croup the thing to do was: "bathe the neck with bear's grease, and pour it down the throat." If you didn't have any bear's grease handy, goose grease was just as good. The standard cure for dysentery was blackberries (there are still some country doctors who recommend blackberry brandy for this complaint). "To eat blackberries is very healthy; tea made of the roots and leaves is beneficial; and a syrup made from the berries is still better."

When the bathroom became the therapeutic center of the house, the standard remedies were kept there in square glass bottles with glass stoppers and labels that were painted into the glass—*Sod. Bicarb., Potas. Perm.*, etc. Sometimes they were stored in the medicine cabinet (to paraphrase Andrew Jackson Downing, "Much of the character of every man may be read in his medicine cabinet"); sometimes they sat elegantly in racks attached to the bathroom wall. Now they are rarely seen, for the simple reason that there seem to be almost no drugs today of a general nature; there is a prescription for everything, or if not a prescription, a patent remedy. It wouldn't, I'd guess, occur to even the most fastidious hypochondriac to keep his (or her) sleeping pills, tranquilizers, vitamins, and headache pills in matching, ornamented bottles.

One cannot overestimate the importance to the changes wrought in the upstairs of the house in the last century of the evolving understanding of health and sanitation and the fight against disease. It has been far more important to the household than the technology that evolved at the same time. One rarely today comes upon advice that one should not sleep with the windows closed; everyone believes it. But Downing fought hard for the idea that proper ventilation should be built into the structure of a house, so that even if prejudice should keep the unwary from opening their windows they would still get proper air to breathe. Miss Beecher and Mrs. Stowe devoted a chapter of *The American Woman's Home* (1869) to "Scientific Domestic Ventilation," in which they praised open fireplaces and damned airtight stoves and hot-air furnaces. They blamed bad ventilation on "the

ignorance of architects, house-builders, and men in general." Both
Downing and Miss Beecher, you will remember, inveighed against
the way young women ruined their health by sitting in overheated
rooms day in and day out without a breath of fresh air or any exercise
—not even the invigorating exercise of making a bed in a well-venti-
lated room.

Little by little the bedroom became a brighter and airier place. The
bathroom became less like a parlor with plumbing and more like a
center of health. Starting in 1869, when the first state Board of Health
was established in Massachusetts, there was a scourge of disease that
led in the next thirty years to the founding of the American Public
Health Association in 1872, to the establishment of one hundred and
twelve medical schools between 1873 and 1890, to the beginning of
open warfare on tuberculosis in 1884. It was in that year that the great
sanitarium for consumptive patients opened at Saranac Lake in the
New York Adirondack Mountains, and millions of Americans became
fresh-air minded. The founding of the National Tuberculosis Association in 1904 spread the word far and wide. America became not only
fresh-air minded but germ conscious. The expression "germ catcher"
began to be heard in place of "dust catcher." Twin beds began to be
looked upon as more hygienic than the traditional double bed. Heavy
draperies were taken down and replaced with lighter, more cheerful,
and more easily laundered materials. Suddenly every householder felt
impelled to have a sleeping porch. From 1905 to 1915 almost no
middle-class household seemed complete without one. They appeared
on new two- and three-story houses, on one-story bungalows, and on
the upstairs and backsides of many Queen Anne houses, whose balconies readily lent themselves to such adaptation. Sometimes the
porches were entirely screened in; sometimes the beds were merely
covered with mosquito netting. Sometimes the porches were roofed
over; sometimes the sleepers were protected from the elements by
canvas awnings. But sleeping out of doors was *the* thing, and it
mattered not at all how bitter cold the weather. In describing the plan
of a rather larger than average bungalow in 1914, *Harper's Bazar* said:

> The porch at the end of the house may be used for sleeping. Provision for
> that luxury is now made in almost every house where out-of-door sleep-
> ing is possible. A few simple cots and some awnings or bamboo curtains
> to keep out the rays of the sun and the possible gaze of the passer-by

are all that are needed. It is, of course, convenient when the porch is just outside the windows of the bedrooms, and still more convenient if the windows are French windows.

The tremendous popularity of the sleeping porch, like the delight that people took in the veranda as an outdoor living room, forecast what has in recent years become the breakdown of the boundaries of the house. Walls, whether glass or brick or clapboard or stone, have become increasingly less important as a means of defining where the indoors stops and the outdoors starts. The bedroom that opens on to a terrace surrounded by a wall to protect it from the view of the passerby is merely a sheltered segment of the outdoors, just as the swimming pool in more and more houses where the climate permits is merely an outdoor segment of the bathroom.

There is no typical bedroom today: it comes in as many shapes, sizes, moods, and manners of decoration as there are women with a will of their own. It is cute or it is tailored, frilly, or forthright, colonial, contemporary, or conglomeration. But by and large it is smaller than it used to be, as most rooms in most houses are smaller. But there is a special reason why the bedroom should have shrunk. The bedroom is still for love and rest, but it is not any longer the general headquarters of the house; it is not an office or a sewing room or a place to receive one's intimate friends, except in those households, now extremely rare, where there are still staffs of servants. The bedroom is not even, any longer, a place for serious illness, as it once was, and it is not a place for death—except accidental death: more fatal accidents occur in the bedroom than in any other room of the house.

There is, on the other hand, a typical bathroom—a cell, compared with the bathroom of thirty years ago, but not as much of a cell as the technologists are capable of. The bathroom stamped out of aluminum that Buckminster Fuller devised and patented in 1940 has not, to my knowledge, ever been mass-produced as it was designed to be, but with the shrinkage of the size of the house and the demand for more bathrooms (ideally, one to each bedroom), the size of the room has shrunk to about a half or a third of the size of the typical bathroom of 1900. The worry about its traps and the efficiency of its units has, however, shrunk proportionately. In most houses the bathroom is an entirely efficient unit and designed in much the same spirit of compactness and efficiency as the kitchen.

However . . .

Every increase in efficiency in the household seems to call forth a compensating desire for nonsense, luxury, and sensuousness. A house, after all, is not merely a machine for living but a place to indulge the whims of the flesh, and in no place can they be more assiduously cultivated than in the bathroom. So there has been a new wave of interest in extravagant bathrooms in the last few years, and in this affluent era the bathroom is, to coin a phrase, the easiest place to put money down the drain. In its most luxurious manifestations it is now warmed by a flickering open fire. Its shower sprays perfume as well as water, or the more masculine scent of pine forests. Its floor is yielding to the touch and is heated from beneath. Its towels are warmed by electrically heated towel racks. Its tub is not a tub but a sunken pool. The sound of running water is tempered with the sound of piped-in music. The "Louis XIV hand-carved chaise pircee (*sic*) (cover for toilet,) white with gold trim . . . $350" is again to be had at such shops as Hammacher Schlemmer in New York, as are "Louis XVI hand-carved cabinet [for washbasin]; white with gold . . . $450." The bathroom, in other words, is trying to reclaim some of its old affinity with the parlor in rich but not "modern" households.

The most important thing that has happened to the upstairs is that it has come downstairs and spread itself out of the house. The characteristic house of our time is a one-story dwelling, though sometimes that story is split on two slightly different levels to give the impression of more variety than it actually has. The expensive modern house designed by an architect rather than a contractor is almost without exception a single-story dwelling, though it may take advantage of the contours and eccentricities of a piece of land and vary in its levels. But whereas the bedroom in Mr. Downing's day had a balcony on which the lady of the house could, if she chose, sit and enjoy the morning sun, today her bedroom opens onto a terrace or a garden, and the wall which divides her from it is glass and revealing, rather than Downing's wall which was concealing. Technology has, of course, made this possible—plate glass and Thermopane glass, air-conditioning, radiant heating, these contribute to the possibility of joining the outdoors to the indoors or, perhaps more accurately, not interrupting the flow of one into the other. But I believe that these technological developments are a result and not a cause of breaking the old conventions of the house.

But that is not the story of the upstairs or of the upstairs come downstairs, and it is only part of the story of today's house and the house of tomorrow. There is no longer an upstairs today, just as there is no longer a below stairs. The leveling of the house is, perhaps, as tidy a symbol as one could find for the leveling of society in our time.

CHAPTER XII

The Living Room
Indoors and Out

> Under the head of living rooms come the
> drawing room, library, smoking room or "den,"
> morning room and and reception room. Under
> gala rooms, the ballroom, salon, and music
> room.
>
> Charles Edward Hooper
> *The Country House*, 1906

In her delightful memoir, *Young in New York*, which I had the
pleasure of reading in manuscript in 1961, Nathalie Dana (Mrs.
Richard H.) in describing the New York house in which she lived
as a small girl in the 1880's said: "The library had the alive welcoming
look of a room that is used all the time. . . . It was called the library
because parlors were out of date and living rooms had not yet become
the fashion."

The living room has gone by a great many names in the American
house and has turned up in a good many odd places in the structure
and under a good many guises. It has been, as the quotation at the
head of this chapter observes, the drawing room, library, smoking room,
den, morning room, and reception room. But that is by no means all
it has been. It has been the sitting room, the study, the family room,
the entrance hall, the recreation room, and it has also been out of doors
as the veranda, the glassed-in porch, and the patio. In the farmhouse
that had a parlor and a kitchen and bedrooms on the first floor, the
living room was a part of the kitchen.

In our time the living room has come to have a specific meaning,
a special aura, and a fairly well-defined use, but before it achieved its

231

present status in the household, it went through many transformations. It had its social ups and downs, its variety of names and schemes of decoration and arrangement, but there was always one room in every house, no matter how simple or how pretentious, that was meant for the family to live in rather than be on show in. Today the living room is not that room, as I suggested earlier in this book; today's living room is really the old parlor in modern undress; it is mostly for show, for entertaining, the one place in the house that is always kept neat against the possibility of the unexpected guest.

But let us look, before we look at today's living room, at what the living room as an idea and an ideal has meant to the American householder and at some of the ways that he and his wife have solved the problems of having a place to relax with their families, to get off by themselves, and to entertain their friends.

In the plans of houses in the 1840's one can occasionally find a room labeled "living room" and it was usually adjacent to the kitchen and was obviously used as a dining room (when the family did not eat in the kitchen) and as a "sitting room." Sometimes there were two "parlors," or a "parlor" and a "dining room," indicated on the plans, but nothing called a "living room." One sometimes encounters a "family room," a term revived since the Second World War after having been long out of fashion, and it served the very same purpose as the present-day family room. There were, to be sure, many houses a century and more ago that had parlors, dining rooms, and living rooms, all three, and some that had libraries, conservatories, salons, music rooms, ballrooms, and sitting rooms besides.

Obviously, the living room in the nineteenth century had none of the status of the parlor or later of the drawing room, but its anonymity reflects the very qualities which endeared it to most people. It was a place, by whatever name it was called, for the family to relax, to putter, to sit in silence, to work; a place to read aloud, to sew, to do homework, play jackstraws, build card-castles on the center table, to have family prayers. It was not a place where anyone felt called upon to put on airs and graces for the benefit of strangers. Callers did, of course, come to this family-sitting-room and were entertained there, but they were apt to be close friends and the atmosphere was a great deal more relaxed than it was in the parlor. Conversation was likely to be practical or gossipy rather than "polite." Behavior in such a room was decorous (manners were not something one filed away in the drawers of the parlor table), but formality was set aside.

The idea that there should be a parlor as well as a room for family relaxation died very slowly. There had to be a place to entertain one's friends as well as formal callers that was free of the helter-skelter of everyday living, a place where one was not likely to find a child's block or stuffed animal half-concealed under the sofa, where the sewing basket did not spill wisps of darning cotton, or where father's smoking stand did not bristle with foul-smelling pipes. ("Foul-smelling" seems always to have been the preferred adjective applied by women to pipes, however sweet.) It had to be a place, as one household writer put it, that was not "too personal, too expressive of the details of a family's life, the details which ought correctly to belong to the individual's own apartment." It should, however, be "the place for family and friends to gather on any and all occasions—a room to live in." Such a room was obviously not the old-fashioned parlor; neither was it the intimate family sitting room. It was something in between that served the purposes of both. As the rigid formalities of the nineteenth century began to give way to more relaxed social amenities, the living rooms of the house were bound to show the change, and they did.

This period of transition from the parlor to the living room coincided with a transition from "gentility" to "graciousness" as the ideal of middle-class social behavior. In America in the last decades of the nineteenth century Society was not only flamboyant in the middle-class extravagance (and occasionally elegance) of its houses and the lavishness of its parties, but it was surprisingly popular and hence influential on the manners of those far less prosperous than the New York "four hundred" and its regional equivalent. There was nothing more attractive to the reader of the daily paper than a peek into the parties of the rich, into their weddings and balls and receptions. The leaders of society provided much the same sort of focus for hero worship that the movie stars did several decades later. Society, for its part, and especially the most ambitious matrons, turned their eyes toward England as the source of what was socially correct and as a hunting ground for titled husbands for their daughters. The end of the reign of Victoria was approaching and the middle-class gentility which she somehow typified was giving way to the more sophisticated attitudes of those who were pleased and amused by the antics of her sporting son, Edward. Urbanity was much admired.

Graciousness is a word one does not encounter in nineteenth-century manners books but one which seems to be indispensable to books of twentieth-century etiquette. There hovers over it a somewhat Lady Bountiful aura of *noblesse oblige* and condescension, and a slightly frozen smile. Graciousness, which is a particularly Edwardian notion of social virtue in America, appears to mean a mingling of the ingredients of formality, mellowness, generosity, openness, privacy, hospitality, and restraint—all qualities that threaten at some point to cancel each other out except in the pages of etiquette books and women's magazines.

It took about thirty-five years for graciousness to emerge out of gentility and for the parlor to fade away and the modern living room to evolve—roughly from the mid-1870's to about 1910.

The looks of America, its size, and many of its manners during these thirty-five years changed radically. The lady in her bustle and the gentleman in his stove-pipe hat no longer sat stiffly in parlors on the edges of their chairs looking at picture albums or "Christian Parlor Books." The hour-glass figure, achieved at a frightful cost of cinching, whalebone, breathlessness, and displaced innards, now thrust the bosom forward and the rear-end backward in a manner that the bodice and bustle only seemed to do. The stove-pipe gave way to the derby, either black or brown, the frock coat to the short, tightly fitting jacket, and the wide ribbon looped several times around a very high collar to the cravat pulled through a gold ring. The derby, in turn, gave way to the straw boater with its silk band of college or club colors in summer, and the wide-brimmed fedora in winter. The Inverness cape was replaced by the long black overcoat with frogs and astrakhan collar. Whiskers, thought the essence of manliness in the 1850's ("Where it can be done without social discomfort . . . the full beard is most natural, most comfortable, most healthful, most expressive, dignified, and beautiful. . . . Shaving renders the face effeminate," said *The Illustrated Manners Book* in 1855), had diminished to the rather full mustache by 1875, and by 1910 most men were smooth-shaven. Women, who in the days of the full beard had ringlets like wood-shavings hanging down about their faces, by 1905 had piled their hair in pompadours that emphasized the thrust-forward figurehead look. Towns and cities had become bigger and nearer together. From 1880 to 1910 the total population of the nation increased by more than 80 percent—from about fifty million to something over ninety million, and people had become more readily and more rapidly mobile. The trolley car joined villages and made them closer to big towns and small cities, and by 1895 there were ten thousand miles of electric transit lines in the nation, and riding the trolley, especially in the open summer cars, became a common means of taking families out of their houses or off their porches for evening excursions. The bicycle craze at about the same time in the nineties put fresh air in the lungs of a good many young women who a decade earlier would not have thought of taking any exercise (Miss Beecher would surely have approved) and, as Marshall Davidson wrote in *Life in America,* "It played a large part in liberating women from the bondage of Victorian fashions in clothes and behavior. To bicycle a woman admittedly had to have legs, an attribute not admitted by earlier standards of etiquette." It also played hob with some of the old notions of chaperonage, though it by no means eliminated "the old dragon." Who expected a chaperon to pump along after a young couple?

In general the rules of chaperonage relaxed between the seventies and 1910. Chaperons were always considered less of a problem in small towns and in the country than in the city, where for a young lady not to be properly chaperoned might well, as in Edith Wharton's *House of Mirth,* cost her her reputation and her future. When "Marion Harland," however, wrote in 1906 that there were few rural communities in which a modified form of chaperonage "cannot occasionally be introduced with advantage," she echoed the concern of many mothers. "Miss Harland" was, in fact, Mrs. Edward Payson Terhune and an editor of *St. Nicholas,* the remarkably successful children's magazine. "The unchaperoned picnic party," she said, "should be stopped. The long country drive of a group of gay young people, with no older person to act as a stop-gap upon spirits that are easily rendered boisterous, should cease." Drives were one thing (and still are); bicycles another. Davidson quotes the census bureau at the turn of the century as reporting: ". . . few articles ever used by man have created so great a revolution in social conditions as the bicycle."

The telephone was one such article, and the automobile, of course, another. In 1900 there were only 1,335,911 telephones in the whole nation to serve homes and business, and most of them had to be cranked. Socially the telephone was still not considered a suitable instrument for issuing invitations except rarely to "an impromptu dinner."

It changed the ways in which women shopped, however, for they could telephone their morning orders to the butcher and the grocer. ("Central," said many women in small communities, "I would like to speak to Smith's grocery, please." Or, "Central, could you tell me the name of the cleaner next to the drugstore?" In Muncie, Indiana, according to Frederick Lewis Allen in *The Big Change*, "the local press warned people that when using the telephone, they 'should not ask for a name but refer to the number list.' ") The telephone also helped to change the customs of "calls" and visiting as it became a friendly and even a gossipy instrument of social intercourse.

The automobile, about whose impact on social customs volumes have been printed, obviously changed the nature of family life and manners far more than either the bicycle or the telephone, though until about 1910 it was still looked upon as a toy of the privileged and sporting classes. Now, of course, it has become almost every man's alter ego, delight, and burden. It quickly turned from a sporting proposition into a rolling living room and, as it was virtually chaperon-proof, into a petting parlor. The clatter of hoofs on dirt roads and cobbles, the tinkling of sleigh bells, and the prevalence of horseflies, so intensely still a part of life in 1900, very nearly vanished in the next fifteen years. The stable became a garage; the coachman became a chauffeur, and finally the car became in its full flowering a seat in a movie theater.

It is not difficult to see why gentility faded away during these years of transition, nor to see why the house and its uses changed so greatly. It was during this time that the reception room, the spacious hall, the library, and the drawing room each enjoyed a time as a center of domestic importance that none of them any longer has. It was also the heyday of the veranda and the sun porch.

One of the first steps in the transition from the parlor to the living room was the arrival of the small reception room, which Mr. Hooper, quoted at the head of this chapter, said was an American contribution to domestic architecture. It replaced the parlor as a room for receiving what the authors of manners books (and probably nobody else) called "ceremonious callers." (In this category one would include such dignitaries as clergymen, young men paying "party calls," and women paying "morning calls" or "dropping cards.") It was also a place for conducting "small business," and therefore, in addition to a few stiff but elegant chairs and a formal sofa, if it was properly furnished, it also had a writing desk and a center table. Hopefully no one had to stay in it for long, though it was the place where many young men were left to cool their heels while they waited for the young lady of the house to grace them with her presence.

In the Queen Anne house, however, the reception room was more than likely to be the hall itself. The hall, you will remember, changed its character from a passageway to a very considerable and very important room when the Queen Anne house became almost universally popular in the eighties and nineties. And as the hall became more important (it was also called the "antechamber" and the "stair hall"), so did the vestibule which separated it from the front door.

The vestibule was considered "a necessary intermediary between the exposure of the street and the protection of the house." Its size varied, of course, with the size and pretentions of the house, and so did its name. (*Vestibule* always means vestibule, a small room immediately inside the front door, but *entrance hall* sometimes means vestibule and sometimes means stair hall. A *foyer* happens only in an apartment, and as the word is pretentious and only half-absorbed from the French, nobody agrees on how to pronounce it.) In *The Woman's Book,* published in 1894, Mary Gay Humphreys wrote: "The vestibule should be neutral ground. In fact, it affords the moment of vantage in which the guest may sum up the mistress of the house in the brass knockers, cleanly kept mats and shining glass, and for the mistress, perhaps, to weigh the importance of the guest. The side-lights and veiled glass are not decorative merely."

Mrs. Humphreys' contemporary, Maria Parloa, considered the halls the best-foot-forward that a house could present. "Let the vestibule and entrance hall," she wrote, "be as spacious as your means will allow. The hall gives character to the house. Nothing in make-up and finish of any other part of the house can atone for a cramped and badly lighted hall. . . . It is the hall that gives the first impression of the home."

The hall became a number of things besides a reception room and a substitute for the parlor. In Mrs. Dana's house, for example, it was big enough to house a sofa and several chairs and an upright piano, and therefore it became the "music room." To the planner, the hall became "a tempting place for an architect to lavish his skill," as one of them said in the nineties, and for the housewife to indulge her most up-to-date taste. It became a place to sit by the fire and enjoy the light that played through the stained-glass window on the stairs. "Nothing so enchants the eye," said Mrs. Humphreys, "as the unreal land of color that lies without and the light within as it is filtered through this beautiful medium."

The furnishing of the hall was a more than minor challenge. It had to be a sitting room, a welcoming entrance to the house, a place to drop things, a passageway. ("They are fortunate indeed who can make the hall not a passage but a place of rendezvous.") It had, ideally, to be both ample and cozy, with a rack for coats and a stand for umbrellas, a cupboard for overshoes (or possibly even a closet), and a small table on which was a silver card tray for visiting-cards. In larger-than-average houses the hall was also a sort of art gallery in which many of the family's proudest pieces were displayed, as they had once been displayed in the parlor. Etchings and engravings seemed most suitable to the walls of the hall and "autotypes of famous works of art" were also considered eminently suitable. Sepia photographs of the two little *putti* from the bottom of Raphael's "Sistine Madonna" were so acceptable as to be nearly unavoidable, and so were engravings of Roman and Moroccan scenes by Alma-Tadema and Gérôme. Mrs. Humphreys recommended "Chinese and Japanese drawings on silk and paper" and on the landing "a niche may perhaps be introduced for a vase of bronze, or . . . a tall clock standing guard by day and night like a faithful guardian of the family welfare. . . . The most beautiful hall lights are those of jeweled glass mounted in brass or in wrought iron."

The library, which was almost universally popular in the nineties, was the next step in the transition from parlor to living room.

The library was fashionable long before the parlor became unfashionable, but one was likely to encounter it only in rather elegant houses. It was considered a proper luxury for a family that could afford both a parlor and a drawing room (or a front and back parlor, as the two rooms were more often called in city houses) to have a library. In Downing's *Country Houses* nearly all of his elegant villas have libraries. The library was a proper ornament for the educated and cultured gentleman and for anyone who aspired to be and could afford to pay for the effect.

"Probably the library, more than any room in the house," wrote the architect H. Hudson Holly in his book *Modern Dwellings* (1878), "reflects the master mind of the household." It was in the library that a man's pretensions were made manifest, even when his interests were not. "One person regards this apartment as simply a place in which to read newspapers, write letters, and keep slippers and dressing gown," Holly continued. "Another's idea is that it is like a museum for bric-a-brac, with showy bookcases and ample shelving for books purchased by the yard, selected according to their backs." (Mr. Holly, who earnestly believed in progress, would be distressed to know that books-by-the-yard is still the mainstay of many dealers in secondhand books.) The ideal library, according to Holly, was what booksellers call a "gentleman's library"—a proper distribution of the classics, books of reference, and other collections, "in which are represented all classes of literature interesting to the general reader."

In most households that could afford one a library was to the parlor what today's "den" is to the living room. (There are distinctions to be made, of course, between den, library, and study. In general, business-men below the level of top management have dens; executives who have prospered and live in expensive houses or apartments have libraries; professional men—doctors, lawyers, academics, clergymen, and writers—have studies.) The library was a "sort of rendezvous for social intercourse," Holly contended, and was "far more cozy and in-viting if arranged like a lady's boudoir." The emphasis was on relaxa-tion and comfort and the family sort of intimacies, not on books.

In the nineties the library changed from a fashionable luxury to a faddist necessity. "Recently . . . ," wrote Oliver Coleman in a manual called *Successful Houses* (1899), "a curious development has been made manifest in which each house of rich or poor alike must have its library." One of the reasons for this, he believed, was "that the making and reading of books has increased until it has become almost of uni-versal prevalence." The new best-sellers that sat on the felt-covered center tables of home libraries under the gas chandelier in the nineties were *Looking Backward* and *David Harum*. *Little Lord Fauntleroy*, published in the mid-eighties, was dog-eared from being read aloud again and again; so were *Uncle Remus*, *Five Little Peppers and How They Grew*, and *Ben Hur*, all of which were published in a single year, 1880. There were magazines for all interests and all ages. There were *Harper's*, the *Atlantic*, *Scribner's*, *Putnam's*, and the *Century*, not only for the thoughtful reader who felt it necessary to be well informed, but for the reader of light essays, literary essays, and interminable serial stories. There was the astonishing *Ladies' Home Journal*, whose editor, Edward Bok, had achieved the miracle of pushing its circulation to almost a million readers, and, of course, there were the farm papers, especially *Country Gentleman*, and fashion magazines like the weekly *Harper's Bazar* and *Peterson's Ladies National Magazine*, and for the children *Youth's Companion* and *St. Nicholas*.

The outpouring of books and periodicals, however, did not change the library into a reading room; it merely changed the sitting room into something called the library because there were so many books and magazines around. "The library," Coleman said, "has become the most unconventional free-and-easy room beneath the roof—the only one whose door is always open and in which the family life is best developed. Books there may be in more or less profusion, but books are only incidental to the room, and merely serve to help the entertainment of those who gather there. The books are for the room, not the room for the books. . . ." To this he added: "Surely the library of today has changed its purpose greatly, yet only in a way to meet the new conditions of our modern life . . . in the largest sense it makes the house a home."

The bridge from library to living room was mainly a semantic rather than an architectural one or one having much to do with changing manners. By the first decade of this century most people who had called their sitting rooms libraries in the 1890's were calling them living rooms. In *Houses for Town and Country* published in 1907 there is a chapter devoted to "The Living-Room" in which the author says: "What we are discussing is the dwelling in which the library and living-room will very often be one and the same. Even in the case of the hard worker with pen or typewriter, the room where his books are kept is usually the sitting-room, he being free to reserve a workroom opening from it, of which he can shut the door and in which he can arrange his thoughts undisturbed and construct the lecture or the article which goes to make him the breadwinner." Writers, presumably, lived in unpretentious houses and had living rooms; more solid and respectable citizens with large houses and substantial investments were, at the same period, very likely to call their living rooms "drawing rooms."

"Drawing room" is an upper-class expression which has now largely disappeared from use and is likely to be heard today only from the lips of men and women who were relatively prosperous young brides and grooms in the Edwardian era. (House manuals for the rich in 1910, for example, used "drawing room" as a matter of course; manuals for the middle classes did not.) Literary men in America have for a long time favored "drawing room" over "parlor" (though during most of the nineteenth century their meanings in the American household were largely interchangeable) probably because *drawing room* is of English origin and *parlor* of French. "Drawing room" is a contraction of "withdrawing room," an expression used in the sixteenth and seventeenth centuries, and it was originally a bedchamber. In the days when a great hall was the center of large manor houses, those who wanted to get away from the brouhaha for quiet conversation withdrew to the sleeping room. Later, a part of this room was screened off, became the withdrawing room, and was used primarily by the female members of the family escaping from men eating in the hall or in the dining room. But there was another function of the drawing room which dates back to its use at the British and French courts as a place to receive guests and for formal receptions. In the American (as in the English) household the nineteenth- and twentieth-century drawing rooms served as both a retreat and a reception room. Unlike the parlor, which never escaped from formality, the drawing room could be relaxed or rigid as the occasion demanded. In *The Country House* (1906) Charles Edward Hooper said: "In the average American home the drawing room serves a twofold purpose, that of the general living room and a room of entertainment, and frequently the drawing room is replaced by the sitting room and parlor; in which case the parlor is used for entertainment and the sitting room as a family room. This arrangement is a good one provided there be no library to retire to. . . . Of late years it has become the custom to speak of the family room as the 'living room' which term is surely appropriate."

Life in a drawing room was somewhat different from life in either a parlor or a living room. It was more formal than the living room and less oppressive than the parlor. "Gentility" in the age of the drawing room gave way to "refinement" and "graciousness" and, at the same time, to more comfortable chairs and sofas, to warmer lamps, to oriental rugs, to a somewhat more relaxed and, at the same time, more sunlit look. No one closed the curtains of the drawing room against the ravages of the sun, as housewives had once done in the parlor. Architects

planned the drawing room in such a way that summer breezes fresh-
ened it and sun could brighten it, even if this necessitated awnings on
the windows to protect the room in the heat of the day. But glistening
tea services placed on a tea table by a maid in a taupe dress and starched
apron, and plates of sandwiches almost transparently thin and *petits
fours* greeted the afternoon caller, the friend asked to drop in for tea,
or the guests invited for a "kettle-drum" or a reception.

In some respects the "kettle-drum" typified the manners of the
drawing room, even though it was most fashionable when the parlor
was still a necessity in every country house and the term *drawing room*
was just beginning to be revived in city houses. The kettle-drum was
made much of in books of etiquette in the late 1870's and the 1880's,
and Mrs. Sherwood in the 1887 edition of her *Manners and Social
Usages* said that no one any longer bothered to put "kettle-drum" on
an invitation for tea; one only put the hour. Everyone took for granted
that it was a kettle-drum. The anonymous author of *Social Etiquette
of New York* had this to say about kettle-drums in 1878:

> A reception may be a very ceremonious entertainment, with elaborate
> and expensive appointments, or it may be very simple and yet altogether
> elegant. The latter style of receiving has borrowed an English name,
> by which it is frequently called, to distinguish it from those more costly
> hospitalities which are becoming less and less fashionable in New York
> every succeeding season. It is often mentioned as a "kettle-drum" because
> it is said to have originated in garrisons, where officers and their wives,
> who have been accustomed to elegances, are compelled to extend only
> the most informal of courtesies, owing to the necessary limitations of
> camp life. They cannot provide sumptuous refreshments and expensive
> table service when they invite their friends upon stated occasions. The
> fascinations which this enforced absence of troublesome and costly
> elaborateness possesses for civilians, who sometimes imagine that they
> are compelled to bear the many burdens of ostentation, have combined
> with the picturesqueness of these social enjoyments in camp to bring the
> "kettle-drum" into general favor with fashionable people.
>
> The name "kettle-drum" signifies to a New Yorker a light entertain-
> ment, with *demi-toilette* [i.e. not dressed for home but not for dinner
> either] for both ladies and gentlemen. It is claimed that a drum-head
> often served instead of a tea-tray at these delightful garrison sociabilities
> in England and the East Indies; and since this informal service of tea
> has become popular in metropolitan society, some of our ladies have
> provided fanciful suggestions of these original afternoon parties in camp.

Sometimes a tiny drum is beaten at intervals in the vicinity of the tea-table, where a lady of the household, or a favorite friend, presides.

Sometimes a bright young lady, costumed prettily as a *vivandière,* sits or stands by the tea-urn as its presiding genius; but these picturesque additions to an ordinary afternoon reception are not to be considered in the light of customs, but simply as pretty caprices, calculated to give vivacity to the entertainment, which any lady may adopt.

Mrs. Sherwood had a less romantic explanation of the kettle-drum. According to her account (and I suspect it is more reliable than the one I have just quoted), the name came from large Victorian tea parties in England "at which people talked so fast and so loud as to suggest the noise of a drum—a kettle-drum, the most rattling of all drums." And she added: "Then it was remembered that an old-fashioned entertainment was called a drum, and the tea suggested kettle, and the name fitted the circumstances."

One of the reasons for the popularity of the kettle-drum, whatever the origin of its name, was that it was a means of getting a great many people together and so of paying one's social debts without going to the expense of a dinner party or the burden of a long, formal evening. In other words, it was the exact counterpart of today's cocktail party, and it became exceedingly popular, so popular indeed, that "ladies had to encompass five, six, sometimes nine teas of an afternoon, and the whole of a cold Saturday—the favorite day for teas—was spent in a carriage trying to accomplish the impossible." It had several advantages over the cocktail party: polite custom provided that one did not stop at a kettle-drum for more than thirty minutes; no one was likely to forget what he was doing and find himself (or herself) standing around hoping to be asked for dinner or to go on somewhere else; tea was a great deal cheaper than even the cheap liquor usually served at cocktail parties. Mrs. Sherwood commented that a kettle-drum cost "nothing but the lighting of the gas and the hiring of an additional waiter," and she applauded tea as a vehicle of entertainment because, for one thing, "To have a gathering of people without the universal oyster was . . . a great relief," and because, "The people who had not money for 'grand spreads' were enabled to show to their more opulent neighbors that they too had the spirit of hospitality." But the kettle-drum was fraught with dangers all the same. Doctors looked upon excessive tea-drinking as "the foundation of much of the nervous prostration, the sleeplessness, and the nameless misery of our over-excited and careworn oxygen-driven people." Many other people, less concerned about health and more concerned with the good life, thought that an even greater peril from the kettle-drum was that it threatened to do away with more civilized forms of hospitality and entertainment.

To them civilized hospitality in the home consisted of the dinner party, the ball, and the evening party with music, the very same entertainments, in other words, that the majority of American men looked upon as the searing price of civilization, the damnation of success and social status. But men had their compensations, some of them. If they were not prosperous they were unlikely to have to suffer the anguishes of formal entertainment, and if they were prosperous they could afford the luxury of a "smoking room" and a billiard room.

"The billiard room," said the author of *The Country House,* "is probably the invention of a woman, designed to keep her strolling spouse in the house evenings." Another architect, however, ascribed its origins to the isolation of the large country estate and the inability of its overlord to find ways to entertain himself in the evenings. Not many houses were designed with a room specifically set aside as a billiard room, with the result that it was usually a room "in some out-of-the-way part of the house, sometimes in the basement, but more frequently in the attic, approached by narrow stairs." Women took not merely a skeptical but a moralistic view of the billiard room. In the first place they didn't like to have the men of the house go off by themselves for amusement, and as billiards was not considered at all suitable for female participation, they felt excluded. Further than that, they thought it a bad influence on the children to have "gaming" of any sort going on in the house, "for fear of giving them a taste for such pleasures." On the other hand, there was no question that it was better that father play at home than go to a pool parlor or even to his club. Architects (all of whom were men, of course) suggested that the solution was to put the billiard room on the main floor of the house near the living room and ask the ladies to play, if they wanted, and the children, too, for that matter. "Where children are strictly kept from games," said H. Hudson Holly in his *Modern Dwellings,* "for fear of giving them a taste for such pleasures, the very prohibition seems to add to the fascination exercised by amusements of this character, and, upon final emancipation from parental rule, they are indulged to excess."

Man's other retreat was the smoking room. In some houses it was just another name for the billiard room and in still others for the den. But some men had their oriental nooks in which to drink their bourbon and smoke their pipes and cigars. It is not easy to remember that less than a generation ago it was customary for a man to ask permission of a woman to smoke in her presence, and that a generation before that no lady (at least no genteel or refined lady) would have thought any man a gentleman who defiled her sweet-smelling parlor or drawing room with the smell of his cigar or pipe. There was, in other words, a valid excuse for a man to claim a smoking room that was his own domain, and as the rarest of tobaccos came from Turkey, what could be more suitable than that the smoking room be a veritable harem of a room?

"The true smoking room," wrote Hooper just after the turn of the century, "with its inviting divans and accessories of far-off Oriental tradition, has gradually evolved itself into the modern den. There are those to whom the parent in all its richness and luxurious ease appeals more strongly than its modern descendant. . . . The true Oriental smoking room is a delight, if it be carried out with some thought as to simplicity and taste. . . . Its entire feeling should suggest the ease of the reclining Turk. Get that effect—in any way, it does not matter how—but get it." As the cigarette became more and more common after the turn of the century and especially during the First World War, women began to smoke as well as men. A lady with a cigarette in 1915, however, was an astonishing sight indeed, and unless she was a visiting foreigner with distinguished credentials, she was very likely to be considered "fast" or worse. Amy Lowell was far better known as a Bostonian eccentric who smoked cigars than as a distinguished poet. When both sexes used "coffin nails," as they were called in 1915, then the reason for the smoking room disappeared. Gentlemen after dinner stayed in the dining room with their cigars and brandy or retired to the library or the den, while the ladies sipped their liqueurs or cordials (a word one hears less frequently now than a generation ago) and smoked their cigarettes in the drawing room or the living room.

The billiard room and the smoking room were progenitors of the recreation rooms of today, and before we get back to the living room proper, let's look very briefly at what they spawned.

The billiard and smoking rooms, as we have seen, were exclusively the domain of men (women had their boudoirs and sitting rooms in which to entertain their women friends), but today's recreation rooms belong as much to women as to men and as much to children as to their parents. In other words, the recreation room is no longer a retreat for rest and quiet; it is a place to make a noise and a mess; if the name "rumpus room" has happily gone out of use, its aura has not. It is there that, in some houses, there is a bar—a miniature, quilted-leather imitation of a hotel cocktail-lounge bar—around which friends gather and where the father of the household becomes a bartender with every convenience of plumbing and refrigeration at his sometimes deft finger tips. Guests sit on bar stools, presumably on the assumption that the illusion of being in a saloon is preferable to drinking peaceably with friends in their living room. Sometimes, especially in houses that emphasize the open plan, the bar is in a corner or segment of the living room, not too far from the "conversation pit." When the recreation room is in the basement, it is more likely to be a room for the children of the family than the adults, and it is equipped with television, record player, and ping-pong table, for it is there that the children can be isolated with their friends and make as much noise as they please. Now that fewer houses have cellars, the recreation room is likely also to be the family room (usually adjoining the kitchen in small houses), so that no matter how much recreation one may get, one has none of the isolation once provided by the smoking room, the den, or the billiard room. The basement recreation room, incidentally, was not the inspiration of an architect or, indeed, of anyone whose primary concern was the livability of the house. It was an unexpected by-product (an example of serendipity) of technological development, but the kind of by-product that had nothing whatsoever to do with technology but a great deal to do with marketing and its handmaidens, advertising and public relations.

According to T. S. Rogers, the author of a practical manual published in 1938 called *Plan Your House to Suit Yourself*, "The basement recreation room . . . started when the American Radiator Company . . . introduced its Red Jacket Heating Boiler." This was in 1926. The American Radiator Company hoped that a bright red jacket would make a spectacular and therefore more salable boiler than the ones the competition was offering. Advertisements displayed pictures of proud house owners showing off their boilers to their friends, and the artists made the cellars that housed them look as attractive as possible by tinting the walls and putting in a chair or two. "Be as proud of your cellar as you are of your living room," the ads said. It was a consultant on sales promotion, C. Stanley Taylor, who suggested making use of the wasted basement space for recreation, and he set up an architectural competition to explore and exploit it. But the basement could not have caught the public's imagination, red jacket or none, if something had not all but vanished from the house which for generations had provided the family with a window on the world about them and ample space for relaxation, gossip, games, and interludes of romance.

"The veranda is perhaps the most specially American feature in a country house," wrote Downing's protégé, Calvert Vaux, in 1857, "and nothing can compensate for its absence."

Downing himself had said: "Verandas, piazzas, bay-windows, balconies . . . are the most valuable general truths in Domestic Architecture." All of them were aspects of the house which looked out and not in and which made the house and its inhabitants, Downing thought, become part of the natural wonders and the man-encouraged beauties of the landscape that surrounded it. In a nation of country homes, when the direct exposure to the sun was looked upon as a danger to be avoided by women, and men had their fill of it during the working day, the cool veranda, with its informality, its comfortable rocking chairs and swings, was one of the most docile and pleasing of rewards. Verandas were prized as "delightful places on which to spend twilight and moonlight summer evenings," as Mr. Fowler of the octagonal house said, and in defense of his own design added: ". . . the advantage of having them *all around* the house is considerable, allowing you to choose sun or shade, breeze or shelter from it, as comfort dictates." Mr. Fowler's arguments had a way of anticipating twentieth-century ideas—in this case Buckminster Fuller's Dymaxion house of 1928 hung on a central mast so that it could be turned to take advantage of the breeze and sun "as comfort dictates."

In a very real sense the veranda was a substitute for air-conditioning. It not only caught the evening breezes, but its vines helped to filter the dust that carriage wheels and horses' hoofs churned up from unpaved country roads. It was a place for exercise as well as rest, and there is scarcely a design for a house from 1840 to 1910 that does not have verandas ample enough if not for a stroll at least for stretching the legs.

"There is nothing, perhaps, that interferes so essentially with the citizen's enjoyment of the country," said the Woodwards in *Country Homes* in 1866, "as the want of facilities for outdoor exercise. It is too hot and dusty to ride or walk before the shower, and after its refreshment has come, it is too wet and muddy. Spacious verandahs shaded with vines, and well-made walks, always firm and dry . . . will give us 'ample scope and verve enough.'"

The verandas of the Gothic Revival house and its contemporaries such as the Tuscan villa and the Swiss cottage were likely to be more formal than the verandas of the Queen Anne house, which were more spacious, more irregular in shape, and more private—more, indeed, like outdoor living rooms in the ways in which they were furnished and used. But houses of no architectural pretensions whatsoever also had their porches where life in the evenings during warm weather lingered and sang and talked until bedtime. Grandmother Brown in her reminiscences of Ohio in the 1820's and '30's tells of her house "of weatherboard inlaid with brick . . . a two-story structure above the cellar" with a "porch that faced the street." This porch, she said, "had a railing around it and a seat against the railing all the way around. It was a resort for old and young. There Ma sat with her sewing. There we all gathered on a summer afternoon."

Life on the piazza was a sort of half-life, neither indoors nor out, neither private nor public. It was not a place to write (papers blew away), though it was a perfectly good place for women's handicraft— for sewing or needlepoint or knitting. It was not a place for confidences, because conversations could be easily overheard, and it was not a place, as Lillian Hart Tryon wrote in *Speaking of Home* in the declining years of the veranda, "to play at any of the healthful or exhausting games which are traditionally known as 'exercise in the open air.'" It was, she said, a place for sociability and indolence, for trifling and idling, a place where no one was called upon to look as though he were purposefully occupied. The veranda was a sort of all-purpose excuse.

In the 1890's there began to be a vogue for converting sections of verandas into glassed-in "sun porches" that were furnished far more informally, with wicker furniture and rattan rugs, swings hung from chains, and hammocks, than an indoor room would be. Very often such an indoor-outdoor room was heated by radiators, so that it might be used all year long. There the indoor garden was installed—palms and ferns in brass kettles, small tropical fruit trees, begonias, and rubber plants, set on wicker stands or hung by chains from the ceiling. There ladies served tea to a few friends when they were being semiformal in demitoilet. "The full value of the sun parlor," said Hooper in 1906, "is hardly appreciated by the majority of home-builders. It is a decided addition to the country house in a temperate climate." Frequently, it was a screened porch in summer and a glazed one in winter. The introduction of wire screening in the 1890's went far to make the veranda more tolerable in the dog days, as it has made the kitchen bearable, and for the same reasons.

The decline of the porch coincided roughly with the rise of the automobile in the second decade of this century. One could get cooler faster by driving in the evening in a car (and the open car was more common than the closed one then), and one could pick one's own view of the sunset or a place for spooning or sparking (it was too soon for necking) and have privacy besides. By the twenties the porch had dwindled to a mere reminder of the old-fashioned porch, and in the Depression years of the thirties it disappeared (indeed, the building industry almost disappeared) except for a sort of truncated front stoop, the only purpose of which was to keep the rain off the postman when he stood at the front door with the morning mail. "I hate to see those desert wastes that were once piazzas," said Mrs. Tryon in 1916. "House after house along any great summer highway, shows its porch, gay with all the trappings of outdoor elegance,—vacant. They have hung their harps upon the willows, and gone a-motoring. . . . But we need the piazza, just as much as ever. There are peace and quiet talk, and the touch upon the soul of a dear familiar view."

"Changes in our social life have been chiefly instrumental in bringing about the large living room of today," wrote the authors of a book called *The Healthful House* in 1917. "It is a combination of family room and drawing room—a formal living room, if you please, or an informal drawing room." In any case, the authors, and almost everyone else, agreed that it was vastly preferable to what the American family had lived with a generation before—a background "composed of hideous 'what-nots,' loaded with meaningless collections of shells and stones; of center tables, with the inevitable photograph album; of cheap, velvet-covered, highly varnished rocking chairs and of stiffly starched, much be-patterned lace curtains." It was, they thought, enough to drive a family to distraction. "Instead of being a constant invitation to a family to come together of evenings, it drove them away—some to the kitchen, some to the dining-room, some to their own rooms to while away the evening, and the young people often to the street."

It is unlikely, to be sure, that Victorian clutter drove very many children out to the streets and, as is implied, to delinquency, but one cannot deny that the revulsion against clutter at the turn of the century was exceedingly strong. This revulsion produced, among other things, a vogue for "Mission" furniture—a foursquare, functional style that looked as though it were made of house timbers and slats and was covered with leather cushions. It also produced a new notion of what was "suitable" ("suitability" became the essence of interior decoration in the days of Elsie de Wolfe and the First World War.) "Suitable" decoration was precisely right for "graciousness" and "gracious living," for it combined elegance with comfort and a sense of "good taste" that was entirely inoffensive and essentially characterless and expensive-looking. It was, in fact, precisely the same kind of "good taste" that still prevails in such stores as W. & J. Sloane of New York or Marshall Field of Chicago, and remains largely unaltered in expensive suburbs like Grosse Pointe or Bloomfield Hills or Englewood or Winnetka. It can, I think, be safely said that no style of decoration or any attitude toward what was "proper" in the looks of the house has ever persisted in America as long as the "suitability" of the Edwardian look. It is a "lady's" decoration, just as the architecture of the period was (and continues to be) a "gentleman's" architecture. It has what is often called rather snobbishly "good breeding."

But if the sense of the suitable has remained much the same for about sixty years (there have been variations on it, of course, such as the "early American" fad of the twenties), the entertainments of the living room have changed greatly. We need to go back beyond the beginning of this century to see what has happened to the ways in which the family has entertained itself and its friends, back indeed to the 1850's, when the first edition of *Hoyle's Games* appeared in this country and made the phrase "according to Hoyle" almost synonymous with "God's truth."

In the 1850's there were, of course, a great many pious souls who looked with revulsion upon any kind of card game as a device of the devil to seduce the innocent into the ways of gambling. But that did not restrain a good many Americans from the progenitor of modern bridge, the game of Whist ("Whist," said Hoyle, "is a well-known game at cards, which requires great attention and silence: hence its name"), or from Casino, Euchre, or Cribbage. Hoyle listed in all fifty games, some of them like "Goff or Golf," as he calls it, outdoor games, and many card games like Pam-Loo, Boston, and Snip, Snap, Snore 'Em ("a very laughable game") which have long been forgotten. Children's games and books about how to play them were plentiful, but none was more popular than Miss Eliza Leslie's *American Girl's Book,* which kept many rainy days from being unbearably tiresome for the young. "I have often regretted," wrote Miss Leslie in the sixteenth edition of her book in 1863, "that so many of the diversions which formerly enlivened the leisure hours of very young people should long since have become obsolete, or only to be found in circles which are yet untouched with the folly and affection of what is called fashion." She recommended games like puss in the corner, copenhagen, stir the mush, and also "Enigmas, charades, rebuses, and conundrums" such as

> *"If I kiss you by mistake,*
> *What war-weapon do I make?"*
> ANSWER: A blunder-buss.

Later in the century Northrup's *Golden Manual* (1891), like many other household books, devoted a chapter to "Home Occupations for Leisure Hours," which opens with the sentence: "There has been a revival of taste in common things, and we care much more than our grandparents about surrounding ourselves with beauty." He recommended the following beautifying leisure occupations to pass the time in the living room:

Embroidery
Making mats of tissue paper
Crocheting
Knitting
Patchwork
Elegant drawn work
Decalcomanie and Potichomanie
Wax flowers
Phantom leaves

Baskets and Wall-pockets
Lace
White embroidery
Making trifles [such as a shaving case for brother]
China painting
Making feather screens

There were other items in his list for artistic activities outside the living room, such as photography, fret-sawing and wood-carving, and collecting ferns. This was before the craze for "pyrography," or burning patterns into wood and leather, that was so popular about the turn of the century.

American women, according to Harriet Martineau, were great readers and spent much of their time sitting by the window or at the center table of the sitting room by a Rochester (or "student") lamp poring over magazines and novels. "All American ladies are more or less literary . . ." she said in *Society in America*. "Readers are plentiful; thinkers are rare." There was also, of course, a good deal of reading aloud in the living rooms of America in the days before radio and television—reading from the Bible, from magazines, and from books of science and of travel—and many fathers took great pride in their skill as readers and performed not without some histrionics. Artistic occupations were most assuredly not for men; to dabble in them was considered effeminate. But drawing was an almost universal leisure occupation of young women, though drawing expertly was a very rare accomplishment among them, according to Miss Martineau, and indeed according to any observer of the handicraft of the last century. Women who were splendid with the needle were clumsy with the pencil and the water-color brush.

Almost everywhere from the seacoast cities to the farthest frontier in America there has always been means of making music, and there has been scarcely a living room by whatever name that has not also been in one way or another a music room. Many pioneers heading for the West in wagons and on canal boats carted their cherished pianos with them. Most Americans agreed with the pious author of *Our Home* (1884), who said: "The money spent for a musical instrument is not thrown away. Every home should contain some such instrument, and there are but few families that cannot afford a piano or an organ. There is something in the nature of music that tends to evolve harmony in the hearts of those who jointly produce it or listen to it."

The spinet, the harp (as much for decorative as musical reasons), and toward the end of the nineteenth century the upright piano and the reed "parlor organ" which had to be pumped by foot were common pieces of living-room furniture. Properly brought-up young women were taught to play a little and sing a little and evenings were frequently spent, when there was company, in showing off their modest accomplishments. David L. Cohn in *The Good Old Days* recalls that in 1886 the United States Bureau of Education reported that seven out of eight pupils in public schools were taught singing and music-reading. It was possible shortly after the turn of the century to buy a Beckwith piano from Sears, Roebuck for as little as $89 (complete with a "Mandolin attachment" which "perfectly reproduces the tones of the mandolin harp, zither, guitar, banjo, etc." If you didn't want this gadget you could have instead "the Muffler Attachment or Practice Pedal, an attachment of great utility as it deadens sound at the will of the performer, a desirable feature during the hours of practice"). Reed organs were a good deal cheaper than pianos, which could, when ordered from Sears, run as high as $165 (the equivalent, Sears insisted, of a $300 or $400 instrument if purchased in a piano store). The best organ that Sears had to offer cost $51.95 and the cheapest, a "Golden Oak Parlor Organ," was $19.90. With the expensive organ went a free stool "with turned legs, brass claws, and glass balls."

Instruments have had a way of going in and out of fashion, and the living room has echoed to a great variety of strings. At the turn of the century the mandolin and the guitar had replaced the banjo in popularity, and the Autoharp was enjoying a vogue among those who wanted to make music but had little talent for it. It was a zither-like instrument and, according to the ads for it, "Anyone— whether he has musical ability or not, can play it with very little practice, and play it well. Thousands testify to its sweetness of tone, which equals that of the highest grade pianos." Such foolproof, even musicproof, instruments have long enjoyed some sort of popularity in America, gadgets on which when one strikes a note a chord comes out; they still do.

The first talking machine was produced by Thomas Alva Edison in 1877-78 and it consisted of a tin-foil cylinder record that was turned by hand. "Those persons who smile incredulously when it is said that the perfected phonograph . . . will sing and play for us . . . at almost no cost, and become a constant source of amusement and instruction," said the *Atlantic Monthly* in 1889, "have forgotten the ridicule they heaped upon the rumor that an American inventor proposed to talk from New York to Chicago. Mr. Edison says that by the beginning of 1890 the phonograph will be far less of a curiosity than the telephone is now. . . . Just at present there is needed a funnel for so magnifying the sound that if the instrument is placed in the center of the table, all persons sitting around can hear." By 1900 it was reported with astonishment that nearly three million disc records were sold in a single year!

The kinds of records that were popular at the turn of the century were not merely music, but vaudeville and minstrel-show skits and turns, the sorts of things that twenty-five years later were the basis of radio programming and fifty years later became the bread and butter of television. There were Negro dialect songs called "coon songs" which had about as much to do with Negro life as Westerns have to do with the life of the cowhand. There were such series as "Uncle Josh"—"Uncle Josh on a Bicycle," ". . . in a Chinese Laundry," ". . . on a Fifth Avenue Bus," and so on—and such items as "An Evening with the Minstrels" (a series of twelve records), and comic Irish songs and Jewish songs and marches and such remarkable tunes as "If You Love Your Baby, Make the Goo-Goo Eyes."

Radio did not turn up in the living room until 1920, when the first broadcasting station in America, Westinghouse's KDKA in Pittsburgh, began to operate to the delight and amazement of families thousands of miles away. Long before KDKA there were thousands of men and boys who had "crystal sets" that they built themselves out of parts they got from electricians' shops, and they made the most minute and painstaking adjustments of the "cat's whisker," which had to find a sensitive spot on the crystal, in order that they might hear wireless Morse code (which meant nothing to most of them) or occasionally a voice from a ship. They sat mesmerized for hours with earphones on their heads, staring into space. Once broadcasting became a reality, however, manufacturers like Atwater Kent began to turn out splendid sets with names like Neutrodyne and Seven-Tube Super-Hetrodyne that were expensive and had horns on top of them for loudspeakers. (Tubes cost, I remember, seven dollars apiece, and my father blew three at once in the 1920's when he had bought a new set and wired it to the storage battery incorrectly. That was before the days when one could plug a set into house current.) Families sat up until all hours of the night trying to get stations that were a long way from home. In New Jersey we were delighted to get Pittsburgh (KDKA, of course), and possibly at three in the morning Chicago might "come in."

Two years after KDKA started broadcasting, the Secretary of Commerce said that there were "over 600,000 persons" with "wireless telephone receiving sets, whereas there were only 50,000 such sets a year ago." By 1931 about sixteen million families had sets that were valued at more than $300,000,000. Today, of course, the number of families that have radios is almost exactly equal to the number of families in America. The phonograph and the radio played hob with the musical-instrument business. Who wanted to listen to an inept young lady sing, or a faltering young man strum a mandolin or make a reed organ wheeze when professional music could be had with the turn of a crank or the flick of a switch?

It is unnecessary here to dwell on the impact of television on the American household. According to the 1960 census 88 percent of all homes in the United States had television sets, whereas in 1950 only 12 percent had them. "Another indication of the continued popularity of television," reported the Census Bureau in August 1960, "is the increase in the proportion of households with more than one set." Eleven percent of all households had at least two sets. By and large, those who lived in cities were more likely to have sets than rural families. It was 91 percent in metropolitan areas as against 82 percent in the country. What this vast prevalence of television has done to American manners, morals, intellects, customs, reading and sleeping habits, cookery, sex, and so on is a constant source of inquiry and speculation, both frivolous and serious, informed and merely inspired, which I see no reason to review or indulge in here. TV has had astonishingly little effect on the looks of the living room (expensive sets are very likely to be put in boxes that are in perfect keeping with Edwardian notions of "good taste"); the TV set is considered most successfully placed in a room where it is least conspicuous, and this may be because it is, essentially, a selfish, demanding, antisocial gadget.

The living room, as I have said before, has become in our time an old-fashioned parlor again in many respects, and in many households. It is not a "living" room at all, but a family showcase, and if it does not look Victorian and hasn't the clutter of whatnots and curio cabinets and wax flowers under glass, it has, nonetheless, a somewhat frozen look because it is not where the family lives and so does not reflect the life and vitality of the family. It is the family's best foot a few inches forward, or sometimes a few miles.

But the "living" room is now not what is called the living room, but something else—a den, a recreation room, a family room. You may remember that in talking about the servant problem I referred to our era as the age of "creeping informality." It is, but that does not mean that we are any more likely to give up the notion that formality is a part of dignity than did the frontier families who as soon as they were able to attach a second cabin to their first one made it into a "parlor." Formality haunts us—we have a respect for order and we wish from the bottoms of our hearts that our children did too. Somehow (we are not quite sure how) they will get it as they grow up, most of them.

In the real-estate section of the *New York Times* in April 1961 there was a hint about formality that may possibly be a straw in the wind. It was a piece headlined, " 'Whoopee Room' of Roaring '20s is Family Room of Relaxed '60s," and it reported a discussion with a development builder. It ended with this observation:

> . . . the recreation room is rapidly turning more formal, too, even in today's crop of split-level houses. It is becoming a second living-room and now is the most likely spot for builders to put the fireplace.
>
> And with this trend, the name is changing as well. In many cases it is designated the family room. If it is relatively small, it is known as the den or study. In higher priced houses it becomes the library.
>
> But . . . this does not mean that the rumpus room is a thing of the past. Having transformed the informal living area into a place to read, sew, or watch television, many home owners are now going back to the basement to add, of all things, a rumpus room.

The further recreation gets from the living room, the more like the old-fashioned parlor that room becomes. It has taken us only about eighty years to come the full circle.

PART THREE

Manners and Style

CHAPTER XIII

Today's House and Tomorrow's

The millions of new homes to be built after
the war will do more than anything else to
heal the scars of war, by bringing families
back together again in the safest and most
comfortable of all havens—the American
Home!

Cecil W. Farrar, quoted in
Small Homes Annual, 1945

On January 4, 1880, the *New York Times* in a column headed
"Scientific Gossip" reported on an event of the year just ended:
". . . With an exceedingly simple and inexpensive apparatus, Mr.
Edison has converted electricity into a light which does not flicker,
which does not require the frequent services of a skilled attend-
ant, and which in quantity and intensity meets the requirements
of domestic life."

To all intents and purposes Mr. Edison had not only contributed
a flickerless light to the comfort of mankind but he had invented
the modern house—the house of switches, effortless heat, unseasonable coolness, humming and sloshing gadgets, and uninterrupted
opportunities for theatrical and musical performances. Electricity
was first admitted to the house from outside generators for the purposes of illumination (battery-operated bells and alarms were not
uncommon before light bulbs), but it was not, at first, a simple
matter of calling in the electric company. Far from it.

Nothing that J. Pierpont Morgan did was typical, to be sure, but
his early determination to have electricity in his house gives one a
notion of what a financier who was also a pioneer was willing to

contend with to be ahead of the populace; fortunately it also tells something of the popular reaction to electricity.

To go back a little, it is well to note that gaslight first appeared in America in 1806 when Mr. David Melville of Newport, Rhode Island, installed it in his house and in the street in front of it. He patented his apparatus (which he had improved) in 1813, and Baltimore was the first American city to install gaslighting in 1818. For several decades, however, gas was a far from satisfactory and reliable source of illumination, as this excerpt from the *Diary of Philip Hone*, December 30, 1836, explains:

> I went this evening to a party at Mrs. Charles H. Russell's, given in honor of the bride, Mrs. William H. Russell. The splendid apartments of this fine house are well adapted to an evening party, and everything was very handsome on this occasion. The home is lighted with gas, and the quantity consumed, being greater than common, it gave out suddenly in the midst of a cotillion. "Darkness overspread the land." This accident occasioned great merriment to the company, and some embarrassment to the host and hostess, but a fresh supply of gas was obtained, and in a short time the fair dancers were again "tripping it on the light fantastic toe."

To this, Mr. Hone added: "Gas is a handsome light, in a room like Mr. Russell's, on an occasion of this kind, but liable (I should think) at any time to give the company the slip." It was, he thought, "illy calculated for the ordinary uses of the family."

Electricity was also looked upon with skeptical glances when it first became practicable. The Middle West was more adventurous about it than the Eastern seaboard, and when Mr. Morgan installed electric lights in his house at 37th Street and Madison Avenue in 1882 there were, according to an Edison Company catalogue of 1883, already six residences in Chicago equipped with private electric plants. (The first general use of electric bulbs was on the steamship *Columbia* in 1880, and there were a number of stores, such as Marshall Field & Company in Chicago, and hotels in large cities everywhere that were bright with them by 1883.) If Mr. Morgan was not the first to have electricity in his house, he was, according to his biographer, Herbert Livingston Satterlee, the first to have his residence "lit throughout with the new light."

It was a nuisance. A pit was dug beneath the stable on 36th Street and in it was installed a little steam engine and a boiler to make the generator operate. Wires from this to the house were carried through a brick conduit and then run through the gas lines so that the gas fixtures were used for both gas and electricity. "Of course," wrote Satterlee, "there were frequent short circuits and many breakdowns on the part of the generating plant." But the human problems were more aggravating to Mr. Morgan than the mechanical ones. "The generator," Satterlee continued, "had to be run by an expert engineer who came on duty at three P.M. and got up steam, so that at any time after four o'clock on a winter's afternoon the lights could be turned on. This man went off duty at 11 P.M. It was natural that the family should often forget to watch the clock, and while visitors were still in the house, or possibly a game of cards was going on, the lights would die down and go out." But more discouraging was the attitude of the neighbors. They complained that the dynamo made an unpleasant noise, and Mrs. James M. Brown, who lived next door, insisted that the vibrations of the contraption made her house shake. So Mr. Morgan "had the machinery taken up and heavy pads of rubber put under it. Sandbags were piled around inside the walls of the cellar to deaden the noise and the vibrations." Mrs. Brown withdrew her complaints about the vibrations and the noise, but she insisted that "fumes from the generator and smoke from the chimney penetrated her pantry and tarnished her silver." As if this were not the last straw, "in the winter when the snow melted above the brick conduit, all the stray cats in the neighborhood gathered on the warm strip in great numbers" and yowled.

Mr. Morgan finally gave in, but in an entirely characteristic way. He put up half the financing (a half-million dollars) for the construction of an uptown power station for the Edison Company, which was already doing business at a downtown station.

The initial reaction to electricity as a means of providing light was rather odd. (Edison's was not the first incandescent bulb; it was the first that promised to be useful in the household. Moses Gerrish of Salem, Massachusetts, made an incandescent lamp in 1869 and electric arc lamps were used in Philadelphia and Cleveland in the late 1870's.) On March 2, 1878, the *New York Times* noted:

> It is only just beginning to be understood that the electric currents of the earth have an intimate connection with a great quantity of things.

. . . Recently it has been asserted that no man can sleep well unless the major axis of his bed, and consequently his major personal axis, corresponds with the position of the axis of the earth. . . . If they [the electric currents] enter a recumbent human being at his feet and pass out his head, he becomes sleepy, while if owing to the wrong position of his bed, they enter from one side to the other, their struggles to get out again produce such a derangement of his nervous system, as to render it impossible for him to sleep.

There is no way to judge what such accounts of the qualities of electricity did to the arrangement of bedrooms, but there were even more horrendous possibilities suggested in the *New York Times*. Someone, the paper reported in January 1878, had devised a secret process which would result in perpetual sunlight and had proposed it to Congress. "What Western girl of any self-respect," asked the *Times*, "would lean on the front gate in broad daylight in company with even the most eligible young man? And what lover, whether Eastern or Western, would have the hardihood to lure his fair cousin to the back piazza or the roof of the house under the pretense of comets and shooting stars . . . ?"

From the point of view of the householder of today, however, the early reaction to the power companies strikes a more sympathetic note.

"Now, there is not the least reason to believe that electricity exerts any better moral influence than gas," said an editorial in the *New York Times* in June 1881, "and we know that when a number of reasonably Christian men form themselves into a gas company, they immediately become pirates of the most merciless and extortionate character. Why should we look for better things from electric light companies? They expect to have us at their mercy and they will be as merciless as the gas men. We shall have electric meters in our cellars that will be as mendacious as the gas meters, and the moment we refuse to pay for 10,000 feet of electricity which we have not used our lights will be cut off and we shall be left to candles and kerosene."

Four years later the *Times* was at it again: "It will . . . greatly dismay the electricity consuming public to learn that an electric meter in use in this city is now charged with having falsely represented that $9.29 worth of electricity was used during last month in a house from which all the electric lamps had been removed for

considerably more than a month." The *Times* blamed the evil performance of electric meters on their close proximity and association
in cellars to those well-known liars, gas meters.

Electricity caught on slowly as a household necessity. Twenty
years after Edison produced a satisfactory bulb, electric fixtures were
still referred to as "burners" and were prohibitively expensive for
most families to install and maintain. In 1899 a writer in *Harper's
Magazine* said: "Now, we are beginning to see that a householder
may choose between gas and electricity." But Samuel Eliot Morison in *One Boy's Boston* recalls that the house in which he was
brought up "was lighted by gas; electricity was not introduced until
about 1910, one of the reasons being that the maids were afraid
of it. Rightly so, too; for if you touched the all-metal light switches
of that era when standing in a tin bathtub, you short-circuited the
works and were lucky not to be electrocuted." One of the accomplishments of electric light that delighted housekeepers, however,
was that closets became much more useful than they had been.
No one dared take a candle into a closet or light it with a gas flame;
electricity made every corner and cranny of it serviceable. As late
as 1920, however, the author of a book called *Lighting the House*
said: "The possibilities of lighting by means of them [incandes-
cent lamps] are incomparably greater than those of open flame,
although gas-lighting has advanced remarkably, considering its in-
herent disadvantages." One forgets how long flames lingered on as
the source of domestic light. In July 1932 the National Electric
Light Association reported that of the 30,500,000 homes then in
America there were still about 10,000,000 whose only source of
light was candles and oil lamps.

Today's house and tomorrow's are, of course, predicated on the
now completely taken-for-granted fact of electric power. Compared
with changes brought about by the discovery or invention of building materials such as steel or plastic or aluminum, or of the great
variety of composition materials, or of structural glass, the contribution of electricity to comfort is overwhelming. Life in the city could
no longer be sustained without it, though life in the country can
be, and indeed occasionally is, if not at a level we would any longer
consider civilized.

But except for the high-rise apartment which depends on electrically powered elevators, electricity has had far less effect on the

architecture in which people live than one might reasonably expect. It has changed the services of the house, has substituted for busy hands and flying brooms, but it has had almost nothing to do with the shape of the living room or the bedroom or the dining room. It has, of course, helped to shrink the kitchen, as we have noted, and made it more like a laboratory in its efficiency than like a room in which people have their being. It has also, by getting rid of the coalbin, cleaned up the cellar, and in many houses eliminated it. It has changed the decoration of houses far less than it might, as most people stick to lamps that are variations on the old kerosene lamp in bases that are vases, or columns, or bowls, rather than accept the attempts that have been made to create fixtures for electric bulbs. Most people find indirect lighting (which was first installed by Mrs. George Westinghouse in her summer place in Lenox, Massachusetts, in 1888 when she put fifteen hundred lights in a cove molding around her drawing room) not acceptably warm in their living and bedrooms, though it is acceptable in bathrooms and kitchens. The "warmth" of light seems to be important to most people, a warmth obviously associated with flame, with the fire on the hearth (the open fireplace is no less cherished for its friendliness today than it ever was, though it has assumed some curious and some primitive shapes), with what the anthropologists call "racial memories." Indirect light, like the light of dawn, is cool; by contrast, most of our houses today, as they were in earlier days of electricity when silk shades were fashionable, seem to be lighted by the last rays of warmth from a setting sun, a pink and golden glow of perpetual twilight. Such conventions of artificial lighting have little to do with electricity but a great deal to do with nostalgias. Mr. Edison would be amused to learn that it is now possible to buy a tiny light bulb that flickers like the flame of a candle.

The modern house and today's house are by no means the same object, as anyone who reads the real-estate sections of the newspapers rather than the architectural magazines knows very well. The houses that are reproduced, for example, in the excellent "annuals" of contemporary houses compiled by the *Architectural Record* are adventurous stylistically and in the uses of materials, in their aesthetics and in their practicability. Some of them have great dignity in their simplicity and elegance while, on the other hand, some are merely doctrinaire in their determination to be modern. This, of course, has always been true of new experiments with architectural style. In this respect the designers of modern houses are no better and no worse than those of the "tasteless temples" of the Greek Revival. The problem of the architect of the modern house is, however, very different from that of the carpenter-builder who adapted a mansion from the plan books of Asher Benjamin or Minard Lafever. The architect today, whatever his convictions, cannot be sure of his client's ambitions, to say nothing of his tastes. The architect today has a doctrine to sell, along with everything else he may want his client to accept in size and convenience and materials. The architect of the Greek Revival house had a presold client, in a sense; he was not concerned with introducing his client to the future or even to the present; he was concerned only with making the past convenient, or as convenient as the Greek style allowed.

This, to a very great extent, is still true of the architects of most of today's houses, for most of today's houses are not architecture in its adventurous or even in its safest aesthetic sense. They are merely shelter of more or less convenience and comfort, more or less flexible, more or less inoffensive to look upon. Today's house, however we would wish it to be, is the development house that ranges from the minimum shell house, an unfinished box with a maximum of do-it-yourself opportunities for its purchaser, to the split-level Cape Cod cottage or the $100,000 ranch house. It is the split-level ranch house; it is the trailer and the "motorized home." It is the row house all over again, now more common in suburbs than in city; it is the suburban garden apartment, the urban luxury apartment sprouting metal balconies from white brick walls; it is the collection of massive, towering boxes, free-standing on little patches of grass, that are immediately recognizable as "public housing." It is the individual unit in the newest species of housing developments—the housing of the aged. These are today's houses, the houses that nearly all Americans move into when they achieve a new dwelling. It is worth mentioning again that less than 12 percent of the new houses built each year are designed by architects for specific clients. Today's housing is part of a package—house, lot, neighborhood—all precooked and deep-frozen, so to speak, and its relation to architecture is very nearly nonexistent.

Let us look then, not at the modern house, which presumably speaks for man's imagination and his hopes for a better life, but at today's house, which merely keeps him warm in winter and dry in wet weather and as private as his income can afford to make him.

Today's house is merely yesterday's house skinned down, its irregular shapes removed, and the remaining shell equipped with gadgets. Stylistically it has come very nearly the full circle from stylelessness to contrived gorgeousness back to stylelessness again. Today's house, as I suggested many chapters ago, is a closer relative of the log cabin than of any kind of architecture that has intervened. Today's house, however expensive, has become a box again, or a series of boxes. Sometimes the box has a sharply peaked roof and is covered with white clapboards, in which case it is called Cape Cod. If it is a box longer than it is wide and has a gently pitched roof, then it is a ranch house. If it is a square box, it is still a bungalow. If it is a two-story box, it is "colonial." If it is two boxes set next to each other but one a little above the other, then it is a split-level. (It can be either a split-level Cape Cod or a split-level ranch.) But like the log cabin it is an architecture built as much to move out of as to move into: it is a way-station architecture. It is the architecture of mobility, not of permanency. When it has roots in the past, as the Cape Cod is supposed to, they are not meant to be real roots; obviously one is not expected to live in a Cape Cod cottage as it was originally lived in; it is a style that is merely meant to be restful to the eye because the eye has become accustomed to it. Its very inconspicuousness is its reason for being. It is comfortable, comforting; nothing about it has to be explained or thought about or looked upon even with affection. It is the safest kind of house; no one has to give his heart to it, defend it, or protect it from the assaults of other people's opinions. It is a machine for living, gift-wrapped.

The same thing is true today of the ranch house in its many variants. It is an architecture so primitive that no one can object to it, except the relatively few people whom architecture excites to pleasure. After the Second World War when, as I have already mentioned, there was a tussle to see what kind of design would dominate domestic building, it was the ranch house that quickly prevailed over all others. Nobody could mind it. It was not experimental enough to be considered "ugly" by even the most conservative, and it was not tricked-up enough to be considered "ugly" by the experimental. It was merely "nice." It was "unobjectionable." It was also "homey," and it was said to be "practical." It seemed to be the only kind of architecture that gave the buyer the illusion of having a house and, at the same time, a semblance of a decent return for its cost per square foot. Like the houses that were built all at once in 1830 in Chicago, turning it overnight from a village to a city, the ranch house has a balloon frame. And like a log cabin it just sits there in its plot, as the cabin did in its clearing, raising its roof no farther to the sky than one-story necessity demands, putting down its roots into the ground only as deep as the crabgrass that surrounds it . . . not a dream house, not even a nightmare house, merely an impermanent dwelling as sheddable as a snakeskin.

There is a growing literature of domestic anguish centered upon the shortcomings of today's house—the thinness of its walls, the lack of insulation and consequent freezing of its pipes, the disappearance of adequate storage space (no cellars and no attics), the fact that roofs leak (they always have), that the windows do not fit their frames or the doors their jambs, that builders are too careless, developers too crafty, that ceilings are too low, building costs and mortgages too high, kitchens too small, bathrooms too few, bedrooms drafty. These matters, and others, have been usefully investigated and deplored at length in books like John Keats's *The Crack in the Picture Window* (1957) and Arthur M. Watkins' *Building or Buying the High-Quality House at the Lowest Cost* (1962). The traps hidden in the small print that have made the purchase of the minimum "shell house" so fraught with dangers for the unwary have been exposed and the exposure and legislation have come to the rescue of these most modest of all home-buyers. There is also a growing literature on the desecration of the landscape, the manner in which planless suburbs and industry-hungry communities are chewing up the remaining open spaces between cities to form urban strips that run for hundreds of miles—from Augusta, Maine, to Newport News, Virginia, or from Detroit to Chicago. For a mobile nation, devoted to the concept of elbow room, both physical and social, we are managing to do our best to deprive ourselves of both. But these are questions that, while they impinge on our domestication at every point, do not need re-exposure here. They are essentially a running fight between "the interests" (which I mentioned earlier as the exponents of real-estateism) and "the consumer."

When the interests and the consumer overlap, however, the conflict takes on a new dimension of reality, a sort of 3-D look. "Architects Don't Care to Live in the Apartments They Design," said a headline in the *New York Times* on April 30, 1961. "Many of the architects who design the apartment buildings going up in Manhattan prefer not to live in them," the article stated. "They live instead in private houses and vintage apartment buildings of the type that are being torn down today to put up the buildings they design." Architects, it appears, like to live in brownstone houses with eleven- to thirteen-foot ceilings, tall staircases, and dining rooms that open into small back-yard gardens. They want dwellings that "offer them the greatest opportunity to exercise their individuality," and the trouble with the buildings they design is that "an apartment house with 'character' . . . [is] economically unfeasible to the real estate developer." Architects find private houses "ideal." "They give you," one of them was quoted as saying, "the large space and intimacy you need." Another architect who lives in an apartment building designed by Stanford White referred to a modern apartment house as a "huge tiny-celled luxury building." "Tiny-celled luxury" certainly ought to be intimate even if it is not private. One is reminded of Dorothy Parker's remark about a tiny office she once shared with Robert Benchley: "If this room were six inches smaller in any dimension," she said, "this would be adultery."

"I remember the nineteen twenties when buildings were well built. Nowadays, when the fellow upstairs rolls a pair of dice you can tell when they come up seven."

"We are forced to put our architectural concepts in the background when we design new buildings. Today's architect is really just a room bookkeeper."

"Home Buyers Get Trading Stamps. Builder in Iowa Offering 100,000 with Purchase of a $14,500 House."

These are the sort of statements the reader of the real-estate pages comes on constantly. Now and then he discovers a real scandal such as the three hundred houses costing from $20,000 to $50,000 in the Canarsie section of Brooklyn that began to sink into the marsh on which they were built. "Foundations," the New York *Herald Tribune* reported on February 1, 1962, "had given way, opening cracks in walls and ceilings; basements were flooded every time it rained, floors had warped, and doors in new $50,000 homes would not open or close." Add to that: "Faulty connection of drain pipes to sanitary sewers . . . ," "Failure to provide proper fireproofing over boilers," and a dozen other "failures" listed in the inspector's complaint, and you get a sense of the character of today's house at its worst.

One finds very little about it in print at its best except in the advertisements of developers and in the pages of "shelter" magazines which, even so, are filled with caveats to the unwary house-buyer or builder.

It is only the gadgets that go into such houses that make them today's houses . . . the gadgets plus the garage. The nineteenth-century house used to put its outbuildings where they belonged, behind the house, and the farmhouse, you will remember, used to string out its various sheds, cold-cupboards, and such, like the tail of a kite. The modern garage, however, has to be where everyone can see whether it is for one car or two (people with three-car garages usually do not let them be part of the house's façade). If, however, one looks upon the car as a household gadget, which essentially it is, it needs a room in the house every bit as much as, say, the furnace. The automobile is a part of domesticity, an extension of it—a means of joining house and shopping center (in other words a supply line), a means of joining town house or apartment with country house, just as a breezeway used to join two log cabins. The car, in other words, is a sort of motorized room which long ago stopped being a luxury, like the parlor, and became a necessity, like the kitchen. Today's house and the automobile are inseparable as a concept and separable as a fact only for a few hours at a time.

The automobile is the most modern thing about most of today's houses. Peculiar and extravagant as the design of many automobiles is, today's car performs most of its functions efficiently, more efficiently than most houses perform theirs. Indeed, it is when the car is performing domestic functions that it is at its best—as mobile nursey, unchaperoned parlor, sun porch. It is at its worst when it tries to perform the functions of a commuter train or other kind of urban rapid transit. But if it were merely mechanical gadgets that made today's house a modern house, then about two-thirds of Americans would live in modern houses. Gadgets, however, do not make the archaic modern any more than they make a house into a home. The modern house is a concept not only of architecture but of the good life; it is not just a means of housing refrigerators, freezers, air-conditioners, garbage-disposal units, and furnaces. Modern architecture is concerned with style, and we shall get to that; at the moment we are concerned with mechanics.

I have in my files two folders, one labeled *The Up-to-date House* and the other *The Science Fiction House*. The former contains examples of some of the more advanced methods of house construction and equipment now in use; the latter bulges with clippings of what manufacturers (rather than architects) think (or say they think) the house of tomorrow is going to be like.

The up-to-date house can be built of steel panels or of aluminum. Tomorrow's house, we are told, will be built of paper (a prototype was built on Long Island in 1961 and looked promisingly durable) or, of course, of plastic, as was demonstrated at the Seattle World's Fair in 1962, and by a Japanese industrial designer, Hikonoske Inoue, several years earlier. In 1962 the president of a chemical company was quoted in the *New York Times* as saying: "Plastics in the building industry will multiply ten times by 1970 and will be accounting for between 20 and 30 per cent of all materials used by builders." He also said: "There appears to be no limit to the development and materials that we can expect in the future."

More and more of today's houses are put together out of prefabricated units—wall panels, trusses, window frames, doors—all of which used to be either tailored by carpenters on the site or were expensively-made "millwork." It is now possible to put up the frame of a four-bedroom, $20,000 house in six or seven hours, a job that used to take two or three weeks. In the last decade there has been a boom in completely prefabricated houses (or "factory-built," as they are also called), especially of the least expensive sorts—houses in the $10,000 class, or nearly minimal housing. Factory-built houses are put together out of sections produced in standard sizes and in large quantities. The requisite sections are shipped to the site, where the purchaser of the house has bought the land and has the cellar dug. The house he gets has a name like his car. It is called a "Fairlane," a "Conway," a "Forreston," or a "Beacon." There are, of course, also more experimental models of prefabricated houses such as the all-aluminum and glass house made in 1961 by Alside, Inc., an Ohio firm, to sell for

$12,000, "exclusive of land," but including "air conditioning, insulation throughout, and a kitchen equipped with a range, dishwasher, garbage disposal unit, food blender, refrigerator and freezer."

The expensive up-to-date house stops with no such conventional gadgets as these, which are now taken for granted except by the most reluctant housekeepers who take a certain nostalgic pride in starting their meals from scratch. Its curtains are drawn by little electric motors; its hall or patio fountains toss electrically circulated water into the air; its pear-shaped swimming pool is electrically heated, as are the towel racks in the bathroom, where a ventilator fan is turned on by the same switch that lights the lights. The lights in the living room, hidden in coves or recessed into the ceiling, may be dimmed by rheostats to suit the mood of the moment. None of this is complex, though some of it is still considered luxurious. Compare such frivolous uses of electricity, for example, with the heating controls that according to the 1960 census were in twenty-four million American homes—the little thermostat—and think what the householder of fifty years ago who had to stoke his furnace (or pay someone else to) would think of the revolution caused by this little gadget in mankind's way of life.

The science-fiction house, at least as it is revealed in my files, offers comparable revolutions to our grandchildren—merely items such as bedcovers that keep one cool in summer as well as warm in winter, spigots that run hot coffee or soda water in the kitchen, incinerators that "dispose of combustible materials—food, paper, cartons and the like—without odor, smoke or ash." There will be, we are assured, "windows that will automatically regulate the intensity of light coming through them" and "an air freshener simulating mountain air or sea breezes that will be diffused through air-conditioning systems." The computer, of course, is expected to play a domestic role. The *New York Times* in January 1961 reported: "In a recent interview, Mrs. Armstrong [of a firm of industrial designers] explained that the home computer would select the daily menu, program cooking, cleaning and laundry chores, locate family members and remind mother of dentist appointments." She added, "The device should free the family for more creative work and play than we experience today." One of the ways it was suggested that the lady of the house might be more "creative" was that "the computer would free a woman to spend half her day preparing an exotic evening meal at which many foods would be *tasted and consumed over a three-hour period"* [Italics mine!].

Television will play a more important role in tomorrow's house, we are told, than in today's. In the General Electric version of the house of the future at the Seattle World's Fair there were no books or magazines; reading matter was recorded on electronic tapes and projected on television machines. Intercommunicating systems within the house and from home to office were equipped with television screens; television will, of course, eliminate not all but many of the functions of the baby sitter.

But more important than the gadgets are the notions that the house will be made up of units that can be added or subtracted at will, rooms like pillboxes that can be attached to existing arrangements of boxes. Furthermore, the standardization of wall, floor, and ceiling materials that could be put together in an infinite variety of ways threatens to make every man his own architect. Nails, we are assured, will be eliminated, and chemical fasteners used in their place, thus making it possible for the homeowner to rearrange or rebuild his house without even the risk of smashing his thumb with a hammer. Nor will he have to paint, paper, or plaster. His building materials, made of plastic, will come impregnated with color and he will have "electroluminescent wall panels which change the color decor of a room by the flick of a switch." He will have "see-through" plastic chairs and will use solar energy not only as the source of heat for the house but to power the air-conditioning and the kitchen equipment.

Forecasts such as these are not, I believe, in the least exciting to today's house owner. They seem to be merely schemes for selling more and different kinds of goods and services and do not seem to promise any better sort of life than the house of today already provides. They do not compare in any degree with the promise held by Mr. Edison's light bulb, "the light which does not flicker." They merely seem like more of what we already have, with even less personality, charm, and humanity. Tomorrow's house, we are told, will provide us with more leisure, so that we can cultivate our minds and eat three-hour meals; the evidence is against our wanting to do either. The apartment house in the 1880's, you will recall, was going to give women "leisure to cultivate the higher intelligence." The three-hour meal was one of the curses of the nineteenth century that everyone was glad to be rid of.

But the gadgets, the mechanization and electrification of the house, have accomplished one major revolution in the domestication of America, and tomorrow's house will, it seems more than likely, force this kind of change still further. The change is suggested in a head-line that appeared in the *Wall Street Journal* in October 1958. It read:

LIFE ON THE FARM
It Acquires More City
Comforts as Farmhouses
Sprout Appliances, TV

"Farmers are losing their identity as a class," the article said. "In the past, they kept pretty much to themselves. Now they're beginning to live like other people."

The farm family now demands and can get precisely the same kind of house that the suburban family has and enjoy all of the same gadgets and what we solemnly call "cultural values." A University of Illinois sociologist is quoted as saying: "Farm life is gradually assuming a character that is typical of many suburban areas." More farmers today have television sets than have telephones; two-thirds of all farm families have TV, 56 percent have telephones. This unques-tionably says something for the independence of farmers, if not much for their cultural values. Mr. Edison and his light bulb and the Rural Electrification Administration, which was established in 1935 to bring light and power to isolated rural areas that were not served by public utilities, have turned the farmhouse into a suburban villa. But further than that, they have turned America into a vast suburb, punctuated by somewhat denser areas of population that we refer to as cities, but which are really concentrations of commerce, construction, and culture that become each year less and less like the living organisms ideal cities should be.

While the values of the farmer are approaching more and more closely those of the suburbanite and his house is becoming more and more like the standard pattern of suburban dwelling, the city dweller is fighting a losing battle for the qualities of the city that he loves. (It is, of course, true that not all suburbs are alike in their values or in their architecture, that a development of shell houses is vastly different from, say, Grosse Pointe or Far Hills. But those who live in suburbs at whatever economic level have something in common that they do not share with those who live in cities by choice.) It does not matter in the least to the city dweller that those who live in suburbs find his values incomprehensible, but he cherishes the privacy that only the large city affords (although it is often bought at the cost of loneliness), the identification with the center from which emanate the ideas that shape the lives of others, the treasure house of the rich, the strange, the aged, the beautiful, the squalid, and the diabolic, that is the metropolis. The cost of enjoying delights considered dubious by suburbanites becomes increasingly expensive for the urbanite. More and more it is true that the only way to live comfortably in a twentieth-century city is to live in a nineteenth- or early twentieth-century dwelling. Such buildings were built by men who, however venal they may have been, or however honorable, understood that the city had to be habitable, and they were bent on attracting people to the city and not on repelling them from it. They were not, of course, any less eager to make a dollar by cutting corners than today's builders and speculators, but they do not seem to have been hell-bent on driving the city dweller to seek refuge from paper-thin walls, malfunctioning services, muggings in corridors, and exorbitant prices for minimal accommodations. It is part of the basic code of real-estateism to make not merely buildings but entire areas of a city become obsolete, to encourage shifts in fashion for residences and for business buildings, and to abandon the unfashionable to deterioration into slums, either human or commercial. It is a pity that the proliferation of gadgets, starting with Mr. Edison's light bulb, has in many ways made the lot of the city dweller more and more difficult in many respects.

The effects of gadgets on urban architecture (and of course on rural architecture as well) has been to relieve the architect of the necessity to use his imagination for the purpose of making the inhabitants of his buildings comfortable. He no longer has to concern himself with spaces that will be cool in summer; he only has to worry if his client can afford air-conditioning. The heat and ventilation of an apartment are no longer his concern; they are the business of the heating engineer. The architect of an apartment building seems to be concerned only with first impressions, not with living. If he installs a fireplace, it is as an ornament and not because the warmth of a fire contributes to sensual satisfaction. Ideally, the number of mechanical contraptions that now perform functions that were once wearisome physical chores should relieve the architect of mechanical details and give flight to his imagination. More than ever before he should be free to exert his talents in the achievement of the third of the three basic qualities of architecture as Vitruvius defined them—"Commodity, Firmness, and Delight." But the fact seems to be that gadgets substitute inadequately for Commodity. In urban construction nothing seems to substitute for the kind of Firmness that separates one man's privacy from another's, and Delight, such as it is, is applied only to the lobby, and then not by an architect but by a decorator. Those who can afford it avoid "luxury" apartments in order to live more luxuriously in reclaimed slums.

But if mechanical gadgets have taken their toll in architectural imagination as it reveals itself in today's home, they have played an enormous role in the process of our domestication. They have made us Sybarites. Mechanical servants such as the automatic furnace, the washing machine, the vacuum cleaner, the freezer, the dishwasher, the refrigerator have made life soft and luxurious for those of us who are not among the third of Americans who live in substandard dwellings. They have provided us with luxurious refinements of comfort and ease and with delicacies for our palates all but undreamed of a century ago. We take for granted as domestic necessities foods and services that in the last century were available to fewer than 10 percent of the population—that sliver on the top of society that could afford to employ large staffs of servants. There is a gadget to replace almost every member of the household staff, or if not replace him (or her) to eliminate his work, or do most of it. Robots substitute for the laundress, the houseman who tended the furnace, the kitchenmaid, the parlor maid, the scullery maid, and so on.

As recently as 1927 there appeared a book by Mary Ormsbee Whitton called *The New Servant*, with the subtitle *Electricity in the Home*. It was a book of more than three hundred pages and contained twenty chapters. The first chapter was called "What Every Woman Can Know about Electricity" and the last, "Training Servants in the Use of Electric Devices." Between these two chapters were information on "When to Cook by Current," "Wired Furniture" (such as tea tables with electrical outlets in them), "Table Cookery," and other matters. Just about fifty years had elapsed between the time Mr. Edison developed his light bulb and the publication of this basic manual for household use of electricity. In her preface, the author said: "One of the most interesting economic changes of the early Twentieth Century [is] the development of all manner of electrical appliances for use within the home, the women of this period learning rapidly to do by machine the tasks which from time immemorial had always been regarded inevitably as hand work." And she added by way of explanation for this phenomenon: "Although the beginnings of this peaceful sociological revolution antedate the World War of 1914-18, undoubtedly its impetus was greatly quickened by the almost total disappearance of the professional household servant during the years following that struggle." One might add that the technological demands of warfare took Bridget out of the house and put her in the factory, and that the vacuum that this created in the household forced technology to respond with machines to take Bridget's place.

What Mrs. Whitton calls "a peaceful sociological revolution" might just as properly be called a technological revolution. One can as easily say that the changes that have been wrought in the house since 1880 are largely the result of the introduction of a new kind of energy into the house to light Mr. Edison's and Mr. Westinghouse's bulbs. But I think we have little to gain here from arguing the question of whether the technological revolution brought about the sociological revolution or vice versa; we know that they came hand in hand. We also know that today's house is a compromise between what technology might do for us if we let it and the requirements of tradition and manners. The house, in other words, could be a far more efficient machine than it is if more people were willing to sacrifice many of the social customs and values to which they attach importance. But social customs change slowly even today, far more slowly than technology. The American home, it is well to remember, is inhabited by a society that takes delight in probing the moon with rockets, but is nonetheless delighted to be able to probe the coals in its living-room fireplace with a poker.

From Soirée to Kettle-drum

"A Domestic Party in Boston, 1855" (above) was not typical; more often the men gathered in one corner of the parlor and ladies in another. But this group, like many, is about to be subjected to the trills of a soprano. Afternoon tea parties (called kettle-drums in the 1880's) were the all-purpose social debt-payers in the days before the cocktail party, an invention of the 1920's.

AN IMPOSSIBILITY.   A ROMAN ST...

Parlor and Rumpus Room

Parlor games a century ago often led to someone's being kissed . . . in notorious pastimes like "spin the bottle" and "consequences." It is doubtful, though, that "blowing the feather" led to many blushes. When television first appeared in the 1940's the beginning of the end of innocent ingenuity about home entertainments was in sight.

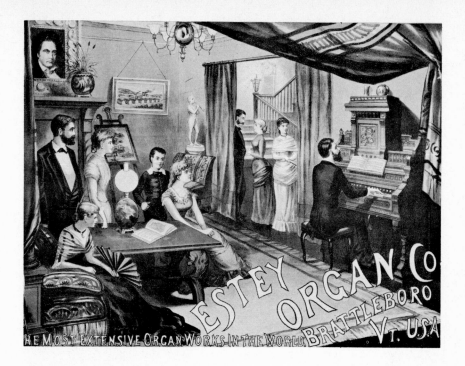

Music to Their Ears

The parlor organ (pumped by foot) and the piano once filled almost every fashionable parlor and many frontier hovels with music, and someone in almost every family performed for friends frozen into silence. Both of these family scenes are from the last years of the nineteenth century. In the one below the spell of home performance is threatened by the magic of a phonograph and its recorded music.

Evenings at Home

Conversation has never been a highly developed or greatly prized American art. In the days of intense chaperonage, lovers flirted across the whist or bridge table as in "Playing the Dummy" by Harrison Fisher in 1907. Today the "conversation pit" is a fashionable architectural device and the one below is meant for conversation. Many such pits are equipped with TV and Hi-fi so that conversation is unnecessary.

LOOK Magazine Pho

Survival of the Fittest

The costumes and the whiskers changed but the problems did not. "The Habits of Good Society" in 1872 and "Buffet Supper" in 1940 reveal man's continuing struggle to be chivalrous and yet avoid starvation in the living room. Since then the same scene has tended to shift to the environs of the barbecue pit.

THE INNER MAN
Buffet Supper

Drawing by Gluyas Williams
Copr. 1940 by The New Yorker Magazine, Inc.

Life on the Porch

The porch was once the center of American summer life—cool in the evenings, private enough but still inviting to passers-by, a place for only the most casual talk, for singing and flirtation. The bower of potted greenery below was on the rear of a New York City house in the 1870's. Above, a honeymoon couple sip the delights of young love and mint juleps on the porch at White Sulphur Springs in the '80's.

Indoors and Outdoors

Little by little the sharp line between indoor and outdoor living has been vanishing. By 1900 the porch had become an outdoor living room where quite formal occasions took place, as above, and many houses had porches that were made useful as sun rooms all year round by glassing them in. The modern house needs neither porch nor sun room. The indoors and outdoors flow pleasantly together.

LOOK Magazine Photo

Domestication in Los Angeles, 1960

CHAPTER XIV

The Americans at Home

The concept of respectability is the enemy of
the concept of style. Respectability is safe
and self-conscious; style is reckless and self-
assured. Respectability worries about what
people think of it; style apologizes to no one.
R. L. in *Art in America*, Spring 1963

"I wonder," a friend said to me not long ago, "if the modern house,
so open, so transparent, so free from dark corners and hiding
places and secrets, is not a reflection of the influence of psychiatry
on our generation."

It was the sort of speculative remark that might have been made
by Andrew Jackson Downing. You will, perhaps, remember that this
book begins with a statement he made as he looked about him
in the 1840's: "Much of the character of every man may be read in
his house."

In some respects, it is possible to find out more about the character
of the contemporary American "every man" from the "modern" house
than from "today's" house. The modern house at its best is a conscientious and imaginative effort to make an environment for today's
family, and to do this the architect cannot fall back on traditional
solutions to familiar domestic problems. The problems of the family
today are not, no matter how nostalgically one may wish to regard
them, quite the same as they were even a decade or two ago. But the
modern house, for all its freshness, its openness of plan, transparency
of walls, frankness of construction, freedom from fussiness, and
unwillingness to draw a line between the outdoors and the indoors,
is full of echoes from Mr. Downing's day and before. The character

277

of the frontier speaks through it just as clearly as the character of "the organization man." The desire for individuality that so puzzled visitors to America in the 1830's because it was so vocal and yet so coupled with belief in conformity is still here. But in many ways it is apparent that the American family has changed and that its aspirations are not what they once were.

Another nineteenth-century man whom we have encountered often in this book and who, like Downing, wrote about architecture, was the phrenologist O. S. Fowler, who started the cult for the octagonal house. "Beautiful birds build tasty nests," he said. ". . . a fancy man will build a fancy cottage, a practical man a convenient house; a substantial man, a solid edifice; a weak man, an illy arranged house; an aspiring man a high house, and a superior man, a superb villa."

I do not intend to practice phrenology on modern houses, though many of them in their different ways are "tasty nests." But I should like to try to draw from their characteristics some generalizations about how America has changed since the days of Andrew Jackson and the first wave of gentility and how in some important respects America has stayed the same.

The most striking, and possibly the most obvious, generalization that one can draw is that one of the traditions of American domestic architecture has finally given in to a persistent fact of American life and disappeared. We have given up what was once so strong a desire of so many American families (and so many politicians) to build for permanence, to establish a family seat which might serve a succession of generations. Almost ten years ago I laughed when the artist Robert Osborn told me that he had engaged a young architect to build a studio for him in Salisbury, Connecticut, and had told him he wanted it made of brick. The young architect refused. "Brick is too permanent," he said. It sounds odd, but it is a reflection of a state of mind we cannot dismiss. He had a valid point, even if Mr. Osborn hired another architect. It has taken, however, a very long time for designers of houses to face the facts of American mobility. The modern house accepts this in its design and makes a virtue of it as "today's" house does not; today's house tries to look like a permanent house, rooted to the ground and to the past, and it accepts the horrid facts of mobility only in the hidden flimsiness of its construction.

We are returning to a basic kind of architecture that one would have thought we had discarded. The new architecture is genuinely a frontier architecture, not, as the ranch house is, a sort of mealy-mouthed adaptation of a kind of architecture once associated with the frontier. The modern house recognizes the fact that the American dwelling is a stepping stone, that it is merely a stop on an incessant journey, and it states this fact quite clearly. Indeed, many modern houses seem to be in motion, their roofs spread like wings, and their bodies hovering just above the ground, not on it, as though they might migrate at any moment. They say frankly what the builders of American houses have always hoped was not true.

Several years ago I visited Richmond and spent many hours looking at the great plantation houses built on the banks of the James River. I was lucky enough to have lunch at Westover, but I arrived there early, too soon to ring the doorbell, and I spent an hour wandering through the gardens, where snow was on the box bushes, and cardinals and bluebirds (it was in January) perched in naked fruit trees. I looked at the house from the river side, its true façade but not the one one sees first; it was a house of tremendous elegance—perhaps, I thought, the most splendid piece of domestic architecture in America. I looked at the barns and the outbuildings, built, like the main house, of brick, and at the circular privy with a fireplace and windows, and facilities for a family of five. Americans were, to be sure, less prudish in the eighteenth century than they became in the nineteenth century and are now.

Westover represents the vanished idea of the house built for the great-grandchildren. "I have settled here," it seems to say, "and I mean to stay here. I am not just a building; I am the monument to a permanent philosophy of the good life." The way of life that Colonel William Byrd II built into his splendid mansion, a rather despotic life but one in which culture and education and a knowledge of the world were insisted upon, lasted from about 1730 until the Civil War. The echo of the way of life is still there, and one cannot help but hear it. But it is an echo from Europe, not only architecturally but in its sureness that a permanent class structure could be taken for granted, that there would always be a landed gentry and a cultured upper class of limited size, but of almost unlimited political and economic power.

The Civil War by no means did away with the concept of building for future generations of the same family; it merely shifted the location from the South to the North, and from an agricultural aristocracy to a new industrial and financial society. The splendid plantation house, set in thousands of acres of cultivated land, lingered, but in poverty; the great princely palace from which its owner sallied forth into the world of financial conflict became the new kind of rich family seat. Colonel Colt, who invented the revolver that bears his name, elected to build himself a villa in Hartford, Connecticut, part Italian and part Turkish, with towers and minarets and glass domes. A little later, when Richard Morris Hunt became America's foremost domestic architect, he built massive châteaux for the Vanderbilts and marble palaces (which were called "cottages") for the Goelets and the Astors and still more Vanderbilts at Newport. They were constructed to stand as their prototypes in Europe had already stood for centuries, and the dates of their erection were carved over the doorways for future centuries to look upon with awe.

And now they are gone, most of them. Gone, that is, as houses. Some, like The Breakers at Newport and Biltmore in Asheville, are museums open to the public—many others are now schools or convents or recreation centers for the employees of large corporations.

Every conscientious effort on the part of Americans to establish a permanent domestic architecture has failed. We have groped our way from one style to another hoping that we would hit on something that might suit us, but how could we expect to find it when we were neither willing to stay still in one place nor on one social level? It was, quite simply, impossible to impose on a highly mobile society the European architecture of a comparatively static society, a society that not only stayed in the same place physically but "kept its place" socially.

The idea of a permanent domestic architecture, grand, solemn, and enduring, had a magnetic appeal for those who had arrived in America at positions of social and financial eminence and who hoped, in the tradition of European aristocracies, to establish dynasties of a sort. It also appealed to those who hoped to achieve eminence by emulating the eminent, not only in the kinds of houses they inhabited, but in their manners, their cultural pursuits, their language, and their means of disposing of (rather than employing) their leisure. While those who had "arrived" (or more properly, the wives of those who had arrived) were imitating the European aristocracy (or in some cases trying to buy it into the family), the *arrivistes* in America were imitating the imitators. As a result, our nineteenth- and early twentieth-century attempts to establish what looked like permanent estates in the grand manner were as pretentious architecturally as they were socially and as little suited to our physical and social restlessness. It was an architecture of mannerisms rather than of style and it was lived in by people to whom etiquette and manners were the same thing.

But even the idea of a simple, unpretentious, but permanent architecture was, as we have seen, more talked about by family reformers and architects and politicians than realized. Whatever an American thought he should believe about the home and its enduring qualities, the fact remained that home, as long as he was on his native soil, was where he was, as much as where he had come from. No home was so dear to his heart that he hesitated to leave it if he could discover one he thought would be better. The society in which he lived and the American dream which guided his ambition were, he believed, always beckoning him forward. It did not occur to him that he was stuck in any special class, and he believed that if he were ingenious enough, lucky enough, and adventurous enough he could escape from his surroundings into more palatable ones. Some men believed they could better their lot with their backs in the wilderness, some that they could push forward with their brains in the universities, or with their wits in the market place, and however many resigned themselves to staying put, there were always spectacular examples of those who moved on, some to catastrophe and some to astonishing success.

How do you house such a mobile society? You house it in temporary buildings, or buildings, anyway, that you would like to think will not become slums—buildings that should be, even if they are not, torn down after a generation.

It seems to me interesting, now that there are no more real physical frontiers in America, that it should be the architecture of impermanence that has won out. The architecture of the economic, spiritual, and social frontier has replaced the architecture of the physical frontier. Even when there is no place to go to, we have elected not to settle down.

We are, taken as a whole, more used to change than to permanence. Nothing surprises us less than what surprised Mrs. Trollope and Dickens so much—a house on its way from one place to another. When we build a house or buy one, the least of our concerns is whether the next generation of our family will want to make it their home. We don't expect anyone to make a family seat out of a Hardoy chair. But changes come so fast in American life that we are scarcely aware of how far-reaching they are. It would take a book (indeed, all too many people, including myself, have taken a book) to outline the changes in our society since the Second World War. But let us look for a moment at a few of the changes in our manners and customs that are, or will be, reflected in our houses.

The young marry younger than they used to a few decades ago, and girls marry at very nearly the same tender ages they did a century ago. They have more children than their parents' generation, oblivious of the fact (or indifferent to it) that the growth of our population is one of the greatest headaches their generation is going to have to face. Many young marriages are now consummated in college, and universities are having to provide housing facilities for young couples. Teenagers, traditionally promiscuous, have become monogamous. The convention of "going steady" threatens to change the sexual mores of the nation, and there are those who believe that going steady will result in an alarming increase in the divorce rate, which has already become alarming because of so many immature marriages. (It would be interesting to know what Harriet Martineau, who was so astonished by the high incidence of abortion in America in the 1840's would think about the incidence of it, and arguments about it, today.) Women are assuming jobs and responsibilities that we have long thought were the prerogatives of men, and men in their turn are taking on a good many chores in the household that as recently as a generation ago would have seemed preposterous as man's work. Shorter working hours mean that more Americans are at home more of the time than they used to be. On the other hand, mother is out of the house a great deal more than her mother was. She is on the road to the supermarket, the station, the school, the church, the PTA, and in many cases she is at her office from nine to five.

This is only a very small part of the picture of change. With the shortage of domestic servants and the wholesale use of mechanical substitutes for their hands, life has not only become more informal, it has also assumed a far less rigid time schedule. Families eat when they please, not when Bridget pleases. With the reversal of the cultural (with a small "c") trade winds (they now blow from California to the East) Americans everywhere have taken to the out-of-doors, to the barbecue pit and the patio, and to dressing themselves in perpetual variations on beachwear. The suburbs, where the outdoor life is pursued the year round, have assumed a place in our national pattern of living that has not only antiquated our transportation systems and local governments, but has threatened to become a brand-new kind of social simplex (as opposed to complex) in which there is no place to rise: the only way up is out.

As our lives become more cluttered and our neighbors come closer, we hear a great deal about "mass" this and "mass" that—about mass culture and mass communications and mass media and mass housing and, of course, about mass production. We hear less about the struggle for individuality, which goes on as usual, and about the nonconformists who are, I suspect, around in just about the same ratio as they always have been. Except for the "beats," whose numbers and adherents began to subside about 1960 after a brief efflorescence in the late 1950's, the nonconformists are neither so noticeable nor so vocal in this period of prosperity as they are when there is economic dissatisfaction. But those who raise their voices in protest against the *status quo* are looked upon with just about as much suspicion by conformists as they have been since the beginning of the Christian era. They may be pilloried, but at least we don't remove their skins or break them on wheels or feed them to lions.

If we did, there would be no such thing as the "modern" house, which does not conform to any mass-production standards of taste, which flies in the face of what is tried and accepted, gives the back of its hand to traditional styles, and in many cases to traditional manners. It has, to be sure, its militantly devoted band of adherents who are often aggressively up-to-date, and who seem as outlandish as their houses to a great many good and useful people who suspect their enthusiasm of being a little tainted with defensive belligerency. Nevertheless, the modern house is a new kind of frontier architecture.

What, in Mr. Downing's words, can we read of the character of every man in the modern house?

The modern house epitomizes (or should), without the curtains of tradition to obscure them, the most up-to-date aspirations of the American family and the ways in which it believes these aspirations for the good life can be practically realized. In a very real sense every good architect is a practicing social scientist. He measures, gauges, and reduces to a formula the social unit for which he is designing, and the formula that he produces (sometimes more "elegant," in the scientist's meaning of the word, than at other times) is a building. What generalities can we discover by applying his formulas to the American at home today?

First, let's look at the children.

There is a tendency in the modern house to return to the nineteenth-century practice of isolating the children from the rest of the house, to establish in effect what was once thought of in large mansions as the children's wing. But in the modern house the children no longer have bedrooms which are also playrooms; they have pigeonholes for sleeping and a "play area" which someday, it is hoped, they will use for teenage riotous living, off there somewhere out of earshot. They are given a place where they can make a mess that will not make a mess of the rest of the house, where they can "express" themselves to their little hearts' content. They are, you might say, provided for, but as Lewis Mumford has written, "the numerous nooks and hiding places, dear to children . . . nooks that gave the young places for quiet dreaming and mischievous eavesdropping on their elders," have gone. Such a statement seems rather sentimental and old-fashioned when we look at the modern house, but it is a fact nonetheless and a reflection of our attitude toward the psyche of the child. We believe in the open mind, in the open plan, in the importance of the facts of life and not of the myths of childhood. In some respects we have given Freud a long white beard and a red cap and made him into Santa Claus. If we are good, he will bring us adjustment for Christmas.

Not that this is unhealthy. What we are doing instead of turning the children over to Nanny (or Mammy), as the prosperous family used to, to discipline and amuse and produce at the children's hour, is to provide them with safe isolation where, at the same time, they can be observed. Now that we are returning (perhaps only temporarily) to the nineteenth-century ideal of the large family, we have to provide a place for children that is not directly underfoot. It is interesting in this context that while the size of the family increases, so do the complaints of many young housewives that there are too many demands on their time. It would, I suppose, be unfair to say that they create the demands so that they can make the complaints; it would be fairer (and probably truer) to suggest that they create the demands because they want to put off as long as possible the moment when they are going to have to fall back on their own intellectual resources to fill their time satisfactorily.

The nineteenth century in some ways seems less far from the modern house than from "today's" house, perhaps because the designer of the nineteenth-century house was concerned with function, just as the designer of the modern house is. The nineteenth-century architect couldn't leave "function" to gadgets; the modern architect doesn't want to. The sensible designer of a century ago, for example, was trying to convince his clients to get the kitchen out of the basement and put it in a convenient, step-saving relationship to the dining room. The modern architect is trying to make it an easy adjunct to the living room, or that part of the living room now called the "dining area." The kitchen is again recognized, even in rather elaborate modern houses, as a center of life, as it was in the old farmhouse. The problem is how to avoid isolating mother from her family and still not have the family eat in the kitchen. This is not merely a reflection of the disappearance of servants from most households; it also apparently indicates that mother again wants to cook and not merely to heat up frozen or canned foods. Cooking has regained its place as a creative function, an opportunity for self-expression. (Among the best-selling books in America, which very rarely appear on the best-seller lists, possibly because so many of them are sold by mail and therefore not reported by bookshops as their fastest-moving merchandise, are cookbooks.) The revived interest in cookery hints at the reversal of a trend; women are becoming more womanly, which will be a relief to a great many men.

In this connection one cannot but be impressed with the smallness of the bedrooms in most modern houses in comparison with the living rooms, which tend not only to grow larger but also higher than they did a few decades ago. The function of the bedroom has been recognized for what it is rather than for what it was in the days when it was a place to loll, a place where a woman could write at her desk in her nightie, or sit by the window and sew, a place to paddle around with hair down and face covered with cold cream without the sense that one must have in the "family room" that one is facing the world. The boudoir is gone except in extravagant houses. Too bad. When the kitchen and the bedroom become adjuncts of the living room, something has been lost, even if something has been gained.

But let's turn our attention to the modern house as a whole, for a moment. Downing, as we have noted, wrote in *The Architecture of Country Houses*, "Verandas, piazzas, bay-windows, balconies, etc., are

the most valuable general truths of Domestic Architecture." They were
all important in the mid-nineteenth-century house, but when we became involved with adaptations of French châteaux and cute little
Dutch houses and half-timbered English cottages and revivals of
colonial houses and "salt boxes" as we did in the early years of this
century, they all but disappeared. We are now recognizing again the
general truths that Mr. Downing thought so important and we are once
more finding virtues in ideas of designing for delight that we had
thought we had outgrown.

In a single issue of the *New York Times* real-estate section in May
1962, were the following headlines for three different stories:

SUN ROOM RETURNS IN EAST SIDE CO-OP

BAY WINDOWS, THOUGH COSTLY, BEING USED IN "VILLAGE" CO-OP

SHINGLE STYLE HOUSE, ONCE FAVORED BY RICH, REAPPEARS

One has only to look at almost any new apartment house or even at
any public housing project to be aware of the revival of Mr. Downing's balcony. In the single house the screened porch, the breezeway,
the patio, or even the back yard, protected from insects by aerosol
"bombs" of one sort or another, has taken the place of the veranda.
The bay window is now the glass wall that gives us the same sense
of being indoors and outdoors at the same time.

But these are by no means the only kinds of projections of old ideas
that are shaping the modern house. "High Ceilinged Homes Are Once
More Finding Favor," the *New York Times* reported on April 1,
1962. It has taken a decade or so for the ideas of some West Coast
architects like Pietro Belluschi, Harwell Hamilton Harris, and John
Yeon, who made living-room ceilings soar again, to reach the East
Coast. The octagonal house has once more turned up on both coasts.
In Hollywood Hills it is a single-story saucer perched on a mast, a sort
of domesticated mushroom approached by a four-passenger cable car,
called a "hillavator." It cost approximately $100,000 to build in 1961.
In the East the houses are not octagons but circles, but their plans
owe just as much to the nineteenth-century octagons that one still encounters in New York state and New England as does the one perched
on a mast. Mr. Fowler would be gratified.

It is an interesting comment on the modern house, I believe, that people who would not think of living in anything so daring during the winter seem to have no hesitation about building a "vacation house" (another name for "second house" or summer "cottage") in the most insistently modern style. There are several obvious reasons for this. Modern architecture appears to insist on a far less formal style of life than a house in one of the traditional styles over which long ago settled an aura of genteel respectability. Vacation houses are open-collar, not white-collar or even blue-collar and certainly not black-tie, houses. It is respectable for the owner of a traditional house to have a modern vacation house, just as it is all right for the owner of a black Cadillac sedan to have a sports car to go to the country club in. The vacation house, furthermore, is a house in which the least distinction is made between indoor and outdoor living. It is a "camp," in the sense that families a generation ago in New York used to talk about their summer places in the Adirondacks as "camps." They were often vast and elaborate establishments, well-equipped with servants, but they always maintained a certain unplastered, roughhewn, and fieldstone-and-log look about them with vast fireplaces surmounted with moose heads. I suspect that people who have modern houses for vacations but live in traditional houses during the winter look upon those who live all year round in modern houses as not quite serious about the business of life.

If many of Mr. Downing's ideas persist, there are other ideas evident in the modern house that would greatly surprise him and that would tell him how America has changed since his time. The façade, for example, is disappearing, and the house, instead of being an inter-ruption in the landscape or an accent in it, has become merely a piece of landscape enclosed for shelter. The denial of the façade, the refusal of the modern house to face the street, could be interpreted as un-neighborly, a turning of the back, but only in the sense that it flouts a convention that most people respect. In some cases, of course, the modern house simply excludes the neighbors with a high stone wall, and in these cases the architect, as I interpret what he is doing, is attempting to provide the kind of privacy that once could be achieved only by a house on many acres of land. If a house is going to be trans-parent, then its privacy must be protected, though once you are inside the wall, the house is an open book . . . a gesture of friendliness almost beyond the call of duty. In some other respects the house behind the wall is very like the nineteenth-century manor house set at the end of a long driveway. It bespeaks not only desire for privacy but for social exclusiveness.

The concern with clutching the outdoors within the walls and with gardens inside the house, speaks, of course, of the urbanization of our society. In the days when men worked out of doors, houses were built to shut away the elements, to keep nature in its place, sometimes enemy, sometimes friend, but always something that had to be coped with. In the modern house nature is a permanent guest. It is also, of course, a substitute for architectural ornament and decoration, a means of achieving variety without having to invent it, of softening without seeming to be a softy, of stopping the eye as it slides over a smooth surface, without violating any architectural doctrines. It often seems to be an answer to the house rather than an expression of it, just as a "playful use of materials," as architects call using a variety of kinds of surfaces in a building, seems to be a way around the problem of dullness rather than a head-on assault on how to provide delight for the eye.

One of the beliefs about the modern house which is usually accepted as gospel by people who do not live in them is that they are, above all else, functional. By functional is meant that they work with a maximum of efficiency and convenience. But if you will look at a great many modern houses, you will discover that convenience is not infrequently sacrificed to appearance. I find nothing wrong with this, even if it does contradict the doctrine preached by many modern architects. You will find, for example, that it is occasionally necessary to go out of doors to get from bedroom to living room. You will find, as I have already suggested, that space has been cut to the minimum in the bedroom in order to provide for a more spacious and luxurious effect elsewhere, where more people will see it. You will find a great many plants that have to be watered and whose leaves have to be wiped. You will find in some modern houses a lack of relaxation in the way the living "area" is disposed that will remind you that the American still hankers for the parlor.

These contradictions in the modern house are to me heartening, because they tell us that the families who live in them are not trying to live entirely rational lives in entirely rational surroundings. This means that people are no longer the creatures of functionalism as so many of the pioneer builders of modern houses were, and that they are aware of conveniences of the flesh worth forgoing for pleasures of the spirit. It seems that the designers of modern houses have struck a blow for eccentricity and experiment, much as their nineteenth-century ancestors did, by trying to reorder their lives in such a manner that the machinery of life does not dictate and circumscribe the fun and disorder of life. A good thing.

It is well to remember, however, that the people who have paid the financial and spiritual price to build modern houses are relatively free spirits. Otherwise they would not have invested their hearts and their bank accounts in this particular kind of frontier architecture—an architecture on a new kind of frontier that is only dimly understood, a frontier of time.

We are just beginning to discover what this frontier is. It is a field of research for sociologists, for foundations, for labor unions, and for management personnel officers. Magazine editors are nibbling at its edges and some are making hay of it. A number of studies have been issued by university presses about it. It is the frontier of leisure, the rapidly expanding void of time that threatens to engulf us . . . the twenty-hour week and the three-day weekend. There is almost no one who does not think that it would be good to have more leisure time, but there is an increasing number of thoughtful people who wonder what it will do to family life, to our culture, to our manners and educational processes and peace of mind. What can be done to make leisure productive? (This is the Puritan point of view. This is what Miss Beecher would have wondered, but she would have had a ready answer, one feels sure). What can be done to make leisure satisfying and not stultifying? (Mr. Downing, who cultivated the mind and the arts of civilized living equally, would have had a ready answer for that.) What will it do to our highways, our national parks, our public beaches? What will it do to our houses?

The nineteenth-century house was the domicile of the sixty-hour and seventy-hour week. It was a house in which the man who paid for it and whose work supported it spent very little time compared with today's householder. He was up and out early, home briefly for lunch, and then home for supper or dinner late. He was early asleep. On the other hand, his servants were up before him, usually, and their workday lasted perhaps fourteen hours. His wife, depending, of course, on the affluence of the family, may have worked all day helping her servants, may have devoted many hours to making clothes or mending or hemming napkins, or to paying calls on her neighbors and sewing for missions or "the poor." If she was rich, her schedule was filled with social obligations and with planning menus, being "at home," or writing the innumerable notes and letters that custom demanded of her. In other words, the nineteenth-century house was lived in almost exclusively by women and children for almost the entire day. If there was an old man at home, too old to work, he rocked his chair in the kitchen or on the porch and did chores that were not too taxing, though the chores that he thought not too taxing might readily kill a fifty-year-old today. (I have a country neighbor who is ninety-one, who gave up chopping his firewood only last summer. His kitchen stove, incidentally, consumes wood in summer and coal in winter, though he could afford an electric range if his wife wanted one.)

The twenty-hour week will inevitably change the looks and character of the houses in which we will live. It will make the house into a new kind of recreation center in which the needs of every member of the family are reconsidered in the light of the new leisure. It will be housing for the intentionally part-time unemployed in a country crowded with people who do their own domestic work, or who hire domestic-service companies to do the chores they don't want to do themselves, who live on relatively small pieces of land in areas that are far more urban than rural, who want to be private but at the same time identified with the community, who want the sun and light by day and protection from the dark by night.

Those who forecast what the house of the future will be are very likely to emphasize how technology will alter our homes and our ways of living, how many devices there will be to spare us from the use of physical energy or intellectual inventiveness. We will be served by robots. Our demands, presumably, will be of the sort that robots will understand.

One can get a far better idea, I believe, of what the house of the future will be by looking at the best of the houses of today, by considering how the architects who are trying to cope with the first hints of the problems presented by the new frontiers of leisure try to solve them.

The architecture of mass leisure, if I read the clues correctly, will have a kind of adaptability that assures privacy when it is wanted—congregation in family rooms, and segregation when the members of the family get to be too much for each other. It will be flexible so that some rooms will come and go as needed (as they do now in really modern hospitals), just as the outdoors will come and go. The kitchen may become a place that mother will be happy to retire to if she has a husband around so much of the time, or it may become the center of family activity . . . but it too will come and go, expand and contract, as the needs of the family change, not just from year to year, but from day to day, or from morning to night. In other words, the house in the new era of leisure will attempt to do in a small space what the great house of the eighteenth century, like Westover, or the villa of the nineteenth century, accomplished by the lavish use of space: provide a relaxed setting for a life of busy leisure.

But of one thing I think we can be reasonably sure. The American architecture of leisure will have no illusions of permanence. However tasty the nests, the horizon will always beckon; the movers will always be prepared to take to their wings, the domesticators will always be on hand to tell them to settle down, the architects to tell them to search for the beautiful, and the older generation to remind them in no uncertain terms that their manners have gone to hell.

Sources and Acknowledgments

The subject of manners is, of course, inexhaustible, but it is also extremely elusive. Because every social act that anyone commits involves manners of one sort or another, every conceivable description of man's behavior and every personal observation is a potential source of information or conjecture about manners. Behavioral scientists attempt to study some aspects of manners objectively, but while I have tried to be objective, I make not the slightest pretense of having been scientific in the accumulation or the sifting or the evaluation of the material in this book. I have quite intentionally used sources that scientifically must be the antithesis of reliable. Whose diary is reliable? Whose travel journal? Whose novel of manners? And how could a book of etiquette be anything but part fantasy? Yet these are the kinds of sources I have used, always allowing for the fact that I was dealing with unreliabilities, impressions, other people's prejudices and flashes of insight. I hope that the results may be at least an approximation of the truth.

As this book does not pretend to be a work of scholarship but, rather, an essay based on the freewheeling indulgence of one writer's curiosity, I do not append a bibliography of the written sources I have consulted. (In many respects my most valuable sources have been conversations with friends and hours spent looking at buildings and pictures.) In the course of reading for this book I have indulged myself by buying a good many of the books, especially books of etiquette, household manuals, and books on house building, that seemed to me to reflect (sometimes with wild inaccuracy, to be sure) the manners and houses of Americans. I know of no adequate bibliography of manuals on the household. Anyone interested in books on manners in America will find *Learning How to Behave, a Historical Study of American Eti-*

quette Books by Arthur M. Schlesinger, Sr., not only instructive but a pleasure. It is also an excellent bibliography, though I dare say Professor Schlesinger has turned up (as I have) some items that he had not seen when the book was published in 1946. The standard bibliography of books on domestic architecture in this country before 1895 is *American Architectural Books* by Henry-Russell Hitchcock. It was originally published in 1946 and was reissued in 1962 by the University of Minnesota Press.

I would like to mention a few other books that I have found especially useful and to whose authors I feel especially indebted. Sigfried Giedion's *Mechanization Takes Command* (1948) is, in part, a remarkable study of the effects of technology on the household. *Domestic Service* by Professor Lucy Maynard Salmon of Vassar College was published in 1897 and is a most illuminating history of who served whom and why in America. It is out of print, of course, and so far as I know there is no recent history which brings the story up to date. Everett Dick's *The Sod-House Frontier, 1854-1890* (1937) is essentially what its title says it is; I depended heavily on it in the chapter "A Far Cry from Architecture." Histories of American eating habits are scarce. I recommend R. O. Cummings' *The American and His Food* (1940) as an excellent and readable study. The most useful general history of American architecture that I have consulted (and used with pleasure) is Wayne Andrews' *Architecture, Ambition, and Americans* (1955). I also have gone back again and again to his book of photographs, *Architecture in America* (1960).

There have been two libraries that have been invaluable to me in the process of preparing this book, and as I do not think that either has been aware of how much I have drawn on its resources, I would like to thank them here for their generous help. They are the New York Public Library (surely one of the great libraries of the world, not only in its resources but in its services and courtesies) and the New York Society Library, of which I have had the pleasure of being a member for many years.

A great many friends have helped me in a great variety of ways. I am especially indebted to Katherine Gauss Jackson for her invaluable help at every stage of this book from the first discussions of its outline to the final dottings of the "i's" and crossing of the "t's." I would also especially like to thank my mother, Adelaide Sparkman Lynes, whose discriminating recollections of her New York childhood brought an era to life for me. My daughter and son, Elizabeth L. Hollander and George P. Lynes, II, helped me greatly with research and with the mechanics of the book. They were imaginative, diligent, and they seemed to be entertained; I am extremely grateful to them and proud of them. If I list others who have helped me, and to whom I am indebted, I am sure to omit someone I would dearly like to include, but I cannot forbear to thank Wayne Andrews, Thomas Hornsby Ferril, John A. Kouwenhoven, John Fischer, Edgar Kaufmann, Jr., Nathalie Dana, Mary Sime West, Hildegarde G. Steimle, John Cook, Simon Michael Bessie, Catharine Meyer, Marion K. Sanders, Virginia Hughes, Eric Larrabee, Walker Evans, Georginia Williscroft, Dale Peters Clyde, Beulah Hagen and Harwell and Jean Harris, all of whom have led me to houses or corners of houses or manners I wouldn't have found for myself. I am, furthermore, greatly in the debt of Cass Canfield for his encouragement, patience, interest, and extremely helpful and generous editorial advice.

I would also like to thank the editors of *Architectural Record* for permission to reprint material in the last chapter of this book, which I had originally written as a preface for *Record Houses of 1957*.

One final thing. My wife says that she has forgotten it (and I believe her, of course), but it was she who suggested the topic of this book in the first place and thereby set me upon a long, entertaining (to me) search into the mysteries of men and houses and manners and styles, an excursion I have enjoyed most of the time and most especially when it has been in her company. To say I am grateful is scarcely to say a fraction of what I mean.

INDEX

Illustrations for this book are not indexed. See list on pp. ix–xii.

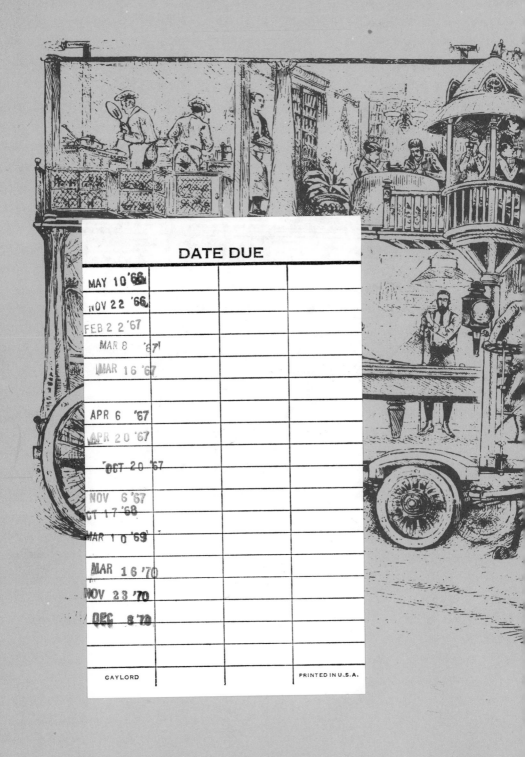

DATE DUE

MAY 10 '66			
NOV 22 '66			
FEB 2 2 '67			
MAR 8 '67			
MAR 16 '67			
APR 6 '67			
APR 20 '67			
OCT 20 '67			
NOV 6 '67			
OCT 17 '68			
MAR 1 0 '69			
MAR 16 '70			
NOV 23 '70			
DEC 8 '70			
GAYLORD			PRINTED IN U.S.A.